THE HOLLYWOOD JIM CROW

Crow

The Racial Politics of the Movie Industry

Maryann Erigha

NEW YORK UNIVERSITY PRESS

New York

NEW YORK UNIVERSITY PRESS
New York
www.nyupress.org

References to Internet websites (URLs) were accurate at the time of writing. Neither the author nor New York University Press is responsible for URLs that may have expired or changed since the manuscript was prepared.

Library of Congress Cataloging-in-Publication Data
Names: Erigha, Maryann, author.
Title: The Hollywood Jim Crow : the racial politics of the movie industry /
Maryann Erigha.
Description: New York : New York University Press, 2018. |
Includes bibliographical references and index.
Identifiers: LCCN 2018020940| ISBN 9781479886647 (cl : alk. paper) |
ISBN 9781479847877 (pb : alk. paper)
Subjects: LCSH: African American motion picture producers and directors. |
African Americans in the motion picture industry. | Motion pictures—
Social aspects—United States—History.
Classification: LCC PN1995.9.N4 E75 2018 | DDC 791.43/652996073—dc23
LC record available at https://lccn.loc.gov/2018020940

New York University Press books are printed on acid-free paper, and their binding materials are chosen for strength and durability. We strive to use environmentally responsible suppliers and materials to the greatest extent possible in publishing our books.

Manufactured in the United States of America

10 9 8 7 6 5 4 3 2 1

Also available as an ebook

CONTENTS

List of Figures and Tables   vii

Introduction: Race Matters in Hollywood   1

1. Representation and Racial Hierarchy   23

2. Labeling Black Unbankable   52

3. Directing on the Margins   82

4. Making Genre Ghettos   115

5. Manufacturing Racial Stigma   141

6. Remaking Cinema   162

Conclusion: Hollywood's Racial Politics   181

Acknowledgments   193

Appendix   195

Notes   199

References   207

Index   215

About the Author   225

FIGURES AND TABLES

FIGURES

Figure I.1. Antoine Fuqua at the premiere of
The Magnificent Seven   2

Figure 1.1. Cultural representation pyramid   25

Figure 1.2. 1963 March on Washington   32

Figure 2.1. Variety headline   58

Figure 2.2. Race of cast and production budgets for
Black-directed movies   70

Figure 3.1. Average production budgets by race of director   96

Figure 3.2. Ava DuVernay at the Ultimate Disney Fan Event   110

Figure 4.1. "She's Back" billboard ad   127

Figure 5.1. John Singleton at a Canadian entertainment cultural
showcase   150

Figure 6.1. Carver Theater in downtown Birmingham, Alabama   167

Figure C.1. Black-directed movies headline cinema in
Athens, Georgia   190

TABLES

Table 2.1. Domestic box office, Tyler Perry–branded films   76

Table 3.1. Racial representation of directors, major distributors   94

Table 3.2. Racial representation of directors, independent /
studio independent distributors   95

Table 3.3. Top-budgeted Black-cast movies by Black directors   100

Table 3.4. Top-budgeted Black-cast movies by
non-Black directors   101

Table 4.1. Black-directed franchise movies   134

Table 4.2. Top-grossing Hollywood franchise movies   136

Introduction

Race Matters in Hollywood

The movie *The Magnificent Seven* (2016), an action/adventure western, starred the veteran actor Denzel Washington alongside the less well-known white actors Chris Pratt and Ethan Hawke. The movie was directed by Antoine Fuqua, who, like Denzel Washington, has a number of successful movies under his belt. Despite their combined experience, there was a hesitance among Hollywood insiders—those with great influence on the decision-making processes in the production of popular cinema—to produce *The Magnificent Seven* for a big budget with Washington starring and Fuqua directing. In the following quotation, Steve details the reasons behind his caution:

> Loved the script—plot, characters all incredibly well written and with Denzel and Antoine it feels compelling. My concern is that *Equalizer* was 36% caucasian and 35% African American. I wonder if we were to look at successful westerns like *True Grit* how much of that audience was caucasian. I honestly don't know but if I had to guess it would be more caucasian and less african american. So if in the last week we're figuring out what audience to double down on like we just did with *Equalizer*, I want to be sure that audience has the elements they need to buy tickets. Do we double down on the AA audience and if so does that audience show up at Westerns in a big enough way to make our number? Or do we push older Caucasian males toward a Denzel / Antoine Fuqua movie and if so will they show up in a big enough way? Obviously westerns pose an initial set of concerns but I'm not sure the pedigree is the perfect fit for the lovers of the genre. And having just been the contemporary, cool, popcorn movie to the *Tombstones* bleak, old fashioned movie—I don't feel as excited about this as id like based on the fiscal layout.[1]

While Steve is a pseudonym for a Hollywood insider, his words and the concerns he voices are real. His momentary praise for the talents of Fuqua and Washington is immediately followed by skepticism for their possibility of success. In particular, he expresses uncertainty about the financial outlook of *The Magnificent Seven* for reasons that appear to be outwardly related to race. Believing that the audience for all western-genre movies skews Caucasian, Steve imagines a predominantly white audience for *The Magnificent Seven*. He reasons, therefore, that the cast and directing should also skew Caucasian in order to capitalize on this target audience, as he puts it, "to be sure that audience has the elements they need to buy tickets" and to be certain "the pedigree is the perfect fit for the lovers of the genre." Here, the *elements* and the *pedigree* implicitly refer to the racial makeup of the cast and director with respect to

Figure I.1. Antoine Fuqua at the premiere of *The Magnificent Seven*, Toronto Film Festival, September 8, 2016. Photo by GabboT.

imagined audience desires. Steve is unconvinced that the genre's key audience (presumably Caucasian males) would "show up in a big enough way to make our number" for a Black actor and director. In other words, he supposes that the combination of a Black actor and director attached to the movie would not gel with white audiences in a way that would drive them in droves to the theaters for a big box-office return.

In a single breath, Steve manages to lump racial considerations with culture and economics in what he perceives to be a perfectly unbiased explanation of market and consumer behavior in a popular culture industry. If his concerns were merely a matter of individual taste, there would be little cause for alarm. However, this racial logic is not uncommon among Hollywood insiders—people who have some aspect of control, input, or voice in the processes of production, distribution, or exhibition of Hollywood movies. Clearly, race matters in Hollywood. On regular occasions, Hollywood insiders such as Steve intertwine race with expectations about profitability and concerns about dollars and cents. Race is a preeminent factor governing decisions about moviemaking, a factor that studio executives consider when determining who should star in or direct a movie and for how much. Likewise, race factors into discussions about where movies should play and to which audiences. Indeed, racial inequalities and hierarchies in the film industry are not simply natural artifacts based on objective assessments of box-office performance. As Steve's remark indicates, race enters the conversation long before the box-office numbers roll in, oftentimes even before a movie script receives the green light for production.

Contemporary U.S. race politics shape film-industry organizations and practices. In the U.S. context, where racial boundaries play a significant role in society, race becomes an integral component for analyzing the organizational logics of the film industry. The Hollywood film industry is not one where race does not matter at all, which would be the case in a postracial society. Hollywood decision-makers embed racial logics in arguments about the economic behavior of markets. A box-office mentality determines scripts, development, green light, and production decisions. Steve's suggestion that the race of the actor and director correlates with box-office returns attaches race to notions of box-office mentality; specifically, he invokes a stain of Blackness that devalues Black stars, directors, and movies and renders Black culture and people economic risks. Linking race to ideas about potential box-office performance happens even before a movie reaches theaters. Overall, movies with nonwhite lead actors and casts—the movies that nonwhites are predominantly hired to direct—are projected to perform poorly at the foreign box office. Therefore, Hollywood insiders justify decisions based on race under the logic that race is a factor that shapes box-office returns.

Making race a basis for hierarchy in Hollywood has direct implications for how people are integrated into film-industry work. The film industry's racial hierarchy harks back to the Jim Crow days, in that one's race marks an explicit criterion for social division. Just as in the Jim Crow days, when race structured daily life, race largely determines the opportunities and outcomes of working professionals in the film industry, from actors to directors. The use of race as grounds for difference has implications for employment opportunities and outcomes for members of different racial groups. For U.S. racial and ethnic minorities, invoking race in decisions about who should get work and in what capacity leads to marginalization, ghettoization, and stigmatization. Movies with racial minorities attached are devalued and deemed inferior cultural products, which has implications for which roles racial minorities occupy and how their careers progress or are hindered in Hollywood. For whites, the use of race in decision-making leads to unfettered privilege and unchallenged immunity from box-office flops. Yet unlike the Jim Crow era, when narratives about innate racial inferiority and superiority were the grounds for stratification, present-day Hollywood couches racial divisions in a market logic that is grounded in economic and cultural explanations for advantage and disadvantage. In effect, we are witnessing a "Hollywood Jim Crow" of sorts, where the communication of ideas about race and value informs inequality and hierarchy in the film industry.

The Hollywood Jim Crow illuminates the process by which racial inequality and hierarchy in Hollywood are socially constructed and outlines the implications for movies and directors. Race occupies a salient position in everyday conversations and business practices within the film industry. As gatekeepers, Hollywood decision-makers actively create and maintain racial hierarchy in how they discuss, conceptualize, package, produce, and distribute movies and in how they stratify movies, actors, and directors. Their actions and opinions shape unequal outcomes that affect the careers and identities of people trying to make a living while working in Hollywood.

Aim of the Book: Making Sense of Race in Hollywood

Every day, numerous press headlines indicate that racial inequality in Hollywood is a popular and reoccurring topic of discussion. Hollywood manufactures racial difference on a global scale, both in front of and behind the camera—though the racial politics of Hollywood, especially processes by which race is made deliberate and relevant in the production and circulation of popular movies, remains underexplored. *The Hollywood Jim Crow* aims to (1) illustrate how the making of racial inequality and hierarchy is a process that is explicitly and deliberately constructed by Hollywood insiders, (2) show how in the popular cinema industry, race and racial considerations are framed around beliefs about cultural and economic value, (3) emphasize the structural underpinnings of inequality and hierarchy in the film industry by forging connections to the Jim Crow system, and (4) demonstrate the impact of racism on Hollywood workers' careers and identities.

Shining a questioning lens on industry culture, practices, and discourses, studies of film-industry production, distribution, and exhibition illuminate the mystique behind the organizing logics of the film industry to unearth answers to nagging issues such as how the industry functions, why decisions are made, and who benefits or loses out in the process. Such studies aim to better understand the inner workings of Hollywood through investigations of its operations, organizations, industrial settings, social relations, creative processes, and/or labor.[2] The making of racial inequality is a process that is pervasive and deeply embedded in all phases of the culture-industry production process—from the production of cultural objects to the relations of labor to areas of financing, marketing, and distribution.

Critical media industry studies, in particular, take a critical look at popular culture, for example, to understand the contours of race and ethnicity in creative industries and cultural production by locating and analyzing national and global sites, discourses, and practices of making race, racial arrangements, racial inequality, and racism.[3] Through

Hollywood cinema, one can examine how racial inequality is made, how the racial order functions, how racial groups are stratified, and how race is embedded into everyday institutional practices in a major culture industry. Within the film industry, specific sites, discourses, and practices facilitate the production and reproduction of racial difference. Of paramount importance is understanding how whiteness operates in creative industries to contribute to racial difference and power.[4] Moviemaking in Hollywood is a global project of establishing doctrines of whiteness and white supremacism. White Hollywood industry workers' racial practices, beliefs, attitudes, and production politics reflect a "possessive investment in whiteness" that contributes to a racialized order.[5] In this manner, white Hollywood workers as cultural intermediaries or cultural brokers can act as gatekeepers who make decisions about cultural products and audiences in ways that create and reinforce unequal racial outcomes.[6] The concrete ways in which Hollywood insiders use racial considerations to make determinations about the production and dissemination of popular movies is underexplored but can reveal how decision-making through a lens of whiteness operates to produce difference. Moreover, little is known about how marginalized racial groups are incorporated into the film industry's elite ranks and how the industry resists racial integration.[7] Hence, investigating the racial politics of the movie industry involves linking creative-industry professions with processes of race-making, whiteness, and integration into ranks of power.

Matters integral to understanding Hollywood's racial production and distribution culture include how ideas about race, economics, and culture are socially constructed in culture industries, how racial divisions of whiteness and otherness are enacted and operate in everyday film-industry practices, and how inequality persists to shape difference and power, film after film, year after year. Race and racial hierarchies are explicitly embedded and institutionalized into decision-making processes about moviemaking—in the employment of workers and in the production, distribution, and exhibition of movies across international markets. As gatekeepers, white Hollywood insiders signify that racial difference has economic and cultural relevance, to shape unequal trajectories for movies and talent, which ultimately affects the careers and identities of Hollywood workers. Racial inequality is rationalized and protected by the structure of the film industry.

Despite the appearance of the U.S. culture industries, such as Hollywood, and their professions and occupations, such as film directing, as venues of solely harmless, feel-good entertainment, they are deeply embedded in inequality making—in manufacturing, reinforcing, and reproducing hierarchies of racial difference. This book reveals contemporary racial structures within organizations and occupations in a major U.S. popular-culture industry: Hollywood cinema. Popular-culture industries are not simply sites for innocuous enjoyment. They are also sites where power structures buttressed by racial inequality are created, reinforced, and reproduced.

The Hollywood insider Steve clearly makes an adamant case for why a Black actor such as Denzel Washington and a Black director such as Antoine Fuqua should not headline a western-genre film. What is somewhat surprising is that his argument, for who should act and direct in a western and for how much the movie should be made, is based on racial logics. While his language about elements and pedigree are race blind, he also directly refers to race, to Caucasian audiences and African American audiences, as a basis for making decisions about the production of movies.

On the surface, this use of direct racial language appears to violate social norms of racial equality, a product of political correctness birthed out of the civil rights era. Although it was law and custom in the United States to use race as a viable justification for unequal opportunities and outcomes of disadvantage and privilege prior to the 1960s, the post civil-rights period ushered in a new era that universally condemned the explicit use of race to exercise discrimination or prejudice. Immediately following the civil rights movement, outright racism was condemned in public society and outlawed through legislation. Racial prejudice and discrimination could be accomplished through covert means but were opposed and countered if overt. Individuals and organizations, if biased, thus adopted implicit ways to covertly signal race, meanwhile producing the same effect of inequality that existed in prior eras.

In the post-civil-rights era, guiding ideologies of colorblindness and postracialism suppose a waning significance of race in shaping life outcomes. Describing how colorblindness is used to advance racial inequality in the twenty-first century, the sociologist Eduardo Bonilla-Silva explains, "Whites have developed powerful explanations—which have ultimately become justifications—for contemporary racial inequality that exculpate them from any responsibility for the status of people of color."[8] Colorblind racism has gained its validity from juridical and legislative systems and has been legally inscribed in areas from college admissions decisions to voting-rights laws. It repackaged social practices that were prominent during the Jim Crow era of race relations to make them appear to be nonracial. Ideas about colorblindness—particularly, that race is no longer a relevant factor in social life—are constructed, disseminated, and used to explain away racial inequality. Most prominent is the use of abstract liberalism, a philosophy that suggests that there is equal opportunity and meritocracy for all, despite opportunities and outcomes being structured on racial grounds.[9] Even further, postracial rhetoric relegates the relevance of race to a distant past. Postracialism is best symbolized by the election of Barack Obama as president of the United States. Born to a white American mother and a Kenyan father, Obama became the first African American and nonwhite president in U.S. history. Soon after his election, however, decades-long societal norms about race that discouraged explicit racism showed signs of waning.

Perhaps the backlash against the Obama presidency prompted a monumental shift in racial norms—from subdued, implicit racism to a bold, unapologetic racism and a rise in overt racial discourse. Some social scientists argue that the image of a Black family in the White House spurred a renewed, overt nationalism among white Americans, one that brought the salience of white (American) racial identity to the forefront and ushered in the election of President Obama's successor: the white Euro-American billionaire Donald Trump (no matter that his mother is an immigrant from Scotland and his grandfather is an immigrant from Germany). In the 2016 presidential election, Trump decisively won every category of white voters (i.e., white women, white men, college-educated whites, upper-class whites, middle-class whites, etc.). Meanwhile, challenges to immigration policies aroused Latino/a Americans' racial and ethnic identities, and threats from state-sanctioned violence spurred Black Americans and Black racial identities to action with groups such as #BlackLivesMatter. In a matter of years, the auras of colorblindness and postracialism gave way to explicit racial relations, discrimination, activism, protest, and violence.

The prevailing societal milieu of explicit race discourse extends its pervasiveness to the film industry, where decisions about film production and distribution have undeniable racial underpinnings. Now it appears that race is no longer a covert force and is increasingly accepted as a means to explain advantage and disadvantage. In a sense, we are back to the Jim Crow days, with race being explicit and racial inequality justifiable. Steve does not use entirely coded language to imply that race should be a major factor in decision-making about movie budgets and productions. His discussion about race—about African American actors and directors and Caucasian audiences—is outright and explicit. Slowly but surely, notions of colorblindness and postracialism are being supplanted by more direct rhetoric. Race is no longer in the shadows but a pivotal characteristic that shapes how Hollywood insiders view prospective movies.

The title of the book, *The Hollywood Jim Crow*, highlights how racial inequality and hierarchy in Hollywood take their cue from the structure of race relations in society. The Jim Crow metaphor describes the enduring structure of racialization, or sorting of groups and individuals along racial lines, that occurs in the film industry today. Jim Crow is an infamous symbol of Black oppression at the hands of whites in the United States. The name originally represented the popular nineteenth-century song-and-dance theatrical minstrelsy stage act in which white entertainers dressed in Blackface, wore tattered clothing, and impersonated buffoons in an attempt to ridicule Black Americans and entertain white audiences. A racial slur, the Jim Crow caricature was a symbol of offense and oppression to Black people in popular culture and the racial imagination.

Informally named after the symbolic minstrel figure, the Jim Crow regime that enforced oppressive government laws and societal customs was enacted in the majority of U.S. states in some form from the late 1800s up to the civil rights era. Under Jim Crow segregation, an ideology of white superiority was used to justify the distribution of privilege to white Americans, while subjugating other racial groups. Jim Crow laws effectively denied equality for Black, Latino/a, Asian, and Native people in America. Buttressed by the 1896 *Plessy v. Ferguson* "separate but equal" decision, Jim Crow laws mandated racial segregation in many areas of social life—for example, within public facilities in schools, housing, transportation, and the military—and granted white Americans sole access to the best of those facilities while relegating other racial groups to inferior facilities. Basing social systems on racial difference and ratifying the difference under the law, the resulting organizational practices created racial disparities of advantages for whites and disadvantages for Black Americans and other racial groups.

In a Jim Crow system, mistreatment of Blacks and privilege of whites is normalized, resulting in the legal discrimination and marginalization of large segments of the population. At earlier points in U.S. history—for example, during periods of Native American colonization, slavery, and Jim Crow segregation—it was commonplace, albeit immoral, to delineate between racial groups to determine outcomes. During slavery, as in the Jim Crow segregation era, biological notions of racial inferiority and superiority were acceptable bases for social divisions. Institutional legacies of racial inequality and difference fester like a sore, untreated wound. Though Jim Crow laws were formally dismantled during and following the 1950s and 1960s civil rights era, systems of racial inequity still remain intact within the United States. On the surface, the dominant racial order in society has evolved over time to encompass several different racial regimes such as slavery and Jim Crow. However, each regime characterized race relations in a similar racialized manner—one that normalizes and lifts white Americans atop a racial ladder and meanwhile marginalizes and sediments Black Americans to the bottom, all within the boundaries of the law.

The basic structure of Jim Crow remains intact in contemporary U.S. society. In the present era, the Jim Crow practices still form the backbone for processes that facilitate unequal hierarchies of racial advantage and disadvantage. Collectively, three basic rules govern the Jim Crow framework. (1) Jim Crow systems operate under a philosophy of racial difference. (2) The systems label and stratify racial groups on the basis of the assumption of difference. (3) The systems produce a result of advantages for whites and disadvantages for other racial groups on the basis of the stratification system.[10] The stratification of racial groups into hierarchical systems engenders grossly unequal outcomes, at times as opposite as freedom and bondage, for whites and Blacks, respectively—resulting in overall positive outcomes for whites and negative, often life-threatening outcomes for Blacks.

The arguments, form, and structure that underlay the Jim Crows of yesteryear are the necessary and precipitant conditions for racial hierarchy in contemporary Hollywood cinematic production. *The Hollywood Jim Crow* shows how inequality shapes representation in the film industry in a way that reinforces ideas of white supremacism. Racial ideology in prior Jim Crow systems helps illustrate the inequality that is pervasive in Hollywood today. Hollywood embodies the racial makeup of the society that it inhabits, exhibiting a racial system that privileges and disadvantages different racial groups, similar to previous racial systems that structure the order and organization of social life. The Hollywood Jim Crow works against African Americans in all the same ways that Black people have been disadvantaged and legally marginalized in everyday life under prior racial regimes within U.S. society—though the present context adds new layers to the age-old practice of racial difference.

In this new era of racial politics, race is explicit in conversations about difference once again, but the reasons for justifying difference have evolved while inequality persists. The Hollywood Jim Crow uses cultural and economic notions of racial inferiority and superiority as grounds for racial difference. An insistence on the economics of the movie business reverberates in discussions about Hollywood. Assumptions about economics guide thinking about cinematic production. Indeed, many people assert that the guiding force and principal aim of the film business is profit, or the bottom line. According to the film scholar Janet Wasko, "the profit motive and the commodity nature of film have implications for the kind of films that are produced (and not produced), who makes them, how they are distributed, and where/when they are viewed. While it is common to call film an art form, at least Hollywood film cannot be understood without the context in which it is actually produced and distributed, that is, within an industrial, capitalist structure."[11] Moreover, Wasko adds that "the commercial and profit-motivated goals of the industry are assumed and rarely questioned."[12] Hollywood's economic logic deserves more careful attention and interrogation, especially as it pertains to the focus on foreign-market profit and the way that race is linked with expectations of profit. This book reveals that this discussion about economics is not far removed from race politics. In fact, the two are linked, often explicitly.

Although the current racial politics dismisses race as purely biological, it nonetheless unabashedly invokes race in other ways. Racial difference in Hollywood is explained away as an outcome of competitive, market forces determined by audience preferences for some cultural products over others. The practice of using biological difference as a proxy for race is reproached for being discriminatory, but meanwhile the act of using cultural or economic justifications as a proxy for race is labeled nondiscriminatory and, more insidiously, an objective fact. Couching racial difference in economic and cultural terms by attributing cultural and economic deficits to racial minorities does not cause immediate social outrage and therefore provides an effective vehicle for perpetuating racism.

Jim Crow racial regimes are connected through their shared assumption of racial difference, labeling of difference, and production of unequal outcomes for members of different racial groups. Following this pattern, Hollywood executives' make allegations of racial inferiority and superiority, legitimate the allegation through labeling, act on the labels, and ultimately marginalize African Americans and privilege white Americans. Making economic rationalizations, Hollywood decision-makers label Black films and directors "unbankable" to advance the assumption that Black films and directors are inferior financial investments at the box office compared to white films and white directors. Due to the "unbankable" label, Black directors and movies with Black characters are disadvantaged in the production process compared to white directors and films with white characters—in a way that imposes limits on the future careers of African American directors. Once the "unbankable" label is established, film companies are freely and legally allowed to marginalize Black films and directors on the basis of the assumption that they are not economically viable investments. The end result is that Black films and directors are prevented from accessing the same markets and privileges as white films and directors. Racial disparities in Hollywood mean more work and visibility for white directors and films and less work and visibility for Black directors and films. These differences for which media become normalized or otherized have abstract ideological implications and tangible outcomes for unequal livelihoods.

Of course, there are notable differences between Hollywood's racial troubles and the racial problems that emerged from slavery, Jim Crow segregation, or even the New Jim Crow of mass incarceration. Fundamentally these prior racial regimes were entrenched on the basis of legal codes and enforced by the federal government—through law, politics, and policing. Slavery, Jim Crow segregation, and mass incarceration were wide-scale systems of social control that were rooted in the everyday lives of all citizens and directly impacted everyone in the nation. The Hollywood Jim Crow, in comparison, might appear to exert only a small sphere of oppression. All (or even most) people do not aspire to become Hollywood workers and, hence, do not experience a revocation of their rights to produce or direct a feature film. Notably, the direct constraints of the Hollywood Jim Crow only apply to creative personnel working in Hollywood and not to the entire nation.

At first glance, the scope of the Hollywood Jim Crow appears to encompass only a narrow, privileged sector of the population—middle- or upper-class professional artisans, many of whom are highly educated. Most Hollywood up-and-comers have relatively privileged and connected lives, though it is unknown whether this is also the case for Black Americans. Apparent financial barriers exist to breaking into film directing. To this point, Spike Lee's grandmother Zimmie Shelton helped fund his first feature film, *She's Gotta Have It* (1986). Robert Townsend put $100,000 on a credit card to fund his first film, *Hollywood Shuffle* (1987), which illustrates the substantial sum of money required even for a small independent movie. Class, capital, and socioeconomic standing play a role in who can access lucrative Hollywood work. Obviously, denying one's rights to be represented fully in Hollywood is by no means equivalent to denying one's rights to use a public restroom or to experience life outside prison walls. In this way, Jim Crow inequality facing the poor, destitute, or otherwise vulnerable and truly disadvantaged populations is qualitatively different in circumstance compared to the inequality that relatively privileged folks encounter.

Nevertheless, the Hollywood Jim Crow's sphere of influence is deceptively larger than meets the eye. Although it is true that the Hollywood Jim Crow does not instigate racial hierarchies among non-Hollywood workers, the ability or inability of workers from various racial groups to navigate Hollywood shapes the quality and content of movies. Besides the relatively few privileged workers who attain opportunities to direct Hollywood movies, global audiences that watch movies are indirectly affected by the film industry's racial marginalization. Representation in the production of cinema allows groups not only to produce movies but also to create and disseminate their own meaning systems for audience consumption. More than mere vehicles for profit, movies are powerful tools for shaping consciousness.[13] Cinema is a forceful piston of an ideological engine that builds consensus around public and social issues. Cinematic messages influence people's views about ideas, social issues, and groups in society; hence inequality in the production and dissemination of movies causes reverberations that echo beyond their origins. Though the racial stratification of Hollywood workers might not affect our lives directly, it shapes our lives indirectly by influencing what images and ideologies are available for consumption and what images and ideologies are withheld from our view. Withholding multiple perspectives from the mass dissemination of cinematic narratives and images facilitates a cultural imperialism—even within the same nation—in which one racial group's perspective dominates cinema.[14] Meanwhile, marginalized groups are denied full citizenship, unable to fully include their worldviews in popular American cultural artifacts. In spite of departures from previous systems of racial hierarchy, the Jim Crow structure still provides a useful framework for thinking about how racial inequality pervades Hollywood, shapes experiences in film-industry work, and, more broadly, conditions our encounters with popular movies. Examining and critiquing racial patterns of inequality in Hollywood, this book attempts to better understand the film industry using the Jim Crow framework in order to make sense of and challenge the film industry's status quo of perpetuating racial myths and disparities.

Approach of the Book

How do industry gatekeepers create and maintain racial inequality? How does inequality affect career outcomes and identities of cultural workers—namely, directors? *The Hollywood Jim Crow* situates the study of racial disparities in Hollywood within a general process to show how inequality in the film industry is embedded into everyday studio operations and practices that facilitate an unequal distribution of rewards.

Who makes movies and the constraints they face in the film industry matter, because movies are so intimately embedded into our daily lives. While other books focus more on independent cinema production and distribution or emerging digital media, this book focuses on the mainstream film industry, commonly known as "Hollywood." Since the early 1990s, the contemporary film industry has been dominated by major global media corporations, which the film scholar Thomas Schatz calls "Conglomerate Hollywood."[15] In 2011, for instance, the major studios controlled 88 percent of market share and grossed over $8 billion in revenue, twice as much as the next 140 studios combined. Movies produced and distributed by the major studios and a handful of large independents hold power and sway over the movie industry with their expansive reach and dominant position in national and global production, distribution, and exhibition of popular culture. A vital component of racial inclusion is the level to which out-groups can access once-exclusionary central institutions and operations.

In particular, this book takes a close look at how racial inequality and hierarchy structure the employment of directors and the distribution of movies in the twenty-first century. Both directors and distributors are central to film-business operations and can provide meaningful insight into Hollywood's racial division of labor and everyday practices. On film projects, directors occupy a central and indispensable role. Though many highly skilled individuals come together to complete a movie, the director occupies arguably the most central role on a film project. The director envisions the final product and is intimately involved with carrying out that vision through preproduction, production, and postproduction.[16] It is common practice that audiences, critics, historians, and academic scholars alike perceive a movie not only as a collaborative enterprise but also as the brainchild of the director's vision—a gesture that acknowledges the director's sizable contribution to the final film, over other cast and crew. Directors' adequate representation in Hollywood holds significance for many reasons. Besides impacting on-screen images, representation for directors results in tangible employment gains. Black Americans' employment in prominent positions of control, for instance, as producers or directors, significantly increases the number of opportunities for Black talent in other positions.[17] Therefore, the absence, underrepresentation, and/or marginalization of directors is troubling in a role that is deemed so vital to the operation of the movie industry. Using the occupation of film directing, this book illustrates contemporary patterns of racial inequality in a major popular-culture industry. It makes strides toward investigating racial barriers in the occupation of film directing and the racial implications of breaking into film's elite ranks.

This story of unequal racial outcomes in Hollywood is told through statistical records, communications between Hollywood insiders, and perceptions of working directors. The book (1) draws on comprehensive industry data on the directors, distributors, genres, production budgets, and box-office receipts of more than a thousand contemporary movies, (2) examines trends in directors' employment on different movies, (3) demonstrates how opportunities, resources, and outcomes in Hollywood are structured by race, and (4) shows how racial inequality is made in the production, distribution, financing, and marketing of movies and in the hiring of labor. Systematic attention to the organizing logics of the film industry reveals a racial division of labor; this book is the first to provide a detailed and systematic analysis of racial divisions of labor in work among Hollywood directors. Furthermore, the twenty-first-century period permits a timely discussion of the state of racial disparities in Hollywood during a post-civil-rights era that has been marked by growing postracial and colorblind discourses. Hollywood's racial politics illustrate how race continues to matter despite public discourses that suggest otherwise.

Specifically, the book compares the career paths of Black directors to other racialized groups in twenty-first-century Hollywood. Out of all U.S. racial minority groups, African Americans have the most representation as Hollywood directors. Therefore, the book focuses on one marginalized racial group in Hollywood, Black directors, in relation to racialized others. Investigating the level of African Americans' inclusion in the film industry particularly necessitates an examination of their access to the facets of production from which they were formerly excluded—the movies and the positions at studios that are most central to film-industry operations. Accessing high-status positions provides financial remuneration that is important to understanding and alleviating racial income gaps—of course, notwithstanding the obvious and pervasive racial exclusion involved in who is permitted to manage large financial investments, own banks, and print and distribute currency.[18] The state of Black inclusion in the contemporary film industry is best evaluated by assessing involvement in areas that are financially lucrative, are central to industry operations, and wield the greatest ideological power.

Beyond statistical numbers, the "deep texts" of production cultures reveal knowledge and power structures.[19] Besides aggregating and tabulating box-office data, a more enhanced portrait of racial inequality in the film industry is achieved by incorporating Hollywood insiders' own views about decision-making in cinematic production and considering directors' perspectives of their work environment. Anonymized communications between Hollywood insiders from a major studio show how decision-makers frame discussions about Black movies and directors. These texts provide rare insight into how people with real power in Hollywood include race in their routine evaluations of popular movies' economic potential and cultural appeal.

Knowledge of how directors, as industry practitioners, understand, make sense of, and explain their positions and practices is also vital to grasp the implications of racial inequality for individual experiences and livelihoods. Because directors' perceptions of racial inequality in Hollywood give greater meaning to the revelations that emerge from the data, the book includes excerpts from press interviews of Black directors. Unlike interviews conducted behind closed doors, these press interviews are an example of "publicly disclosed deep texts," accounts that are self-consciously created for the general public to consume.[20] In exchange for promotion of directors' films on blogs and websites, directors grant interviews to media outlets, which in turn publish these interviews to generate increased site traffic or user views of the web content. During the interviews, directors discuss their past and upcoming films and their work lives within Hollywood—which sometimes leads to conversations about race and gender challenges. These narratives help to properly situate the quantitative data on movies within the deeper qualitative context of directors' experiences, in effect, enriching the complex story that is embedded in the data in order to illustrate how directors make sense of and even sometimes successfully navigate the Hollywood Jim Crow in the face of widespread inequality.

Overview of the Book

Central to understanding the Hollywood Jim Crow is discovering how film-industry workers create, reinforce, and reproduce racial patterns of difference over time. Undertaking an institutional analysis of race in the film industry, this book examines the plight of Black directors and their movies, highlighting the places that Black movies and directors occupy in Hollywood cinema and how other racial groups are treated in relation to their plight. The chapters that follow examine the quotidian practices and effects of racial inequality in the film industry, rituals that confine the production and circulation of movies directed by racial minorities.

Chapter 1 outlines various facets of representation—symbolic, numeric, civic, and hierarchical—that are important in cultural and cinematic production. Cinematic images are disseminated globally, carrying symbols of progress that hold value for underrepresented groups. Numeric representation embodies the quest for increased proportional representation via employment opportunities for workers from racially marginalized groups. Civic representation demands cultural citizenship and belonging in a nation's popular cultural artifacts. This chapter also gives an overview of Black directors' representation in Hollywood and considers concerns beyond numeric, civic, and symbolic representation. Racial hierarchies in cinema dictate what kinds of movies directors take on and where their career paths lead. Looking at hierarchies of representation provides a useful metric for grasping how racial divisions characterize labor in Hollywood and what steps can be taken toward achieving racial equality.

The next chapters detail the repressive institutional race politics that structures directors' work in Hollywood. Each chapter is devoted to unfolding the multiple layers of the Hollywood Jim Crow: assumption of racial difference, marginalization, segregation, and stigmatization. The chapters disentangle (1) how Hollywood insiders create and rationalize racial inequality using cultural and economic frames, (2) how racial hierarchy penetrates the careers of directors and the production of movies, and (3) how racial inequality shapes the identity, self-presentation, and character of group progress.

Chapter 2 illustrates how Hollywood executives and insiders label Black films and directors unbankable at the box office, suggesting risk and uncertainty around their potential for profit, especially at the foreign box office. Ironically, the assumption that "Black is unbankable" goes against the conventional logic of creative industries that "all hits are flukes" and that "nobody knows" what creative products will succeed or fail.[21] Armed with the "unbankable" mythology, Hollywood decision-makers devalue Black films and directors, for example, by attaching smaller budgets to Black-cast movies and attaching larger budgets to racially mixed and white-cast movies. Although films overperform and challenge the "unbankable" myth, perceptions that Black directors and films are unbankable trap them into limited trajectories. Overall, African Americans are employed and contained on the basis of this pretext of limitations on Black movies and directors.

Chapters 3 and 4 further highlight institutional efforts to disadvantage Black directors, through marginalization and segregation. Chapter 3 illustrates the ghettoization of Black directors outside of big-budget and major-studio distribution. Movies in these areas generally have white stories, ideologies, casts, actors, and directors.[22] Some directors, such as Tyler Perry, do manage to find success directing a number of films. Still, they are usually limited to small or medium budgets due to their tendency to direct Black-cast films, which are undervalued in Hollywood. Even when directors such as Tim Story and Antoine Fuqua direct films with white or racially mixed casts, they still encounter racial ceilings, never approaching the level of whites' inclusion. In contrast, studio executives give white directors the leeway to leap from small-budget projects to big-budget projects (or even to receive big budgets at the onset of their careers in cinema). However, this same leap of faith is rarely, if ever, granted to Black directors, due to their ghettoization in Hollywood. Moreover, white directors experience the privilege of bigger budgets when directing Black-cast movies compared to the budgets that Black directors of Black-cast movies receive. What is more, the fact that Black-directed movies typically get little to no distribution in foreign markets further exacerbates their marginality in the film industry.

Besides existing disparities between opportunities and resources for Black and white directors, gender also shapes women's and men's experiences in different ways. In the eyes of Hollywood decision-makers, race and gender doubly impact Black women's perceived capabilities. Their representation is limited to only a sporadic presence behind the camera. The career trajectories of the few who have found some modicum of success give voice to the understudied population of Black women who work on major studio productions and to the constraints that hinder their advancement.

Segregation in genres, as discussed in chapter 4, is yet another factor that contributes to incomplete integration and distance from the inner circles of Hollywood. For Black directors, integration happens only in some areas of work and not others. In contemporary Hollywood films, Black directors are overrepresented in the music genre. Meanwhile, the music genre locates Black directors in literal and figurative genre ghettos. Many music-genre films are situated in urban ghettos and center on themes about violence, poverty, and drugs. Music-genre films also record the smallest average production budgets compared to other genres such as sci-fi, action, and comedy. Black directors are sparsely included in financially lucrative areas of directing, for instance, on sci-fi movies or on tent-pole franchise films—movies that are of substantial importance to the operation of the film industry and to the career success of individual directors. Even when African Americans have similar qualifications to or in some cases more experience than white directors, they rarely direct these commercially lucrative motion pictures. When they do direct franchise movies, they more often are hired on less popular films with comparatively small budgets. Distance from high-status positions that are central to Hollywood film production ultimately undermines the commercial success of Black directors and their movies. Underrepresentation on tent-pole franchise movies prevents them from achieving a level of commercial success that would make it difficult for studio executives to refuse their demands for more financial resources to create popular cinema.

Chapter 5 considers how the Hollywood Jim Crow shapes the presence of Blackness in popular cinema. To a large extent, the act of labeling Black unbankable resembles the attempt to paint a picture of a "Negro Problem," which the pioneering sociologist W. E. B. Du Bois detailed in his early writings. Hollywood insiders conjure up a stigma around Blackness and suggest that Blackness in movies is in need of reform. Reacting to the "unbankable" judgment, some directors face pressures to transcend race and to neutralize Blackness in their movies or in conversations about their movies. To avoid the negative consequences that result when studio executives label a movie as a "Black film," they implement multiple strategies: attracting crossover stars, adding white characters to casts, featuring multiracial casts and postracial themes, or referring to films as "universal." Directors endeavoring to integrate into Hollywood encounter unique obstacles. Testimonies from directors reveal that as they plunge deeper into the core of Hollywood—making films with big budgets at major studios—they are increasingly discouraged from making films with Black casts or themes. Hence, the typical Black Hollywood director's oeuvre starts with movies with Black casts and themes, and then, as his or her career progresses to more financially lucrative movies, shifts to films with multiracial or white casts and nonracial themes. On the surface, African American directors are seemingly integrated into the film industry. However, with Blackness stigmatized, directors find difficulty expressing their ideal narratives and inscribing their own visions into the dominant cultural canon. Some people argue that this predicament undermines the very purpose of integration, a movement that initially set out to gain Black representation not only in participation but also with regard to the inclusion of Black cultural content, perspectives, and meanings. At the stage of commercially lucrative blockbuster movies, Black worldviews, ideologies, and identities are, in large part, systematically, consciously, and symbolically excluded from the screen.

Chapter 6 considers approaches to reenvision cinema in order to overcome the adverse effects of the Hollywood Jim Crow. One plan of action is to advocate for racial-minority participation in key positions. This involves closing racial disparities related to working at major studios, directing big-budget movies, and occupying decision-making positions. Another viable path toward equality involves greater investment in filmmaking outside of Hollywood. This path requires directors to place emphasis on forging youth film cultures and striving to create ways to "remake cinema" removed from Hollywood's governance. In particular, it calls for the revival of Black owned and operated organizations that support film production, distribution, and exhibition. The chapter details the goals, shape, and components of a Black cinema collective. Through organization, planning, institution building, and technological education, directors can orchestrate a Black cinema collective to circumvent the Hollywood Jim Crow and produce a diversity, number, and scale of movies without having to rely on financing from Hollywood studios. The revitalization of a Black cinema collective could serve as an impetus to curb racial inequality within Hollywood and include narratives it currently marginalizes or excludes. That is, if the burgeoning Black cinema industry becomes successful, it could put pressure on Hollywood to diversify in order to remain competitive as a producer of movies about Black people.

The conclusion contains a summary of the book's main findings. Implications of the Hollywood Jim Crow are pertinent not only to comprehend how race matters in a popular culture industry but also to grasp how racial hierarchies operate in other spheres of social life—and to ameliorate their impact.

1

Representation and Racial Hierarchy

Members of the exclusive Academy of Motion Picture Arts and Sciences—mostly white-haired white men over age sixty (and a few select others)—annually convene in an auditorium for the Academy Awards ceremony, held to commemorate the highest achievements in the American film industry. Red carpets, four-piece tuxedos, black bow-ties, and glittering designer gowns adorn the evening, which despite its grandeur, usually passes with little fanfare for Black directors, for whom few nominations and even fewer wins are rather the norm. When the presenters tear open their sealed envelopes to announce "and the award goes to . . . ," the phrase completing the sentence is rarely the name of a narrative-feature-film director who is Black. In fact, since the first Academy Awards ceremony was held in 1929 through the arrival of the twenty-first century, the Academy had yet to award any feature-film director of African, Latin, or Asian descent. For all the faint praise of symbolic nominations, the pinnacle accolade had evaded even the best of them.

Only recently has the Academy formally recognized movie direc-tors of African, Latin, or Asian descent. For Black filmmakers, the 2014 Academy Awards ceremony marked a historic turning point when Steve McQueen, who is British born and of Grenadian descent, won the cov-eted Best Picture Oscar for *12 Years a Slave* (2013), which he directed and coproduced. Eighty-five years after the inaugural Academy Awards ceremony, McQueen's victory marked the end of a long drought at the podium for Black-directed films. *12 Years a Slave* chronicled the life and tribulations of Solomon Northup—a man who was kidnapped, sold into slavery, and held in captivity for over a decade. By the movie's end, Nor-thup has regained his freedom. Coincidentally with the accolade, Holly-wood sought a liberation of its own. To some people, the dismantling of a racial barrier for Black directors signified a departure from a history of nonrecognition.

Despite the movie's clear merit, its victory at the Academy podium was far from being a shoe-in. In fact, some Hollywood insiders, who hold positions of influence and control in the movie industry, thought that the racial demographic of the voters would deter McQueen's film from receiving the shining crown. As a case in point, before the Best Picture Award was settled, Laura, a Hollywood insider, expresses doubts about the likelihood that white men in the Academy of Motion Picture Arts and Sciences would support a movie such as *12 Years*. She voices this observation in a correspondence to Hollywood executives and other insiders:

> "12 Years" is truly a brilliant film with a compelling story. . . . This film is made by a Brit that exposes the darkest "hidden history" of America, exposing a cruel and brutal segment of our white society. These planta-tion owners are as terrible [as] the Nazis, who are the only "acceptable" cinematic villains. The Academy's experience of watching this film is not pleasant. Some will not see it . . . yet, because of the violence. Eventually they have to, to vote. If they put it in their dvd, they may fast-forward or turn it off. So, will they vote for a Best Picture so difficult to watch? Many others who have seen it tout the brilliant filmmaking but are a bit embar-rassed by the story and more importantly did not "enjoy" watching it. My point is . . . is this the story American cultural bell ringers want to send around the world as the "best story" in the best picture? I think the voters are patiently waiting for an excuse to vote for another film. In their hearts, they are uncomfortable sending a global message from a Brit that we are or were terrible people.[1]

As this quotation reveals, race is a defining characteristic of Holly-wood that matters in film-industry workers' deliberations about movies. Laura points out the whiteness of Hollywood as an industry. In her cor-respondence to several Hollywood insiders, she refers to "our white so-ciety" and self-consciously feels that after watching the historical drama about U.S. slavery, viewers at home and abroad would conclude that "we [whites] are or were terrible people." She believes that white Academy voters such as herself would be hesitant to award a movie that envisions white Americans as cinematic villains, that showcases white-on-Black violence as a "cruel and brutal" yet integral and enduring mechanism of American race relations, and that depicts a narrative of Black suffering that is downright unpleasant for most whites to relive. Laura's quote demonstrates how easily criteria besides sheer filmmaking (even filmmaking described as "brilliant") enter into decision-making about what kinds of movies receive recognition during the annual ceremony. Race and racism are explicit factors governing how Hollywood insiders contemplate and evaluate movies. In Hollywood and in the Academy of Motion Picture Arts and Sciences, representation is important for members of all racial groups to equally impress their opinions and subjectivities on crucial decisions in cinema.

Key aspects of representation in a culture industry can be visualized in the "cultural representation pyramid" shown in figure 1.1. At the bottom of the pyramid are symbols and images. A reminder of the slogan "if you can see it, you can be it," both images and symbols typify visible monikers of representation that indicate early signs of inclusion in popular culture. Recognition at the Academy Awards and other

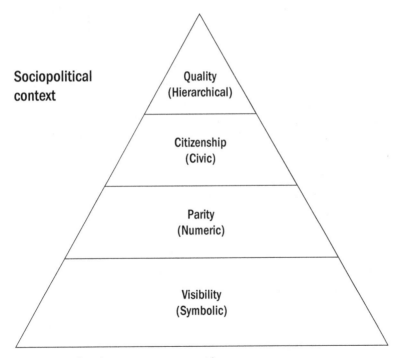

Figure 1.1. Cultural representation pyramid.

awards ceremonies is a form of symbolic representation. Images and themes in movies also provide racial symbols of inclusion.

Once a group has established visibility in symbols or images, its members might subsequently pursue advocacy for numerical representation. Fighting for representation in numbers, groups emphasize demography, usually in the form of landing roles in films or attaining adequate employment in jobs. The threshold of representation might be tied to the group's population share. Struggles for numerical and symbolic representation is ongoing, and the goal may take a long period of time to attain—if parity, or something like it, is at all in reach. Meanwhile, numerical representation promises greater presence on-screen and behind the camera. Symbolic and numerical representation, however, can be present but with little real improvements toward alleviating inequalities. Symbolic representation, for instance, could be only superficial yet not substantive. Despite an appearance of harmonious inclusivity with visible symbols, more telling signs indicate there are further layers to the story. Like symbolic representation, numerical representation is meaningful, but further dimensions of representation can be more insightful for understanding and alleviating racial inequality. Scholars and observers should critically examine representation in Hollywood under a microscope that goes beyond symbols and numbers.

Having achieved some improvements in numerical and symbolic representation, groups can stake citizenship claims in the dominant cultural canon. For example, Spike Lee's *Do the Right Thing* (1989), about racial conflicts on the hottest day of the summer in Brooklyn, New York, was inducted into the National Film Registry in its first year of eligibility for the honor and was deemed "culturally, historically, and aesthetically significant" by the U.S. Library of Congress.[2] As voting members of the Academy, Black directors have a hand in influencing whose movies are memorialized during the Oscars as national cultural artifacts.

Presumably, the last goal for attaining representation in cultural production is to occupy positions of power. In such positions, groups can control cultural output and steer flows of workers into and out of positions on cultural projects. Therefore, beyond the numbers of directors present or absent behind the camera or the number of victories at awards podiums, rethinking representation to look more closely at qualitative measures of institutional representation—especially access to lucrative positions of influence—is a way to investigate in more depth how racial inequality happens in Hollywood. An institutional analysis of the contemporary race politics of representation in the film industry would need to be located in the dimension of hierarchical representation. Hollywood insiders, who have the power to shape cinema from within the industry, structure film production around unequal racial hierarchies and justify inequality using statements that value and privilege white movies and directors over Black, Asian, and Latino/a movies and directors. This Hollywood Jim Crow racial hierarchy, in which outright expressions about race matter for the sorting of individuals and films in the movie industry, privileges whites at each level of the cultural representation pyramid, whereas African Americans and other marginalized racial groups find underrepresentation at each level. For film directors, racial disparities span what kinds of movies they direct, which movie genres are prominent, how much movies cost, and which studios are involved. Hierarchical racial representation has implications for individual careers and for the broader impact that directors and their movies can exert on global societies.

Symbols of progress, numbers of people in jobs, markers of cultural citizenship, and placement in positions of power and prestige reveal multiple levels at stake in the complex struggle over racial representation in the film industry. All this happens within the nation's sociopolitical context. The nation's racial context, for instance, plays no small role in shaping groups' access to each level of representation. The racial climate determines which groups are most likely to be employed and to occupy positions of power just as much as it influences whose cultural citizenship rights are realized or dismissed and what images become commonplace occurrences or rare anomalies. Examining various measures of representation provides a new look at racial inequality in Hollywood, while new reasons to explain away those inequalities circulate among those who are positioned to protect their advantage.

Symbols of Progress

Steve McQueen's win was quickly followed by other victories for Black talent behind the camera. In fact, the 2017 Oscars ceremony was a landmark year of firsts for Black workers in technical, behind-the-scenes positions in cinema. They received an uncharacteristic barrage of recognition in nominations and awards. An unprecedented four Black directors were nominated for Best Documentary Feature: Ava DuVernay for *13th*, Roger Ross Williams for *Life, Animated*, Haitian-born brothers Raoul Peck and Hebert Peck for *I Am Not Your Negro*, and Ezra Edelman, who ultimately won Best Documentary Feature, for *O.J.: Made in America*. Barry Jenkins, for *Moonlight*, became only the fourth Black director in Academy Awards history to receive a directing nomination. African Americans also received nominations in film editing and cinematography. What is more, the 2017 Oscars marked the first occasion that three Black-cast movies were in consideration for the top honor of Best Picture. Three Black producers received Best Picture nominations: Denzel Washington for *Fences* (2016), Pharrell Williams for *Hidden Figures* (2016), and Kimberly Steward for *Manchester by the Sea* (2016). Ultimately the Barry Jenkins–directed *Moonlight*, an adaptation of Tarell Alvin McCraney's novel *In Moonlight Black Boys Look Blue*, took home the Best Picture win.

Upon the announcement of victory, smartphones fanned the room. Blinking lights from the handheld gadgets captured the moment on video. Barry Jenkins accepted the award to raucous applause from a crowd of cheerful, teary-eyed onlookers with mouths agape. With a look of wondrous disbelief, he stepped up to the microphone and uttered, "Even in my dreams, this could not be true. But to hell with dreams— I'm done with it, because this is true. Oh, my goodness."[3] The momentous energy was palpable throughout his speech. Fists pumped toward the ceiling. Clearly, something of magnitude had been accomplished, something beyond expectations, and it felt good.

Via symbolic gestures such as Academy Awards accolades, Black directors can influence audiences and effect change through their creative works. The producer of *Moonlight*, Adele Romanski, a white woman, spoke about the symbolic power of the Best Picture victory for uplifting young African American teenagers: "And I hope even more than that, that it's inspiring to people—little black boys and brown girls and other folks watching at home who feel marginalized and who take some inspiration from seeing this beautiful group of artists, helmed by this amazing talent, my friend Barry Jenkins, standing up here on this stage accepting this top honor."[4] In an essay in *The Root*, Danielle Belton describes the exchange of inspiration and admiration that took place at the African American Critics Association Award Ceremony when, prior to the Oscars' Best Picture Award, John Singleton presented an accolade to Barry Jenkins for *Moonlight*. Belton writes that "probably one of the most deeply affecting moments during the awards ceremony was when acclaimed director John Singleton (*Boyz N the Hood, Baby Boy*) could barely mask his pride and admiration for a man he admitted he hadn't met, but felt he knew through his art: fellow director Barry Jenkins, the auteur behind independent film *Moonlight*. Singleton was presenting an award to Jenkins for *Moonlight*. Jenkins, in turn, thanked Singleton for inspiring him through his work on *Boyz N the Hood*, Singleton's first, groundbreaking film."[5] Before ever meeting in person, they engaged each other through their films. Movies and images are symbolic vehicles that shape audience perceptions and exert influence beyond the screen.

As a marginalized group in Hollywood, Black Americans have a restricted ability to control their own self-images or to challenge disparaging stereotypes about themselves—stereotypes that not only influence individual people but also shape crucial social factors such as politics, racial attitudes, and treatment by authority, namely, employers and law enforcement. The capability to create images for mass consumption comes packaged with the power to effect change. Cinema can be a vehicle for both racist and antiracist ideologies. Hence, cinema can serve to counteract racist ideologies with progressive ones. With inadequate representation behind the camera, Black Americans are less able to shape the minds of viewers or create mass-disseminated cinematic images that effect change with regard to social issues around race relations in the United States, such as mass incarceration and police brutality.

In the post-2000 era, the wheels of integration into the Academy Awards also turned for Asian and Latino/a directors. Twice, Ang Lee won Best Director—for *Brokeback Mountain* (2005) and *Life of Pi* (2012). On the heels of Ang Lee's achievements, two directors of Latin descent, both Mexican, won Best Director: Alfonso Cuarón for *Gravity* (2013) and Alejandro González Iñárritu for *Birdman* (2014) and *The Revenant* (2015). For *Birdman*, Iñárritu also won Best Picture. Implanting seeds of retreat from a racist past, these victories provided the arsenal for one to believe, or at least hope, that Hollywood would turn a new leaf toward a long-awaited future of racial inclusion.

By and large, film directors' symbolic acceptance in the Oscars aligns with Hollywood's public reputation as a liberal-leaning industry. Across the broad spectrum of Hollywood professions, actors and executives alike have been linked to this liberal moniker. For instance, Bruce Davis, a white American and former executive director of the Academy of Motion Picture and Arts and Sciences, once described the Academy as "overwhelmingly made up of liberal actors, writers, directors, and producers."[6] Hollywood celebrities are also commonly associated with liberal political involvement. To name a few, Beyoncé Knowles, 50 Cent, Jennifer Lopez, Brad Pitt, Ben Stiller, Will Smith, and Jada Pinkett Smith publicly supported the Democratic Party or donated money backing Democratic politicians.[7] In 2003 alone, Hollywood companies donated over $30 million to Democratic politicians and contributed substantially less, $10 million, to Republicans.[8] Part of the film industry's liberal image stems from key players' advocacy for liberal groups over conservative groups.

Beyond individuals, Hollywood movies have also garnered a reputation for portraying liberal themes, bolstering the perception that the industry upholds ideals of racial tolerance. In the midst of intense racial tensions in the United States, Hollywood social-problem films of the 1950s and '60s assumed progressive stances on social issues about racial inequality and, in doing so, spearheaded a national dialogue on race relations with such movies as *Guess Who's Coming Home to Dinner?* (1967), which featured an on-screen interracial romance between Sidney Poitier and the white actor Katharine Houghton. Beginning in the 1970s, progressive fictional portrayals depicted African Americans as leaders of the nation, preceding change in the general society. Indeed, before the community-organizing senator of Illinois, Barack Obama, became the forty-fourth president of the United States, numerous African American presidents preceded him in popular culture: James Earl Jones in *The Man* (1972), Tommy Lister in *The Fifth Element* (1997), Morgan Freeman in *Deep Impact* (1998), Terry Crews in *Idiocracy* (2000), Chris Rock in *Head of State* (2005), and Dennis Haysbert and D. B. Woodside in the Fox television series *24*. Through taking progressive stances on social issues, Hollywood offered themes and characters that not only purged the old dispensation of racial exclusion but also provided symbolic gestures of liberalism.

Just decades ago, a dogged racial exclusion and invisibility plagued representation of racial minorities in Hollywood. In fact, the history of racial exclusion in Hollywood exceeds the level of exclusion in other industries such as music or television.[9] Accolades for directors of color at the Academy Awards, political advocacy for the Democratic Party, and movies provoking conversations about controversial racial issues point to a symbolic inclusion for racial minorities that gives the appearance of a growing, albeit gradual, racial progress—as if presenting the case that a history of the film business once plagued by racial inequality is being supplanted by a more liberal future that fosters egalitarian ideals. Nonetheless, obvious questions follow: How could a film industry that appears to be so racially liberal be the constant subject of racial inequality? How does racial inequality persist within an American society that outwardly condemns racism and within a Hollywood film industry that presents a liberal public face?

Symbolic representation of racial minorities presents a public face of the U.S. film industry as a liberal entity. As the scholar of American popular culture Eithne Quinn writes, "there was a prevalent view among whites that the [film] industry, despite glaring evidence to the contrary, was basically racially progressive."[10] The appearance of growing symbolic inclusion can be deceiving. Despite the semblance of greater inclusivity, this portrait of a liberal Hollywood contrasts sharply with the lived realities of racial minorities working in the film industry. Progressive on-screen images or conspicuous awards ceremonies can obscure stagnant behind-the-camera working conditions for racial minorities.

Number Crunching

Ossie Davis, the director of the second-ever Black-directed film distributed by Hollywood studios, *Cotton Comes to Harlem* (1970), highlights one recurring concern about representation in cinematic production: that employment is important to secure jobs. Davis says, "there is from time to time a big brou-haha—sometimes it gets quite excitable—over whether or not a white director can really ever make a film truly representative of black lifestyle and black culture. This question, in my opinion, is more about jobs—and ultimately about power—than it is about race."[11] In the film industry, work is a necessary step, first, to secure a livelihood and, second, to exert control over images in popular culture.

As Ossie Davis emphasizes, representation is largely about jobs. Adequate representation for directors has direct gains with regard to employment outcomes. Gainful employment in any major industry, including culture industries, is vital because for African Americans as a group, employment levels are persistently lower than for every other racial group. For example, in September 2015, the Bureau of Labor Statistics reported a huge racial employment gap for young adults between the ages of sixteen and nineteen, with a 31.5 percent unemployment rate for African Americans compared to a 13.9 percent unemployment rate for white Americans. For men and women twenty years old and over, African Americans likewise had more than double the unemployment rates of white Americans, 9.2 percent compared to 4.4 percent.[12] Even these numbers drastically underestimate the gap between Black and white unemployment, since they do not include incarcerated citizens, of which African Americans are disproportionately overrepresented.[13]

Closing the racial gap in unemployment requires effort from all sectors, including entertainment industries. Yet popular culture industries such as Hollywood are rarely included in discussions about places where

Figure 1.2. 1963 March on Washington. Courtesy of National Archives.

African Americans have been historically overlooked in employment and where significant efforts to increase Black employment can be made. Hollywood still has much work to do with its inclusion of African Americans in all positions in cinema. The Hollywood workforce includes a range of jobs beyond directors: set designers, gaffers, office workers, lab technicians, visual artists, colorists, and carpenters, to name a few. Major culture industries, therefore, should not be overlooked in efforts to close the racial employment gap.

Beyond images and gestures characterized by symbolic representation, numerical representation is preoccupied with questions of demography and parity, measured by proportions and employment numbers. The central aim of equality becomes to make the proportion of African Americans in Hollywood equal to or greater than their share of the general U.S. population. In this vein, sociological research has highlighted racial inequality in the occupational careers of African American writers, actors, and directors.[14] For instance, studies by William and Denise Bielby and Darnell Hunt and colleagues have concluded that African American writers are well underrepresented in relation to the U.S. Black population. Recent studies have thoroughly documented various aspects of minority underrepresentation and marginalization in film directing, concluding that Black directors are underrepresented in relation to Blacks' proportion of the U.S. population and are otherwise marginalized in the profession.[15]

A number of academic studies have demonstrated the significance of employment in power roles for other positions on film sets. Employment of African Americans in prominent positions of control, especially as Hollywood directors or producers, increases both the number of work opportunities for Black talent behind the camera and the number of on-screen speaking roles for Black actors. In a 2014 study of the one hundred top-grossing movies of the year, Stacy Smith and colleagues found that when no Black director was behind the camera, less than 11 percent of characters on-screen were Black; however, when a Black director was behind the camera, 46 percent of characters on-screen were Black. The presence of a Black director increased the number of Black actors more than four times over.[16] The director Tim Story describes his efforts to diversify acting roles: "I make it a point to do those movies where I can actually put Black people as well as Latinos in those parts."[17] In addition, Chris Rock explains how he personally uses his platform to provide opportunities for entry into work for other African Americans: "I try to help young Black guys coming up because those people took chances on me. Eddie [Murphy] didn't have to put me in *Beverly Hills Cop II*. Keenen Wayans didn't have to put me in *I'm Gonna Git You Sucka*. Arsenio [Hall] didn't have to let me on his show. I'd do the same for a young white guy, but here's the difference: Someone's going to help the white guy. Multiple people will. The people whom I've tried to help, I'm not sure anybody was going to help them."[18] By Story's and Rock's estimations, as well as through the testimonies of other Black directors and film scholars, the best advocates for African Americans' employment have always been, and perhaps will forever be, other Black workers on the job.

In positions of influence on movie sets, Black Americans in larger and more powerful roles are able to advocate for and demand inclusion for Blacks in other positions. Their involvement facilitates a process by which they can break down color barriers on historically "lily-white" film crews, trade organizations, and technical unions.[19] Underrepresentation in directing jobs leads to decreased opportunities for Black Americans in the workplace, which means less authority in the decision-making process and fewer profits.

More African Americans working in Hollywood would mean greater control over images that travel to audiences worldwide.[20] Hollywood exerts a widespread domination of mass dissemination, production, distribution, and exhibition of popular culture in both American and global markets. According to the cultural theorist Stuart Hall, dominant groups monopolize control over public communication and therefore over public meaning and cultural influence in society.[21] Dominant groups, which are best positioned to use cinema to serve their own interests, encode cinematic texts, for instance, to shape public events and to reinforce their ideologies. In contrast, marginalized groups are not generally well situated to create and disseminate their own meaning systems through popular movies. As it stands, marginalized racial groups exert little control over the production and content of cinematic images that are consumed by mass audiences. However, it is important for racial minority groups to penetrate all levels of the film industry in order to harness power and control over global media systems.

Representation in cinematic production and distribution is essential because directors hold immense power to influence what images come across our television and movie screens. Hollywood plays an important and critical role in the creation and dissemination of ideologies through images, narratives, themes, and genres. Calling cinema "a mind molding art form," the director Neema Barnette stresses, "There are some of us who are storytellers who understand that film is the strongest political tool that we have. Some of us got into the art form because of that, and I'm one of them."[22] Barnette reflects on cinema as an art form that possesses unparalleled strength in its ability to move and affect audiences across the world, even in the face of new digital and communication technologies. Through the medium of cinema, film directors, as drivers of vehicles that influence and affect thoughts, perceptions, self-esteem, politics, and policy, play an important role in disseminating, legitimating, and rationalizing worldviews.

This is not to suggest a unidirectional relationship between movie directors and audiences that is uncontested; audiences also play a role in interpreting movie messages. For example, viewers heralded the decision to make a female reboot of *Ghostbusters* (2016), but many were unimpressed that the only Black female character (played by Leslie Jones), who is also the only nonwhite member of the Ghostbusters team, was the only nonscientist of the group. Instead, she played the role of a transportation worker. Jones responded to critics on Twitter: "Why can't a regular person be a Ghostbuster? And why can't I be the one who plays them, I am a performer."[23] On the one hand, viewers felt that the role kept Black women circumscribed into their narrow box of roles in mainstream cinema. On the other hand, the role brought the lived experience of workers to light through Jones's performance.

As cultural objects, movies can be interpreted and evaluated in various ways, sometimes in manners that contradict intended meanings. Audiences embrace some portions of media and reject others. Social experiences and characteristics such as race, gender, class, education, political affiliation, religious affiliation, and locale also structure how people make sense of movies, often depending on how much a social category is privileged in a film. Besides individual readings, social-group interactions and dynamics can lessen or intensify evaluations of movies and movie characters.[24] Even though audiences exhibit control over how they react to movies, cultural producers and creators, such as film directors, set the stage for what cultural objects are available for consumption and interpretation. Controlling this sphere of fictional reality gives cultural workers vast authority over the imaginings that the majority of audience members devour uncritically at leisure. The director of *Meteor Man* and *The Five Heartbeats*, Robert Townsend, remarks, "Films are powerful. Images are powerful—they can travel around the world. . . . Even though [*Hollywood Shuffle*] was my first film, it gave me an education on the power of images."[25] No doubt, directors' presence or absence behind the camera helps shape what images are seen and what images remain invisible. But more than creation of images alone, representation in film directing is a measure of power to execute one's vision of art and life in an influential culture industry.

Discussions around the politics of representation emerge in decisions about who should direct movies showcasing Black issues or icons. August Wilson, who wrote the play *Fences* and optioned the movie as a feature film before his death in 2005, said that he wanted a Black director to helm the film adaptation: "I declined a white director, not on the basis of race, but on the basis of culture. White directors are not qualified for the job. The job requires someone who shares the specifics of the culture of African Americans."[26] Besides Wilson, other directors believe there is something more to directing movies of cultural or historical significance beyond technical proficiency. John Singleton chose not to direct a studio biopic about the late rapper Tupac Shakur, posting on Instagram,

> The reason I am not making this picture is because the people involved aren't really respectful of the legacy of Tupac Amaru Shakur. . . . [Tupac's] real fans just know I am still planning a movie on Tupac. . . . It doesn't matter what they do mine will be better. . . . Tupac was much more than a hip hop artist. . . . He was a black man guided by his passions. . . . Of most importance was his love of black people and culture. . . . Something the people involved in this movie know nothing about. . . . Real talk! How you gonna make a movie about a man when you suing his mother to get the rights to tell his story?! They have no true love 4 Pac so this movie will not be made with love!"[27]

Both Wilson and Singleton are tuned into the rampant misrepresentation and stereotyping of African Americans that occurs on U.S. screens. For Wilson, knowledge of culture is paramount in the execution of movies about African American communities. For Singleton, love and appreciation of Black culture and people is a key ingredient in making a movie that is not only antiracist but also respectful of popular Black artists. The intentions, awareness, and empathy of the director make a difference in the outcome of the film and portrayals of characters and stories.

The assumption underlying most calls for increased representation of marginalized racial groups is that more representation would lead to more humanizing images on-screen. Although directors' presence or absence behind the camera does not necessarily mean that less stereotypical or more multidimensional and complex racial representations are sure to follow, there is reason to believe that people of color behind the camera would improve on-screen images. For example, Robert Townsend remarks, "When you look at my career, I've tried to stay on course in my mission to uplift people of color."[28] Black Americans' employment in high-paying and lucrative occupations in a competitive industry such as Hollywood holds immeasurable weight for the well-being of broader communities beyond the benefits it bestows on any single individual.

Cultural Bell Ringers

Another pressing concern is how underrepresentation in the film industry undercuts rights to citizenship. Citizenship rights are additional facets of representation in Hollywood that deserve recognition. Assessing the level of representation in media is one method of gauging a racial group's access to cultural citizenship, which includes standard components such as voting rights and free speech but also the right to produce and be recognized in a nation's dominant cultural myths, narratives, and images.[29] In this sense, African Americans have been disenfranchised during Oscar season when the film industry votes for the highest awards for creative talent of the previous year.

Awards ceremonies are as much cultural as they are political and geopolitical. Awarding a movie with an Oscar sends a symbolic message to people across the globe. Earlier, we heard one Hollywood insider, Laura, lament that *12 Years a Slave* might send out an "uncomfortable" global "message" that whites in America "are or were terrible people."

She called Academy of Motion Picture Arts and Sciences members "American cultural bell ringers." Symbolically, their awards function as a sounding board that calls attention to certain art works and, in doing so, labels some movies and not others shining examples of American culture. Laura recalls, "The Academy consists of approximately 6,000 white 60-year-old-men who are educated, experienced filmmakers who take their voting power seriously. They are all fiercely patriotic and very aware of our day by day international standing politically and culturally."[30] Laura's mention of fierce patriotism demonstrates how movies, beyond their significance as individual art forms, embody national cultural representations and are intended to speak to the world about the American cultural canon. Interestingly, Academy voters understand that their movie choices should reflect the nation's "international standing politically and culturally." Part of regular business practice in the film industry involves deciding what movies travel to other parts of the world, with foreign-market distribution determining the relative ease or difficulty movies have in entering international markets. Those subjective assessments, which are racially skewed to favor whites and disadvantage Blacks, demonstrate the immense power that Hollywood insiders possess to define what counts as American cinematic culture on a global scale.

Having few voices in Hollywood and little representation in the Academy of Motion Picture Arts and Sciences, African Americans are unable to vote in proportional numbers for industry awards, which play an integral role in enhancing visibility and bolstering careers. A *Los Angeles Times* survey of 6,028 Oscar voters in 2012 showed that 93 percent of Oscar voters were white. Future predictions project the Academy membership to be 89 percent white, at its *most* diverse outcome, by 2023—which still means that Black, Asian, Latino/a, and Native Americans, who currently stand at 36 percent of the U.S. population, collectively would have only 11 percent of Academy votes.[31] With few Oscar ballots, these groups have diminished rights to representation in the voting process for the film industry's annual awards ceremony.

On several occasions, the dearth of racial minorities recognized at the movie industry's annual awards ceremony has raised protests, in both the physical and virtual worlds. During the 2015 ceremony, the hashtag #OscarsSoWhite became a trending topic on Twitter, as social-media users reacted to the dearth of Black, Asian, Latino/a, and Native

American nominees.[32] Some Academy members did not empathize with the calls for inclusion. In response to the #OscarsSoWhite controversy, one disgruntled white female Academy member ranted anonymously, "When a movie about Black people is good, members vote for it. But if the movie isn't that good, am I supposed to vote for it just because it has Black people in it?"[33] With criticism and approbation for popular cinema come high levels of subjectivity—which is all the more reason why it is important that African Americans and members of other marginalized racial groups realize their rights to include their subjectivities on decisions made in the Academy Awards program in particular and in Hollywood more broadly.

Methods of acquiring membership to the Academy, and thus attaining voting power, are problematic, in that they privilege whites who have existing connections to Hollywood and to the Academy. Directors and other creative personnel can become members by receiving an Oscar nomination, getting a recommendation from two existing members, or getting an endorsement from an Academy membership committee or staff. Barriers to entry make it difficult to achieve racial equality in Academy representation.

Recent amendments to the voting rules have led to more diverse incoming cohorts, though diversity in leadership at the helm of the Academy of Motion Picture Arts and Sciences also affects who is able to vote for awards and ultimately shapes who is nominated and wins. Cheryl Boone Isaacs was the first African American president of the Academy, elected in 2013 to serve for four consecutive one-year terms. During her tenure, she prioritized increasing diversity in the Academy, inviting a record 683 people, 41 percent of whom were racial minorities. During this wave, more Black talent received invitations to join, including several Black directors: Keenan Ivory Wayans, Dee Rees, Ice Cube, Ryan Coogler, and others. The viral #OscarsSoWhite hashtag of 2015 described an extreme lack of diversity, with white actors receiving all twenty acting nominations. Subsequently, as a result of critical changes in the Academy's organizational structure, with an infusion of people from various racial backgrounds as members of the Academy with voting power, Academy nominations and awards have become more diverse.

The sociologist Darnell Hunt lauds the changes that have taken place to enable a more racially inclusive awards program and organization.

Hunt says, "The Academy is now talking about the issues in major ways as opposed to apologizing for them, which is what they had done prior to that. They actually made some changes in terms of the voting rules, and they've been bringing in much more diverse new members every year, and a lot of that was under [Cheryl Boone's] leadership. There's no question she's made an impact. The question is, will [the Academy] continue to move in this direction under new leadership, and will they continue at the same pace?"[34] Black representation in key leadership positions proved to be of immense importance for achieving greater recognition at the Academy Awards. Boone's leadership demonstrates that racial representation has tangible outcomes with regard to opportunities for people of color. It remains to be seen, however, whether the momentum for inclusion can continue after Boone's tenure as president comes to an end and other presidents preside over the Academy.

Cultural citizenship includes the right to participate in shaping a nation's cultural narratives. The ability to contribute to the nation's dominant cinematic cultural narratives is as much an inalienable claim to citizenship as is any other right. However, Jim Crow systems result in marginalized groups' loss of basic citizenship through political disenfranchisement. Barriers to attain equal rights to produce popular cinema resemble exclusions from citizenship that characterized the experiences of Black people during previous Jim Crow eras. Lacking the capabilities to contribute to cinematic expression in an ideal fashion, African Americans achieve only an incomplete cultural citizenship and belonging in the United States.

Black Directors: Then and Now

The quest for representation in Hollywood for Black directors has run the gamut from full exclusion to a growing inclusion. Throughout the vast majority of the twentieth century, African Americans were barred from directing Hollywood films. In the onset of the American film industry and the Hollywood system, African Americans were excluded as directors at major Hollywood studios. Barred from the mainstream film industry, African Americans such as Oscar Micheaux and Spencer Williams labored outside Hollywood studios, starting independent film companies and disseminating "race movies"—films that, from the 1910s through the 1950s, centered on Black themes, featured Black casts, and targeted Black audiences.[35] Some producers especially stood out from the bunch. During the silent-film era, Bill Foster's Chicago-based Foster Photoplay produced short films such as *The Railroad Porter* (1912) and *The Fall Guy* (1913). Soon after, the Universal Studios actor Noble Johnson founded the Lincoln Motion Picture Company, which likewise produced short films, its first being *The Realization of a Negro's Ambition* (1916).[36]

Following the production of short films, African Americans ventured into feature filmmaking. By far, the most prominent filmmaker during the silent era was Oscar Micheaux, who in 1918 started the Micheaux Film & Book Company and in 1919 directed the first feature-length film by an African American filmmaker: *The Homesteader*, a film adaptation of his second novel. Over the course of his prolific career, Micheaux made twenty-six silent films and seventeen sound films.[37] In the late 1920s, however, Black cinema's progress faced strong obstacles including the depletion of financing in the time of the Great Depression and a lack of resources during the transition from silent to sound films. Still, independent Black filmmaking and race movies thrived up until the 1950s, with filmmakers such as Spencer Williams, who started the Lincoln Talking Pictures Company. Despite early filmmakers' successful careers outside Hollywood, all the while, Black Americans remained entirely excluded from directorial work within mainstream film companies. Like the racial order of the broader society, this situation was bound to change in the coming decades.

During the 1940s, the top priority for Black Americans in the film industry became the push for integration into Hollywood. These aspirations followed a growing integration ideology of antidiscrimination rhetoric, spurred by African American troops fighting for equal treatment in the armed forces during and following World War II.[38] Increasingly, African Americans brought pressure on institutions to end racial discrimination and integrate schools, communities, and workplaces. Led by the Hollywood chapter of the National Association for the Advancement of Colored People (NAACP), African American directors challenged their exclusion from white Hollywood companies.[39] Advocates lobbied to improve the on-screen portrayal of Black characters and to increase the behind-the-camera presence of Black creative talent on mainstream films. African Americans also participated in letter-writing campaigns, picket lines, protests, and boycotts to advocate for film-industry jobs on-screen and behind the camera. This activism during the civil rights era orchestrated the entry of Black directors into Hollywood in the post-civil-rights era.

Since the end of the civil rights era, African Americans have gained increased access to directing films at Hollywood studios. With Gordon Parks Sr.'s film adaptation of his novel *The Learning Tree*, he became the first African American to direct a Hollywood film, for Warner Brothers, in 1969. Yet amid the 1960s era of social-problem films, on-screen fictional advancement far outpaced behind-the-camera working conditions for racial minorities. During the 1970s Blaxploitation era, Melvin Van Peebles directed *The Watermelon Man* (1970) for Columbia, Gordon Parks Jr. directed *Superfly* (1972) for Warner Brothers, Ivan Dixon directed *Trouble Man* (1972) for 20th Century Fox, and Michael Schultz directed *Car Wash* (1976) for Universal Pictures—to name a few who pioneered entry into Hollywood.

Whereas before the 1960s, there were no Black directors in Hollywood, by the 1980s, African Americans accounted for between 2 and 3 percent of film directors, according to Directors Guild of America membership. Subsequently, the 1980s and 1990s brought about what the film scholar Ed Guerrero calls the "Black Film Boom"—a spike in directing, with Hollywood studios optioning independent works of Black filmmakers for commercial release.[40] This group of commercial independent trailblazers included Spike Lee, the writer/director of the 1986 romantic comedy *She's Gotta Have It*, about a woman and her three lovers; Robert Townsend, the writer/director of the 1987 satirical comedy *Hollywood Shuffle*, about stereotyped roles for Black folks in show business; and John Singleton, the writer/director of *Boyz N the Hood* (1991), about the lives of three young men in South Central Los Angeles.

Black women also gained access to Hollywood film directing, beginning with the Haitian-born Euzhan Palcy, who directed *A Dry White Season* (1989) for Metro Goldwyn Mayer (MGM). Years later, the Miramax film *Just Another Girl on the I.R.T.* (1993), a coming-of-age story about an adolescent girl in Brooklyn, became the first mainstream film released to theaters that was written and directed by an American-born Black woman, Leslie Harris. In 1994, Darnell Martin's *I Like It like That*, for Columbia, became the first Black-female-directed film distributed by a major Hollywood studio. Martin's entrée into directing was followed by that of other Black female directors. In 1997, for example, Kasi Lemmons wrote and directed *Eve's Bayou*, a period drama that followed a mystical Louisiana family during the 1960s. Three years later, Gina Prince-Bythewood wrote and directed the popular sports romance *Love and Basketball* (2000). By the 2000s, the percentage of Black directors had nearly tripled to between 6 and 8 percent and also included a number of female directors.[41] In just a few short decades, Hollywood became more inclusive of Black directors. The pendulum of Hollywood film directing swung from complete exclusion to growing inclusion.

Still, directors and audiences witness an unsteady number of Black movies in theaters. Tyler Perry, known for his Madea comedies and dramas, describes this pattern as waves of Black movies that come and go: "Hollywood always has a wave, and in these waves comes films about people of color. It's just a wave that happens and once it crests, it goes away. Back in the nineties there were lots of movies about African American people, then I come along for many years and it's only me out there."[42] Over the years, there has hardly been a strong, uninterrupted output of Black-directed movies in theaters. Rather, there are ebbs and flows, highs and lulls. The media researcher Stacy Smith and colleagues report no meaningful change in the percentage of Black directors of top-grossing films between 2007 and 2013. In fact, only 6.5 percent of the one hundred top-grossing films in 2013 had Black directors: Malcolm D. Lee's *Scary Movie 5* and *Best Man Holiday*, Tyler Perry's *A Madea Christmas* and *Temptation*, McQueen's *12 Years a Slave*, Lee Daniels's *The Butler*, and Antoine Fuqua's *Olympus Has Fallen*.[43]

Beyond the sheer inconsistency in the presence of Black directors behind the camera of Hollywood motion pictures, these trends also reflect that when the film industry as a whole takes a hit and the total film output for all studios decreases, racial minorities receive the hardest blows and suffer the most in lack of employment. This harsh reality is consistent with other studies that report that Blacks are the first to be fired from companies when business subsides.[44] At any rate, their level of representation throughout the history of Hollywood remains below their 13 percent share of the general U.S. population.

Despite an overall promising increase in African American participation in film directing over the past decades, the problem of racial inequality in the film industry remains a constant fixture in contemporary public discourse and among scholars of film, media, communications, sociology, and economics. Film professionals, content creators, activist groups, critics, and audiences also sense problems amid progress. Accusations of racial inequality and discriminatory treatment still remain prominent, and the subject of racial representation has not departed from the minds and platforms of activists seeking a Hollywood reformation. With no palpable movement toward reaching parity for African Americans in recent years, the industry's racial disparities impede progress to achieving full equality in cinematic production. However, improving numbers alone cannot alleviate Hollywood's extensive race problem. The missing piece is taking sustained and persistent action to diversify critical positions of power.

More than Mere Numbers

Though the directing profession still remains largely and disproportionately white, those who believe Hollywood is alleviating its racial woes point to the numerical and symbolic progress as evidence of a commitment to promises made in the spirit of the familiar civil rights rhetoric—that slowly but surely, in the words of the soul singer Sam Cooke, "change gon' come," eventually. To a great extent, the vision of change that has been articulated is a change of numbers or demography. The sociologist Herman Gray reports that demography became an essential point of reference following the push for representational parity in media industries. To assess representation and monitor its effectiveness, the salient benchmark became literally counting the number of workers in jobs.[45] Scholars and industry professionals turned their focus to the issue of employment and unemployment, to the question of how many workers occupied each space. The central site for contestation and regulation naturally became a numbers game.

Even while representation in the film industry matters a great deal for directors, the interpretation of behind-the-camera representation has focused almost exclusively on a single dimension—numerical representation—and ignored other ways of conceptualizing representation. Calculating numerical representation, studies have assessed the level of inequality or equality primarily on the basis of the percentages of people present or absent. On these terms, the key measure of progress in Hollywood directing is the addition of more directors from underrepresented racial groups behind the camera, while the key obstruction to integration becomes the problem of underrepresentation.

Framing the debate about inclusion into Hollywood solely in binary terms of representation (presence) and underrepresentation (insufficient presence or absence) raises problems. If the primary issue is underrepresentation, then the singular resolution to racial inequality is increased representation. By this standard, true integration would be realized when African Americans and other underrepresented racial groups have reached parity with regard to their proportional representation in the U.S. population. In other words, once the proportion of Black directors of Hollywood movies reaches 13 percent, all inequality would be overcome. However, it is problematic to make a leap to equality from mere parity in numerical representation. Framing the debate as an either/or issue—either presence and inclusion or underrepresentation and exclusion—elides the key problem at hand. Many scholars and observers would agree that demography is a necessary but insufficient factor for adequate representation in cinematic production.

Indeed, Gray problematizes the idea of using diversity as a proxy for inequality. Namely, diversity is a sociocultural goal, while inequality speaks to a multitude of components: a specific history of exclusion, the vicissitudes of protest and unrest, and an ultimate mission of gaining access and equality. The sole reliance on demographic representation and the quest for greater diversity holds dear the assumption that becoming more diverse—achieving social parity via increasing numbers—would alleviate inequality in the film industry, redress stereotypical images and content, and usher in social justice.[46] Adequate demographic representation is required to achieve diversity and is an important aim in and of itself for reasons of employment and citizenship, but demographic parity alone is insufficient to achieve equality.

While some measure of progress is captured through increased representation—if there are greater numbers of Black, Asian, Latino/a, and Native people working in Hollywood—only tackling the issue of numerical underrepresentation would not eradicate *all* racial inequality within Hollywood directing. Demography alone tells us little about the contours of directing careers, as numerical representation does not take into account qualitative differences that directors experience within their workplace environments. Numerical representation alone cannot explain whether there are qualitative differences in the movies Blacks and whites direct, a difference that in no small part facilitates racial disparities in career trajectories. Merely relying on numerical representation can result in observing progress that is more symbolic than substantive. African Americans can appear to have a greater presence in Hollywood, but upon closer inspection, their presence could remain only marginal to core film-industry operations. Having racial minorities occupy key decision-making positions is important to their prosperity in the film business. As Cheryl Boone's leadership in the Academy illustrates, executive position matters in the opportunities generated for racial minorities. In cinema, what is being green-lit, by whom, and with what kinds of production budgets matter a great deal. These kinds of details cannot be captured by measuring demography but require a finer prism through which to examine the full spectrum of representation.

As studio executives in positions of power, African Americans are influential in bringing movies with Black casts, stars, and directors to audiences. For one example, Devon Franklin worked as a studio executive at Sony Pictures and MGM. At MGM, he worked on movies such as *Be Cool* and *Beauty Shop*. As senior vice president of production for Columbia Tristar Pictures for Sony, Franklin worked on *The Karate Kid* reboot, starring Jaden Smith, and *The Pursuit of Happyness*, *Hancock*, and *Seven Pounds*, starring Will Smith. In addition, at Sony, he developed and supervised movies that were geared toward the urban and faith-based markets. He worked on the faith-based hit movies *Not Easily Broken* and *Jumping the Broom*, both produced by Bishop T. D. Jakes, as well as *Heaven Is for Real* and *Miracles from Heaven*. Few executives from racial-minority backgrounds exist in Hollywood. The chief executive at Warner Brothers, Kevin Tsujihara, is a rare Asian studio executive in Hollywood. Just as white studio executives bring white movies to audiences, integrating the executive ranks would likely lead to more racially diverse movies on-screen.

Beyond inequalities of numerical representation, further obstacles to equality persist for Hollywood directors such that increased representation behind the camera cannot single-handedly close the racial inequality gap. There is no denying that Hollywood has made progress, since its exclusionary years before the civil rights era, toward greater inclusivity of African Americans in film directing. Yet it is premature to suggest that Black directors who do break into the film industry automatically experience work conditions on par with white directors working in the industry. Rather than asking how many racial minorities occupy direct-ing positions, the more telling question is: How do the work experiences of directors from different racial backgrounds differ from one another? To allow for a more complete and complex understanding of obstacles to equality for film directors in twenty first century Hollywood, it is nec essary not only to monitor the demographics of representation but also to understand recurring patterns of representation that result in racial hierarchies and unequal outcomes. Besides visibility and demography, other metrics for progress—such as access to lucrative opportunities and ample resources—are important for assessing inequality in film-industry work. Examining the hierarchical level of cultural representation, as it relates to who occupies what types of positions in Hollywood, gives a more refined portrait of privilege and power in the director's chair.

Hollywood Black directors encounter an enduring racial inequality that is a direct product of the society that they inhabit and in which they work. In order to thoroughly investigate how racial inequality oper-ates in Hollywood, it is first vital to comprehend how racial inequality operates within the larger American social context. Racial hierarchies of privilege, power, and oppression have been prevalent in the United States since the nation's inception. Racial inequality was built into the fabric of the United States, residing deep within the bones of the nation's social practices, pastimes, and organizations, while creating a kind of racial skeleton undergirding social life that shapes interracial relations among members of various groups.

In the early centuries of American social life under the prevailing sys-tem of slavery, to name one racial regime, white Euro-Americans trum-peted an ideology of white superiority and Black inferiority in order to justify hundreds of years of enslavement of Black people. During slavery, the social order stratified whites and Blacks, labeling the ma-jority of whites "free men" and the majority of Blacks "chattel slaves"— forced laborers brought in chains from African coasts across the Atlantic Ocean to become the property of free whites. With regularity, African people were subject to inhumane treatment and brutality of savage proportion—lynchings, whippings, rape, and killings at the hands of white Europeans who were themselves newly arrived on North American shores. The system of slavery not only relegated African Americans into inferior positions in society but also perilously threatened their life chances. On the other hand, the slavery era reserved advantaged positions, with privileges of property ownership and inalienable rights to life, liberty, and the pursuit of happiness, exclusively for whites. Entirely on the basis of racial membership, whites and Blacks were subjected to unequal treatment and outcomes. Nationally enforced laws and practices solidified persistent racial inequality, while weakening African Americans' ability to fully participate in society.

Though the capitalist enterprise of American transatlantic slavery has ended, the centuries-long American system left behind an ingrained institutional legacy. The institution was formally dismantled, yet the disparate distribution of material resources and social conditions along racial lines was merely reproduced in other forms.[47] The orchestrated social divisions between racial groups in the United States, along with the lawful discrimination and marginalization of African Americans that initiated during slavery, were manufactured in other ways even after slavery was officially abolished. Soon after slavery, the era of Jim Crow segregation bore its institutional legacy, once again establishing relations of domination and subordination, of privilege and disadvantage, between racial groups.

The organization of Hollywood is not far removed from the operation of racial inequality within the larger American context. Racial hierarchies prevailing in Hollywood privilege or disadvantage creative workers. In the face of obvious gains in proportional representation, racial inequality still persists in the film industry. Although Black directors have increasing access to Hollywood directing compared to earlier decades, the Hollywood Jim Crow prevents them from attaining full integration into the directing profession. The Hollywood Jim Crow creates obstacles to the advancement of Black films and directors, in the same racially hierarchical fashion that has disadvantaged African Americans during each era of U.S. history. Notions of representation in Hollywood are inextricably attached to the profit motive. Predetermined cultural and economic rationalizations made on the basis of race shape the projected value of popular cinema. Hollywood insiders perpetuate the myth that Black films and directors are unbankable, or unprofitable, and that they draw smaller audiences compared to white films and directors. As a result, Black directors face marginalization, segregation, and stigmatization that limits the scope and progress of their careers.

In the racialized film industry, resources and opportunity are distributed along racial lines, such that Black directors experience disadvantages compared to white directors. Rarely do Black directors obtain lucrative, high-status positions. The Hollywood Jim Crow thwarts them from achieving true equality in the motion-picture industry. Race divisions in the film industry have real consequences in the form of barriers that obstruct access to jobs and constrain the scope of American images and worldviews that are disseminated around the nation and the globe. Images from Hollywood are thought of as embodying American cinema, yet this slice of the American cinematic pie omits or obscures whole racial groups. The portrait of a liberal Hollywood and a complete integration for African American directors, as well as for Asian, Latino/a, and Native American directors, is thus far a fairy tale without a happy ending.

Despite the film industry's outward projection of equality, racial disparities persist. Hollywood liberalism appears to display what the sociologist Christopher Winship calls a *veneer of consensus*, a mere surface appearance that differs from the true reflection that lies beneath the surface.[48] By this view, Hollywood's liberal front is emblematic of complete racial integration only superficially, while beneath the surface lies a racially conservative industry that remains monopolized by white men. Although substantively this book focuses on film directors, this lens of hierarchical representation can be used to interrogate how inequality works in other creative professions off camera, from writing to producing. Rethinking representation to closely examine the quality of work within a systemic U.S. racial hierarchy provides a comprehensive way to assess progress toward racial equality in the film industry and beyond.

* * *

Representation in a popular-culture industry involves the interface among creative workers, media organizations, movies, and audiences around the globe. The character of representation takes on different forms. Representation is as much about securing jobs and depicting images as it is about having one's voice heard, being counted, and belonging in a nation. Images and award recognition constitute a symbolic form of representation that stands for something beyond sheer numbers. Representation in the form of numbers ranges from seats around a table of decision-makers to people behind and in front of a camera. Both symbols and numbers are common ways of thinking about representation as a form of demography—counting the tangible presence or absence of racial minorities in a particular medium.

Representation for directors behind the camera has proven benefits. Studies have shown that diversity behind the camera with people in positions of power leads to more diversity in front of the camera with on-screen characters and actors. On a day-to-day basis, representation for a film director in the movie industry means a job, which provides a paycheck and an income that grants the cushion to afford a lifestyle; to support family, friends, and community members; and to build wealth. An absence of regular, well-enough-paying jobs denotes financial and likely other related hardships and economic instability. However, representation can, and often does, take on other forms that are less tangible in measurement. Citizenship is an integral component of representation, as presence in the film industry allows for groups to contribute to a nation's cultural narratives and myths, a form of cultural citizenship.

Insufficient representation in the production of popular movies leads to multifaceted disadvantages. For racial minorities, underrepresentation impedes their ability to disseminate perspectives and ideologies, ultimately having their stories and viewpoints told from others' lenses while obscuring their visions. Underrepresented, they are able neither to sustain careers nor to advocate for work opportunities for other talent. Whose stories are or are not told has social, psychological, economic, and political implications. The history of Black directors in Hollywood reflects their ongoing struggle for adequate representation in the U.S. film industry, a struggle over symbols, images, jobs, citizenship, and more.

Most critics of Hollywood consider demography as a first-order proxy, not the whole picture of inequality. Rethinking representation beyond presence in numbers allows us to interrogate how racial hierarchies further impede opportunities, outcomes, and belonging in cinema. Looking at hierarchies of cinematic representation means exploring where and under what conditions directors are employed, including their films' genres, production budgets, and distribution arrangements. Understanding the complex layers of representation—symbolic, numeric, civic, and hierarchical—is vital in making sense of why racial inequality in Hollywood directing matters and how the effects of racial inequality go beyond any individual director to reverberate in entire communities.

Despite the growing presence of Black Americans in film directing, systemic racial inequality remains embedded within the organizational practices of the film industry. The result is that although Black Americans have surely come a long way, making bold strides into film directing, still, more progress remains before Hollywood can truly be called liberal and until full integration and equality are achieved.

2

Labeling Black Unbankable

About the action thriller *The Equalizer* (2014), starring Denzel Washington, the Hollywood insider Billy surmises, "In general, pictures with an African American lead don't play well overseas."[1] In his correspondence with a white studio executive, he further elaborates, "[The studio] sometimes seems to disregard that a picture must work well internationally to both maximize returns and reduce risk, especially pics with decent size budgets. . . . Casting [Denzel Washington] is saying we're ok with a double if the picture works. He's reliable at the domestic [box office], safe, but has not had a huge success in years. I believe whenever possible the nonevent pictures, extra 'bets' should have a large inherent upside and be made for the right price. Here there isn't a large inherent upside."[2]

In just a few sentences, Billy launches several objections to casting the well-known, two-time Academy Award–winning actor Denzel Washington in a movie with a "decent size budget." Using a baseball analogy, "we're ok with a double if the picture works," he suggests that a film starring Washington could at best only reach second base, with the most opportune scenario falling well short of a home run—a huge box-office success. Billy puts forth the argument that "a picture must work well internationally" to warrant a big budget and then regards Washington as "safe" and only "reliable at the domestic" box office but not dependable to deliver international success. Billy appears to use economic rationalizations to justify why movies starring Black talent, even a known star such as Denzel Washington, must "be made for the right price," for small budgets. Such a strategy, he claims, would "both maximize returns and reduce risk." After all, "there isn't a large inherent upside" to casting Washington. These statements are a telling example of how Hollywood insiders make race-based judgments that constrain movies with Black actors and directors and reward movies with white actors and directors based on biased perceptions of box-office potential.

By labeling white movies as economically superior to movies by or about racial minorities, Hollywood insiders offer market and cultural rationalizations to buttress practices of racial inequality. In this same manner, Jim Crow–era norms legalized disparate treatment for racial groups built on assumptions of racial difference that privileged whites and disadvantaged Blacks. The expression of racial difference is as overt in the twenty-first century as it was in the nineteenth century, except now it is couched in economic and cultural logics, so as to be resistant to accusations of racism and discrimination.

Drawing on opinion surveys of white racial attitudes in the post-civil-rights era, the sociologist Joe Feagin and colleagues find evidence that whites make individual, heartfelt denials of racial discrimination to absolve themselves from racism despite making racist remarks and taking racist actions. The researchers call these narratives "sincere fictions." In their words, "sincere fictions [are] personal ideological constructions that reproduce societal mythologies at the individual level. In such personal characterizations, white individuals usually see themselves as 'not racist,' as 'good people,' even while they think and act in anti-Black ways."[3] Billy similarly employs sincere fictions to absolve himself of racial bias, despite racist, anti-Black comments. When asked directly, "Are you saying *Equalizer* shouldn't have been made or that African American actors should be excluded?" Billy insists, "I am not saying *The Equalizer* should not have been made or that African American actors should not have been used (I personally think Denzel is the best actor of his generation)."[4] The intent here is to commend Washington and the hiring of African American actors in an attempt to appear antiracist, though his earlier criticisms suggest otherwise.

Sincere fictions also arise in the characterization of foreign audiences. The Antoine Fuqua–directed *Equalizer* grossed an estimated $192 million worldwide, nearly four times its $55 million budget, about half of which (an estimated $101 million) came from the domestic box office—though the amount did not meet Billy's box-office revenue expectations that 65 percent of ticket sales (rather than *The Equalizer*'s 47 percent) should come from the international box office. Billy extends an ostensibly heartfelt denial of personally advocating for racial discrimination, to instead blame foreign audiences: "I believe that the international motion picture audience is racist."[5] In other words, Hollywood does not want movies with Black talent to receive small budgets; rather, international audiences, with their weak support for Black talent, are forcing the industry's hand. The argument shares a striking similarity to a remark that the Columbia Pictures industrial relations director Howard Fabrick made decades earlier regarding unionization and racism: "I'm the last guy in the world who would try to maintain that Hollywood has clean hands in the question of minority group employment. . . . But it's not the fault of the studios. The real question for the Justice Department to handle is challenging a union seniority structure that has for twenty years prohibited a studio in hiring in the manner it might, in all good conscience, want to."[6] Sincere fictions allow individuals, and even entire industries such as Hollywood, to blame outside parties for racial-minority underrepresentation and marginalization. Meanwhile, individual behaviors and production practices continue to promote anti-Black business strategies.

When emails between Hollywood insiders were leaked onto the internet, the contents incited anger from observers around the world. Many labeled the statements proof that Hollywood was mired in racism. Indeed, conversations between studio executives, producers, and other decision-makers expose the ways that seemingly harmless everyday conversations can serve to buttress structural racism and racial hierarchies in the film industry. Billy's statements about Denzel Washington serve as a window into understanding how racism operates in the film industry and why Black talent and movies suffer a race penalty under the Hollywood Jim Crow that marks Black movies and directors as economically risky, brands them as culturally unappealing to foreign audiences, and then uses these grounds to marginalize, segregate, and discriminate against Black productions and talents.

Whereas colorblindness and postracialism rely on race-neutral language, arguments, and rationalizations to justify racial discrimination, the Hollywood Jim Crow uses explicit racial language, arguments, and rationalizations. Hollywood insiders outwardly liken whiteness to culturally preferred movies and better financial investments. They reproduce racial hierarchies but blame culture and economics for their disproportionate assignment of rewards and disadvantages along racial lines. The logic goes that racial difference should be tolerated because, for the film business, race has meanings for profit or loss in the cultural marketplace. Equality and morality pale in comparison to the all-knowing bottom line.

Generally, Hollywood executives display a blanket lack of enthusiasm for the profitability of movies with Black talent. Marked as economically inferior to movies with white casts or lead actors, movies with Black casts or lead actors are assumed to possess an inherent disadvantage that stems from biased perceptions that place disproportionate weight on foreign-market revenue and cast doubt on Black movies' and directors' profitability in overseas markets. Black movies and directors are assumed not to perform well—especially among foreign audiences—and are therefore labeled unbankable, not expected to return huge profits at the box office. Hollywood insiders allege that there is no real discrimination against Black directors and movies, only a focus on what strategies will make money and increase profits. The rhetoric is not race related but about marketability, defined as the ratio of commercial success to budget.[7] When a Black film gets a small budget, studio executives contend that the allocation of little funds to Black directors or films is attributed solely to the notion that prior Black-cast films or directors did not make money (though this myth is factually untrue) and, thus, that future films are likewise not expected to return huge profits.

The "unbankable" label affects a movie's marketing strategy. Hollywood executives conceive of small, specific audiences for "Black films" and large, general audiences for "white films" that often go racially unmarked. In turn, Hollywood executives envision raced, segmented audiences and thus heavily market Black movies to Black audiences. What transpires is a self-fulfilling prophecy: raced marketing plans reinforce the perception that Black movies are unbankable to non-Black audiences. Other racial minorities are similarly deemed unbankable compared to white actors and directors. Ironically, the rationale that Black films are unbankable operates against the conventional logics of cultural industries, which normally suggest that it is impossible to predict which cultural products will succeed and which will fail.[8] In contrast, the economic and cultural rationalizations put forth by Hollywood decision-makers suggest that Black films are not expected to succeed or to achieve the level of success of white films. Meanwhile, movies with white directors or casts that perform poorly at the box office are excused. Even in the face of counterevidence, demonstrated by movies with Black directors or casts that perform well and are profitable at the box office, Hollywood still applies the "unbankable" label to Black films and directors, which artificially limits their production budgets and decreases their potential commercial success at the box office.

Raced Movies, Imagined Audiences

Hollywood insiders perceive movies as racial entities. Movies with predominantly Black, Latino/a, or Asian casts or lead actors are thought of in terms of their racial makeup, while movies with predominantly white stars are marked invisible. In this way, whiteness is seen as normal and general—just the way movies are—and Blackness is framed as particular, different, and other. Race-making in the labeling of movies is evident in the way Hollywood insiders think of a movie's similarity to other movies and its promotion to audiences.

Hollywood insiders label movies by race when they compare the box office and audience reception of similar films. When a new movie is on the horizon, usually a "comps" analysis of comparable films gives a range of expected performance criteria based on the outlook of similar recent films that have already debuted at the box office. Generally films are matched by genre and expected audiences, yet another key criteria used to develop lists of comparable films is race—of the star(s), cast, or director. Comps for the Black-star crime thriller *No Good Deed*, starring Idris Elba and Taraji P. Henson, were Tyler Perry's *Temptation: Confessions of a Marriage Counselor* (2013), a Black-cast movie, and the crime thriller *The Call* (2013), which starred Halle Berry and Morris Chestnut.[9] Even while movies of the same genre are being selected, comparable films are also matched along the racial composition of the cast.

At times, race even trumps genre in comparing similar movies. For the Black-cast romantic comedy *About Last Night*, comparisons used were *Think Like a Man*, *Best Man Holiday*, and *Ride Along*.[10] Both *Think Like a Man* and *Best Man Holiday* are romantic comedies starring African American casts, but *Ride Along* is an action-genre movie that stars two Black actors and has a Black director. Similarly, comps used for *Think Like a Man Too* were again the original *Think Like a Man*, *Best*

Man Holiday, and *Ride Along*.[11] Race of the cast is explicitly used to compare movies even when the genres do not match.

Even on potential projects, race is taken into consideration in assembling comps for the movie's projected outlook. For a potential *Harlem Globetrotter* movie, about an exhibition basketball team entertaining audiences through theater, tricks, skills, and comedy, comps listed were *42*, *The Butler*, *Red Tails*, and *Glory Road*, all historical movies featuring story lines with Black characters in feature roles—though only *42* and *Glory Road* are sports movies, baseball and basketball, respectively.[12] The primary commonality across all films is Black men breaking barriers in historical times, whereas white movies about sports are not perceived as comparable movies for the *Harlem Globetrotter* project. Evidently, race is an important factor when conceiving comparable movies. The selection of comparable movies is one stage where race is made relevant in the minds of Hollywood decision-makers.

Concerning the movie *About Last Night* (2014), the Hollywood insider Harry writes, "About Last Night again makes good strides forward with our core African-American demographic."[13] He goes on, "Over the next few weeks we will put everything in place so that we are the must-see event for African-American women, and we are tied inextricably to Valentine's Day. . . . On this film African-American females were always our core, and the hope is the comedy will appeal to guys enough that they're interested as well, or at least it's an easy compromise."[14] Although *About Last Night* is a romantic comedy, as Harry's correspondences make clear, the Black cast of the movie, including Kevin Hart, Michael Ealy, Regina Hall, and Joy Bryant, takes precedence over the genre in marketing the movie. More than all women, African American women are the focus of this advertising campaign.

A pattern becomes evident among Hollywood decision-makers in which, first, movies are branded "Black films" on the basis of their Black casts, as demonstrated in figure 2.1. Second, Hollywood insiders create segmented audiences for these films through targeted marketing campaigns that selectively single out African American audiences. The consumption of "Black films" is heavily pushed along the lines of this segmentation. Black-film reception is steered to Black audiences. Besides an occasional push to gain more Latino/a audiences, there is little effort on behalf of Hollywood studios to market Black-cast films for wider audience reception.

Figure 2.1. Variety headline: "Friday gives life to black niche films." Photo by Kimberly Cecchini, Montclair Film, May 7, 2017.

Similarly, the Hollywood insiders view Latino/a casts as a means to attract Latino/a viewers. For example, Harry writes that *No Good Deed* "features Kate del Castillo, a Mexican actress. . . . [that] on its own is not enough to guarantee commitment but we will try to use her as a conduit to speak to Hispanics who are fans of thrillers." The racial logic goes that a Hispanic actor should draw Hispanic audiences. Hollywood executives target narrow audiences in marketing campaigns for Black- and Latino/a-cast movies. Meanwhile, in a circuitous logic, Hollywood decision-makers retroactively blame these movies for not generating enough interest from broad audiences.

Marketing efforts are extensive. Hollywood studios regularly employ market-segmentation techniques to categorize movie audiences by race, gender, age, or other categories, to strategize how to reach audiences of particular demographics. For example, Hollywood decision-makers categorize audiences into "females under 25," "teen boys 12–16," "African Americans," or "Hispanics"—though generally whiteness is unmarked and invisible in these categorizations. Advertising and promotion expenses are important because they represent funds spent to persuade audiences to buy or watch a movie. Common advertising methods include television spots, articles in trade publications, sneak previews, and promotions in theaters. Unpaid media attention via publicity campaigns, paid promotions and advertising, giveaways, contests, trailers, movie previews, internet promotions, awards ceremonies, festivals, trade press, critic reviews, and other promotional events are all aimed at driving public interest in a movie. Companies develop marketing strategies for particular audience demographics. Studios hire market-research companies to run focus groups and perform test screenings with exit interviews in order to ascertain predictions of viewers' awareness and likelihood of seeing movies.

In the case of Black-cast movies, there is little attempt to drive public interest from broad audiences. The imagined audience for Black-cast movies in the minds of Hollywood decision-makers is first African Americans and second Latino/as in the United States. African Americans are thought to be the core audience for any movie with Black stars. Typically, Black-cast movies are marketed to African American audiences on radio or on network, cable, and reality television programs that feature African American hosts or actors. Black-cast movies are also marketed during National Basketball Association (NBA) and National Football League (NFL) games. Hollywood insiders shape marketing campaigns around audience demographics. The focus of marketing Black-cast movies is what programs are presumed to be of general interest to African Americans. The programs during which ads run reflect the target demographic.

Similar to *About Last Night*, the marketing campaign for *No Good Deed* was targeted to primarily Black audiences. Programs listed for the *No Good Deed* advertising campaign demonstrate an unmistakable focus on African American audiences. The Hollywood insider Claire announces,

Per last week's . . . discussion, the team was able to secure a minimum of 20x :60s in key African-American programming. We did both national syndication and cable inclusive of the following programs:

Queen Latifah
106th & Park

Apollo Live
Love Thy Neighbor
Preachers of LA
Snapped
Sisterhood of Hip Hop
Atlanta Exes Premiere
Love & Hip Hop Finale
Hit the Floor Finale
K. Michelle: Rebellious Soul
Braxton Family Values
Peoples Court
Judge Mathis

We're still pushing and may turn up even a little more. That's the status for now, thanks.[15]

Targeted programs included popular reality television featuring Black talent and programs with Black hosts. As the *No Good Deed* advertising strategy illustrates, Hollywood insiders perceive segmented audiences for Black-cast movies. They specifically target African Americans in media campaigns for Black-cast movies. In addition to the programs Claire mentions, *No Good Deed* ads also appeared on the Black Entertainment Television (BET) Awards, college football, NBA, NFL, TV One, Oxygen, Oprah Winfrey Network (OWN), Lifetime, Lifetime Movie Network, *Details* magazine, *Ebony* magazine, *Live with Kelly and Michael*, Steve Harvey (radio), and Tom Joyner (radio).[16] Studio workers also advertise Black-cast movies on the network WeTV and shows such as *Single Ladies* (with Queen Latifah) and *Being Mary Jane* (with Gabrielle Union) that feature Black actors in prominent roles.

In addition to television and radio, online campaigns for Black-cast movies are heavily targeted to African Americans. Digital campaigns are common on Facebook, Twitter, Instagram, and Vine, with concern for generating millions of social impressions and using online influencers to steer traffic. While the television ads tend to include predominantly African American shows, the targeting for online campaigns is even more pronounced. In another correspondence regarding *About Last Night*, Harry writes,

> We have 17 roadblocks this week across African-American lifestyle and entertainment properties (Essence, BET, Gossip, Styleblazer, MediaTake-out, VH1) and targeted media on broader entertainment sites (Pandora, Tumblr, YouTube & Facebook). We have a Facebook stunt running now targeting African-Americans age 17+, which should reach 95% of that demo on Facebook. . . . We've had a great response thus far, with many people eager to share their support for the film. Digital media launched into full swing this week with hits across BET.com, Complex, Global Grind, VH1, The Urban Daily, Interactive One, Hello Beautiful, Facebook, Twitter, You-Tube, Tumblr, and more.[17]

Blogs, social media, and websites provide studios with virtual sites to extend their targeted marketing campaigns to select demographic groups. *About Last Night*'s promotion included a BET Instagram sweepstakes in which participants uploaded photos referring to different themes in the film, in the hope of winning a grand-prize trip to Los Angeles. Harry writes, "This week we're kicking off the branding campaign with a Facebook stunt, which will reach 100% of African-American females age 13–49 on Facebook, delivering 6MM impressions in 3 days."[18] African American women are a key demographic for Black-cast movies, and social media enables studios to reach them in large numbers.

Besides Black audiences, Hispanic audiences are another racialized group to which Hollywood decision-makers explicitly cater. For example, the Hollywood insider Ralph writes to fellow insiders Jonah and Meg, "Josh Gad speaks fluent Spanish so don't even think I'm not going to be maximizing that asset. He's going to Miami for a press day and he's going to do intros and VO [voice-over] for all our spots in Spanish as well and we are going to push them to all Hispanics on Facebook like we did on NGD [*No Good Deed*] and Equalizer. 53M Hispanics. We are gonna woo them like they ain't ever seen and it's gonna be MUY BUENO!!!!"[19] Using the Spanish language and social media, Hollywood executives daydream of courting the entire U.S. population of Hispanics, potential moviegoers who they hope can increase their bottom line.

On occasion, Hollywood insiders extend advertising campaigns for Black-cast movies to other racial minority groups, especially Latino/a audiences. Regarding media efforts for *The Equalizer*, Claire articulates a strategy to go "deep with incremental African-American and

Hispanic-focused media,"[20] including live reads on Steve Harvey's and Tom Joyner's radio programs and focus on African American television networks such as BET and Bounce and Hispanic radio and television such as UniMas and Estrella TV. The *No Good Deed* campaign also catered to Latino/a audiences. According to Claire, "We are targeting African Americans, skewing female. We also have a layer built in for the Hispanic audience/females."[21] Black-cast movies tend to receive marketing to Hispanic and Black audiences, but Hollywood decision-makers rarely deliberately extend their advertising campaigns beyond U.S. racial-minority audiences. Given that there is little effort to establish wide viewership for Black-cast movies, audience segmentation and targeted marketing campaigns erect a pronounced hurdle for Black movies to jump over in order to be marketed to broad audiences.

As various advertising campaigns demonstrate, there is often a strategic decision to narrowly target African American and Hispanic audiences for Black-cast movies. In the minds of Hollywood decision-makers, the imagined audiences for Black-cast films are African Americans and not general audiences of all races. Next, they consider Hispanics as a second demographic to target. Essentially, studio executives envision that these movies would appeal to less than one-third of the U.S. population and suggest that only small pockets of foreign audiences would find them interesting enough to patronize. Following the logic that heavy marketing to African American audiences, if successful, should presumably lead to more African American audiences patronizing Black-cast movies, the on-the-ground campaigns hit major U.S. cities with large Black populations. In one instance, Harry acknowledges, "We plan to leverage our huge cast for a whole range of great publicity hits throughout this campaign, and our hard working actors and actresses will be traveling to New York, LA, Detroit, St. Louis, Houston, Memphis, San Francisco, Chicago, Miami, DC, and Philadelphia."[22] It should come as no surprise, therefore, that the result of millions of dollars' worth of racially targeted marketing would draw audiences that, by design, overrepresented African Americans.

The mainstream media parrot Hollywood's racial logic of Black movies performing well among some audiences and not others. In a *Los Angeles Times* article about the movie *No Good Deed*, Oliver Gettell writes not only that the film performed well among women of all races but that "the film was also popular with African American moviegoers and performed especially well in large cities including New York, Los Angeles, Dallas, Chicago, and Atlanta."[23] It is no coincidence that large cities with pre-dominantly African American residents were precisely the targets of the studio advertising and promotion campaigns. The success of movies in those metropolitan areas and among Black audiences is in no small way related to where the money goes to create awareness about films. This circuitous logic that Black-cast movies do well in the cities and among the audiences where advertising dollars are focused raises the question: If marketing campaigns were structured differently and targeted elsewhere, for instance, to foreign markets, would patterns of success also change?

Using race and strategically targeting specific racial demographics, Hollywood insiders socially construct audiences for movies. A Black-cast movie that performs extraordinarily well with Black audiences per-haps reflects an effective marketing campaign and likely an entertaining film, to boot. Instead, the interpretation becomes that Black-cast movies *only* attract African American and (sometimes) Hispanic audiences. The origin and directive of the marketing campaigns are conveniently forgotten, though it is highly likely that the imagined audience and the racially imbalanced marketing to target those potential viewers shape the actual audience.

"We're All Chained Together"

"I applaud the success of every Black film. When a Black film hits, that rises all ships. When a Black film flops, that hurts us all. We're all chained together, whether we like it or not. All of us have to root for each other's successes."[24] In this quote, the director Reginald Hudlin advances the idea that one commercially successful Black film breeds many others, while a film that does not perform well hurts the perceptions of economic viability for all Black films. Several directors have echoed this thought, advancing the idea that one successful film could give studio executives greater con-fidence in Black directors' financial returns, thereby encouraging them to make other, similar movies. The filmmaker Russ Parr suggests that all movies with Black characters, themes, or stars—even unrelated films—are nonetheless connected: "A big problem in Hollywood [is] they put us all in the same box. If a Tyler Perry film comes out and doesn't do well, you won't see a Black film for four or five months."[25]

In other cases, directors link the success of particular films or directors to more opportunities for all African Americans. The film director David E. Talbert recalls that the production of his movie *Baggage Claim* (2013) was inextricably linked to the success of Tim Story's *Think Like a Man* (2012)—both are romantic comedies with ensemble Black casts. Talbert explains how Fox Searchlight green-lit *Baggage Claim* in 2010 but then put production on hold until after the success of *Think Like a Man*.[26] Tyler Perry makes a similar remark linking the success of movies with Black stars to opening doors for African Americans: "The thing that caused this dam to break was the success I had for a while but the thing that changed it was the success of *Django Unchained* and *Think Like a Man*. When those movies did that well everything Black got green lit in Hollywood, that's what happened and here comes the wave. As long as they're doing well they'll be here, but as soon as they fall off, we'll go through another lull and then maybe up again."[27] In the same manner, Reginald Hudlin suggests that a successful film with a Black character in an atypical role might lead to the acceptance of similar characters: "I'm working on a big kick ass film and hopefully that success will encourage people to make more movies about Black heroes."[28]

The rhetoric of unbankability has caused Black directors to develop a sense that their individual success stands for more than their individual career gains. In light of the "unbankable" label, they put forward the notion that success matters not only for their individual ability to gain work directing another movie but for the presence or absence of other Black directors and movies. They predict that studio executives group all Black movies together in such a fashion that the success of one movie impacts the odds that studios will take a chance on another, in a domino effect. But if one flops, if one domino fails to catapult the next into motion, the entire industry puts the production of a whole slate of Black films on hold. Industry insiders' communications reveal that they rationalize the practice of linking together the fates of Black movies, for example, the way they assemble lists of comparable movies to develop marketing strategies and predict box-office performance.

Black directors give the success of their films a higher purpose that is linked to the making of future films, appealing to Hollywood's capitalist bottom line. They express optimism that favorable box-office performance could influence studio executives' acceptance of Black movies, while also encouraging studios to make similar movies. By demonstrating that their films are profitable, worthy investments, directors make economic and financial arguments that justify why more Black movies should be made. The logic goes that their success with a film with a Black cast, lead, or theme will enable studio executives to open their eyes and understand that Black movies actually do make money and are very bankable.

However, success does not translate for Black directors as it does for white directors. Unfortunately, hits do not appear to "rise all ships." While it is true that Black films and directors are "all chained together," it does not appear to happen in the way that directors hope. In spite of their successes, they are all chained together as unbankable. Black directors and racial minorities generally bear the burden of "the mark of the plural," a phrase referring to how the mores of white supremacism group all oppressed communities together, particularly with regard to negative outcomes.[29] Failure, especially, is pluralized in a way that any individual negative trait is cast on the entire swath, in this case of African Americans. In contrast, Black success is not uniformly applied to all. Contrary to the way that failures and negative traits become group stereotypes, success is viewed as an exception and not the rule. In the face of multiple box-office hits, Hollywood insiders still label Black movies as unbankable and risky.

A successful Black movie or even a series of successes does not change the overarching mentality guiding how film-industry executives handle Black movies, nor does it change the film-industry production practices that constrain them to low production values. Pertaining to Black movies, the mark of the plural explains how white studio executives view failure (especially in overseas markets) as a norm for Black movies and thus judge all Black movies negatively on the basis of a single failure. In the eyes of studio heads, when Black movies are successful, their box-office performance stands apart from other Black movies. Always the film is said to have performed better than expected. Even after a series of successful performances of Black movies in theaters, studios do not give due credit to these performance through sizable increases in production budgets. Expectations of failure for Black movies remain constant despite several successes.

To be sure, the mark of the plural exposes a double standard for Black- and white-cast movies. For Black films, the myth claims, *Hollywood executives do not necessarily want to exclude Black films and directors, but their films are unsuccessful.* Yet when a white film performs poorly at the box office, Hollywood insiders do not write it off as flopping due to its white cast.

The "unbankable" label for racial minorities conveniently ignores the numerous white movies that routinely flop at the domestic and foreign box office. Hollywood insiders insist that films directed by or starring racial minorities are unbankable. Yet no small number of movies directed by or starring whites have poor box-office showings and fail to recover their initial budgets at the box office. These are just a few examples:

- The Fox Searchlight movie *Demolition* (2016), directed by Jean-Marc Vallee, grossed $2 million domestically on a $10 million budget.
- Louis Leterrier's *The Brothers Grimsby* (2016) cost $35 million to make but only grossed $6.8 million domestically and an estimated $25 million in all markets—still $10 million below its budget.
- David Koepp's *Mortdecai* (2015) grossed an underwhelming less than $48 million in all markets, an estimated $40 million internationally and $8 million domestically on a $60 million production budget. Koepp's *Premium Rush* (2012) also did not make back its $35 million budget in box-office returns, earning an estimated $31 million worldwide.
- The director Pete Travis's *Dredd* (2012) grossed $35 million in all markets, an estimated $13 million domestically and $22 million internationally, on a $50 million production budget.
- Warren Beatty's *Rules Don't Apply* (2016) took in less than $4 million in all markets but was made for $25 million.
- *That's My Boy* (2012), a Sony-distributed picture starring the white actor Adam Sandler, grossed only an estimated $59 million worldwide, less than its $70 million production budget.
- Greg Mottola's *Keeping Up with the Joneses* (2016) made just under $15 million domestically and under $30 million in all markets, $10 million less than its $40 million budget.
- *Popstar* (2016), directed by Akiva Schaffer and Jorma Taccome, took in less than $10 million in all markets but was made on a $20 million budget.

None of these movies with white directors and white casts, to name just a few, performed well enough domestically or internationally to recoup the initial investment. None of these movies was bankable at the box office. The examples of white-directed, white-cast movies that perform poorly at the box office—both domestically and internationally—are plentiful. Yet failed films with white casts and white directors are not rendered unbankable due to the whiteness of the production. They are not penalized in the same way that studio executives penalize movies by and about racial minorities. Hollywood insiders do not attribute whites' underperformance to race, in the way they treat movies with racial-minority directors and casts.

Studio executives never lament, *Those white films never do well at the box office. We should stop investing in them.* Instead, Hollywood operates under a norm that presupposes that white movies always have the potential of bankability, even when numerous movies with white casts amass little profit at the box office or even go straight to DVD, as do most films that lack racial diversity. In placing the onus of Hollywood's dearth of Black movies and directors on Black people themselves, the success myth (that hits will raise ships) blames the victim and transfers the burden of proof to the racially marginalized group—to prove that their movies are worthy of financial support—whereas this burden of proof is never thrust on whites in Hollywood.

Hollywood's double standard that Black movies are unbankable violates the expectation of uncertainty and predictability generally thought to characterize the production of culture. About creative industries, the economist Richard Caves describes one logic that defines creative products across industries—whether in music, book publishing, or film—that "nobody knows" if a creative product will succeed or fail.[30] Likewise, the sociologists William and Denise Bielby posit that "all hits are flukes," to describe the randomness and unpredictability of successful media programs.[31] These statements very well summarize the conventional wisdom of cultural products, such as movies, which suggests that success in popular-culture industries is difficult, if not impossible, to predict. Although this is the agreed-on rule for cultural products, when it comes to movies with Black casts or stars in the film industry, Hollywood decision-makers venture to proclaim the opposite: that they know with certainty that these films will not succeed, that they are, according to one Hollywood insider, a double at best. This subjective predetermination of the fate of Black movies inverts the rule of conventional wisdom that "all hits are flukes" and "nobody knows" what will succeed or fail. Under the Hollywood Jim Crow, where Black is marked with inferior status, organizational practices and industry operations are guided by the assumption that movies with Black stars, casts, or directors will not be hits. The racial logic that Black films are unbankable and that the success of one film or many films does not change the perception of the majority negates the notion that success breeds more success. Along the lines of the Hollywood Jim Crow, "everybody knows" Black movies will not perform well *enough* domestically or well *at all* overseas.

These kinds of assumptions impact the employment of Black directors and the conditions under which they are able to make movies. Economic arguments about actors, films, and directors are used to influence what movies get green-lit and for how much, how movies are marketed and promoted, and how movies perform at the box office. As a result of the economic and cultural "unbankable" label, studio executives locate Black directors away from the industry's major studios and high-profile movies, arguing that they are not sure bets to generate huge profits at the box office. Ultimately, arguments about Black directors and films shape directors' career trajectories in ways that facilitate disadvantage for African Americans, legally disenfranchising them within the film industry's labor market.

Obama Likes Black Movies

In another series of emails, Meg, a studio executive, and Richard, a producer, exchange jokes about what then-president Barack Obama's favorite movies would be. According to them, since he identifies as African American, he is sure to appreciate only movies with African American casts. Meg writes, "Should I ask him if he liked *Django* [*Unchained*]?" referring to the slave-era western released to theaters in 2012. They also suggest that Obama liked *12 Years a Slave* (2013), the antebellum memoir about a captured and subsequently freed Black man; *Think Like a Man* (2012), the contemporary romantic comedy with an ensemble Black cast; and *The Butler* (2013), the historical drama about an African American man who diligently served in the White House under eight white U.S. presidents—all movies featuring Black themes and actors in prominent roles. To conclude, Richard throws another movie into the mix: "Ride-along. I bet he likes Kevin Hart."[32] Their conversation is indicative of a larger pattern: African Americans gain work on cinematic projects only if the themes, characters, or content directly relate to African Americans or racial minorities.[33] Otherwise, they are seldom selected to participate.

The filmmaker, actor, and comedian Chris Rock makes a similar observation, in reference to screen actors, that Hollywood executives hire Black talent only for specific, usually race-related roles: "Now when it comes to casting, Hollywood pretty much decides to cast a Black guy or they don't. We're never on the 'short list.' We're never 'in the mix.' When there's a hot part in town and guys are reading for it, that's just what happens."[34] Rock remarks that African American actors are rarely in consideration for open calls but only when there is a particular request for a Black actor. The same argument—that studio executives seek out a Black director only when they have a particular movie with a Black cast, lead actor, or race-related theme in mind—appears to hold some validity for film directors. For instance, Marvel Studios sought out a Black director for the superhero movie *Black Panther* (2018)—ultimately settling on Ryan Coogler, the director of *Fruitvale Station* (2013) and *Creed* (2015). Black directors are generally hired on movies with Black casts or leads, yet they are largely not under consideration for the vast majority of directing jobs, those with white casts or leads. They are rarely involved in talks about or hired to direct lucrative tent-pole franchise movies. Since Black cast-movies are precisely the movies that Hollywood labels unbankable and devalues, African Americans become relegated to primarily directing movies with low production values, setting them up for paths of economic disadvantage in the film industry. The initial assumption of racial difference in cultural and economic value that governs the Hollywood Jim Crow leads to disadvantaged outcomes for African American directors of Black-cast movies.

Sorting African Americans in specific areas of work is unique neither to the film industry nor to media institutions. Employers sort employees onto different tasks and into different positions on the basis of various factors besides skill; race often plays a role in determining who gets what opportunities in the labor market.[35] In Hollywood, race influences one's assignment to movie projects. On television programs, for instance, African American writers are predominantly ghettoized to write only for characters or shows featuring Blacks or racial minorities. On the other hand, white writers in television are not similarly ghettoized; they are employed to write for all parts, no matter the racial background of the character.[36] Hollywood decision-makers envision whites as universal contributors, while African Americans are expected to contribute only to programs about racial minority groups.

Similar to how Black television writers are almost exclusively employed to write for racial-minority-cast shows or to write for racial-minority characters, film-industry executives tend to hire Black directors almost exclusively to direct movies with Black lead characters, casts, or themes.[37] The assumption is: *Of course, Obama would work on Black movies, because he is Black. What else would be appropriate?* Figure 2.2 shows the race and cast for 124 Black-directed movies released to theaters between 2000 and 2016. More than half of the movies that African Americans

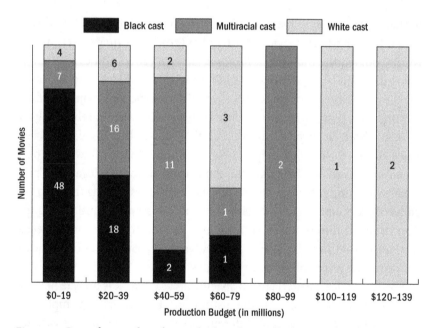

Figure 2.2. Race of cast and production budgets for 124 Black-directed movies, 2000–2016. Production budgets in millions. Data on production budgets from Boxofficemojo.com and IMDb.com. Includes movies distributed by Sony, Universal, 20th Century Fox, Paramount, Buena Vista, Warner Brothers, Miramax, MGM, Focus, Lionsgate, New Line, Fox Searchlight, and Sony Screen Gems.

direct have entirely Black casts, while more than 80 percent have Black or multiracial casts that feature African American actors in leading roles. Meanwhile, white directors and writers are employed to direct movies or write for television shows and characters for any program regardless of the themes, lead characters, or cast's racial composition. As discussed in chapter 3, whites also direct movies with majority-Black casts and with some of the most popular and commercially successful Black actors attached, such as Will Smith, Eddie Murphy, and Martin Lawrence. Not only does this assignment give whites a wide range of opportunities for employment and African Americans a narrow range of opportunities, but it also constrains African Americans to working on movies that studios regularly devalue, label unbankable, marginalize, and ghettoize.

Hollywood's investment in ideologies that privilege whiteness comes through in the organizational structure of cinematic production.[38] The overwhelming whiteness in Hollywood necessitates that studios prioritize white directors who make movies about white people and culture over Black directors who make movies about Black people and culture. Thus, Hollywood executives place a smaller economic value on movies with majority-Black casts, themes, and characters compared to movies with majority-white or multiracial casts, themes, and characters.

As shown in figure 2.2, most movies that African Americans direct are Black-cast movies with small budgets. The budget ranges for Black-, multiracial-, and white-cast movies are quite distinct. Nearly all Black-directed Black-cast films have budgets less than $40 million. Generally with a Black cast, directors can make only medium-budget pictures at best. In contrast, more Black-directed movies with multiracial casts fall into the $20 million to $60 million budget range, an indication that if Black directors desire to work on bigger-budget pictures, they must do so apart from making films with Black casts (a point that is elaborated on in chapter 5). Meanwhile, movies that are budgeted at or over $100 million have majority-white casts. Overall, there appears to be a tiered system for movie budgets on the basis of the race of the cast. To direct films with bigger budgets, typically, African Americans have to direct films with few Black characters—with multiracial or white casts—while films with Black casts receive considerably smaller budgets. The economic logic used to justify this racial disparity has to do with perceived audience preferences. Decision-makers insist that Black-cast movies will not perform well overseas and will only perform well domestically among Black audiences and occasionally Latino/a audiences.

The music-genre film *Be Cool* (2005), directed by F. Gary Gray, featured a multiracial cast, with Andre Benjamin and Cedric the Entertainer alongside the white actors John Travolta, Uma Thurman, and Vince Vaughn. In contrast, the music film *Drumline* (2002), directed by Charles Stone III, starred an all-Black cast. Both movies grossed $56 million at the domestic box office. However, *Be Cool* was made on a $53 million budget, while *Drumline* cost only $20 million to make. In the domestic box office, *Drumline* made nearly three times its budget, while *Be Cool* only matched its production budget. However, the multiracial *Be Cool* received more marketing, promotion, and distribution overseas, which boosted its international box-office performance. In a similar fashion, *Stomp the Yard* (2007), a Black-cast dance movie—directed by Sylvain White and starring Columbus Short, Meagan Good, Darrin Dewitt Henson, Brian White, Laz Alonso, and the rhythm-and-blues singers Ne-Yo and Chris Brown—also experienced great success at the domestic box office, grossing $61 million on a $13 million production budget, thus grossing almost five times its budget. Yet *Stomp the Yard* experienced little marketing, promotion, and distribution in international markets, despite its immense popularity in the domestic market. As these movies demonstrate, the "unbankable" label artificially limits Black directors' production budgets, commercial success at the box office, and career trajectories such that Black directors who direct movies with Black casts or themes see their films made with small budgets, released in few theaters, and offered paltry, if any, overseas distribution.

As an example, Tim Story's Black-cast movies received far less financial support compared to his films with multiracial casts. Set in a barbershop on the South Side of Chicago, the Black-cast comedy *Barbershop* was made on a $12 million production budget yet grossed more than $75 million at the domestic box office—thus grossing more than six times its budget. The film starred the rappers Ice Cube and Eve, the comedian Cedric the Entertainer, and the actors Anthony Anderson, Sean Patrick Thomas, Keith Davis, and Michael Ealy. Story's Black-cast ensemble romantic comedies *Think Like a Man* (2012) and *Think Like a Man Too* (2014) had $12 million and $24 million budgets, respectively. *Think Like a Man* grossed more than seven times its budget, with over $91 million at the domestic box office, while the sequel grossed well over twice its budget, at more than $65 million at the domestic box office. In contrast, Story's action comedy *Taxi* (2004), starring the hip hop entertainer and actor Queen Latifah and the white comedian Jimmy Fallon, was made on a $25 million production budget but grossed only $36 million at the domestic box office. Meanwhile, the multiracial-cast *Fantastic Four* action films were Story's biggest budgeted films, at $100 million for the 2005 film and $130 million for the 2007 sequel. Depending on the cast of the film, different budgets are allocated for production. In this case, Story's Black-cast films were undervalued compared to his films that had multiracial casts. Some of the disparity, especially with *Fantastic Four*, is due to the blockbuster superhero genre compared to comedies, which are usually smaller budgeted. However, a relevant question is also why superhero films are rarely all Black. For decision-makers, Black-cast films are devalued compared to white-cast films. Quite possibly, Hollywood decision-makers rationalize that Black audiences will flock to Black-cast movies no matter how much is invested in them, so they opt to make them for less to increase profits. That Black movies are precisely the projects on which African Americans are most likely to work means that they are deeply disadvantaged by the "unbankable" label throughout their careers.

Snubbed Home Runs

In another email thread, the comedian-turned-actor Kevin Hart requests remuneration to compensate for his efforts using the social media platform Twitter to market his star vehicle, the ensemble romantic comedy sequel *Think Like a Man Too* (2014). In turn, a white Sony executive, Dan, calls Hart a "whore" for asking for money.[39] For Dan, the idea that *Think Like a Man Too* should receive more money for marketing and promotion seems ludicrous. Due to the "unbankable" label, studio executives are reluctant to invest large sums of money in movies with Black casts, leads, or directors, artificially limiting their production budgets and commercial success at the box office.

On several occasions, numerous Hollywood insiders commend Kevin Hart's efforts to promote his movies, with special emphasis to suggest that he goes above and beyond expectations. Regarding promotion for *About Last Night*, Harry remarks, "Online we have a lot going for us on this film, as that is the best forum to showcase the raunchy comedy that makes this film unique. It is also where we can leverage Kevin's immense social following. This week we will combine these assets to launch the 'Hallmark' :60 on YouTube and World Star, with Kevin promoting the piece to his fans. . . . We had Kevin and Regina [Hall] record a video that plays at the end of every word of mouth screening, where they encourage everyone to go on social and talk about how great the movie is."[40] In a similar fashion, another Hollywood insider, Peter, reports on a successful promotion via social media, "[Kevin] put Hallmark card on his Facebook and it has 300k hits in 20 minutes."[41] Harry also commends Hart's promotions on social media, saying, "We'd be here all morning if we were to lay out all the online efforts, but it suffices to say anything Kevin touches turns to clicks. Whether it's on twitter, Instagram, or promoting the videos we release, Kevin and his army of followers are with us every step of the way."[42] Fervent admiration for Hart's promotions unofficially crown him the hardest working man in showbiz.

Besides social-media promotions, insiders are also impressed with Hart's extensive on-the-ground campaign on various television shows, magazines, and programs. For *Think Like a Man Too*, Hart was featured in *Parade, GQ, Elle,* and *People*. For *About Last Night*, Hart appeared on *Ellen, Kimmel, Dancing with the Stars,* and *The Grammys*. Harry writes regarding the success of *Think Like a Man Too*'s premiere, "No doubt part of this great debut is due to our TNT NBA Round 2 Playoff promotion featuring Kevin Hart impersonating all four of the Inside the NBA hosts."[43] The evidence is clear that studio executives and Hollywood insiders believe Hart works hard to make his movies as successful as possible. However, studio executives still complain about the notion of investing more money into Hart and his productions; his movies are still subjected to a ceiling in advertising and promotion due to their Black casts.

It is true that in some cases, as in the case of *Think Like a Man*, commercially successful Black movies are green-lit for sequels. However, a previous commercially viable Black film rarely leads to Hollywood executives showing confidence that future movies will perform well enough at the box office to justify a considerable increase in their production values—hence the strong rebuke of Kevin Hart's request for more money. Overall, the result of the "unbankable" label is that successful movies with Black casts and directors are overlooked. Instead, their collective fate is predetermined. For many studio executives, the success of Black movies hardly diminishes the imagined risk that accompanies them. Information of success does not defog the discriminatory lens through which Black movies are deemed "a double" at best and never a home run.

The narrative of unbankability crumbles in the face of box-office numbers. Distributed by Universal, Jordan Peele's *Get Out* (2017) was widely successful. The horror flick about a young man's nightmarish encounter with his white girlfriend's family at her parents' secluded estate in the woods grossed over $175 million at the domestic box office and over $78 million at the foreign box office on a $4.5 million budget. Also distributed by Universal, Malcolm D. Lee's *Girls Trip* (2017), which starred Queen Latifah, Regina Hall, Jada Pinkett-Smith, and Tiffany Haddish, was the year's best performing live-action comedy film in the domestic market. The comedy about friendship and romance during four women's trip to the annual Essence Magazine Festival grossed more than $115 million on a $19 million budget. The only Hollywood superhero movie featuring a Black cast, the action/adventure movie *Black Panther* (2018), about battles for power within the royal family of a futuristic African nation, shattered the box office, making an estimated $1.3 billion worldwide.

The claim that Black movies and stars are unbankable belies the facts that they are, indeed, quite bankable. Observing this reality, a 2015 *Variety* article stated that although "films with African-American leads topped box office charts for five consecutive weeks in August and September . . . Hollywood continues to act stunned by the power of black audiences. . . . Perhaps it's time to retire the shock-and-awe charade."[44] One of the films leading the box office during this time was F. Gary Gray's *Straight Outta Compton*, a biopic about the hip hop group NWA that made more than $160 million at the domestic box office on a $28 million production budget. Especially given the small budgets of Black movies, they often overperform at the box office. In the domestic market alone, *Compton* returned more than five times its production budget. Evidently, statements that Black movies do not make money at the box office run contrary to actual box-office receipts.

For years, Tyler Perry movies, propelled by Perry's multiyear distribution deal with Lionsgate, have also demonstrated that movies featuring

Black casts and themes can perform quite well at the box office. Table 2.1 shows the domestic box-office gross of Tyler Perry–branded movies, films that Perry produces, directs, writes, acts in, and owns.[45] Collectively, his movies grossed $867 million at the domestic box office, an average of $51 million per film. Accounting for much of Perry's success, his Madea movies—*Diary of a Mad Black Woman* (2005), *Madea's Family Reunion* (2006), *Madea Goes to Jail* (2009), *Madea's Big Happy Family* (2011), *Madea's Witness Protection* (2012), *A Madea Christmas* (2013), and *Boo! A Madea Halloween* (2016)—grossed an average of $64 million at the domestic box office, compared to an average of $42 million for Perry films in which Madea is not the central character. Perry's greatest commercial success, *Madea Goes to Jail* (2009), earned $90 million at the domestic box office. Except for *Single Mom's Club* (2014), notably also his film with the most racially diverse cast, all of his movies grossed

TABLE 2.1. Domestic Box Office, Tyler Perry–Branded Films, 2005–2016

Year	Film	Gross ($, in millions)
2005	*Diary of a Mad Black Woman*	50.6
2006	*Madea's Family Reunion*	63.2
2007	*Daddy's Little Girls*	31.3
2007	*Why Did I Get Married?*	55.2
2008	*The Family That Preys*	37.1
2008	*Meet the Browns*	41.9
2009	*I Can Do Bad All by Myself*	51.7
2009	*Madea Goes to Jail*	90.5
2010	*For Colored Girls*	37.7
2010	*Why Did I Get Married Too?*	60.1
2011	*Madea's Big Happy Family*	53.3
2012	*Good Deeds*	35.0
2012	*Madea's Witness Protection*	65.6
2013	*A Madea Christmas*	52.5
2013	*Temptation: Confessions of a Marriage Counselor*	52.0
2014	*Single Mom's Club*	16.0
2016	*Boo! A Madea Halloween*	73.2

Note: Box-office estimates compiled from Boxofficemojo.com and IMDb.com. *Diary of a Mad Black Woman* was directed by Darren Grant. Tyler Perry directed all other films listed.

upward of $30 million. On the basis of reported numbers, the average budget for a Tyler Perry film is $16 million, which means that on average his movies' box-office performance is more than triple their production budgets, while the Madea-franchise movies make four times their production budgets. Furthermore, *Madea Goes to Jail, Madea's Family Reunion, Why Did I Get Married?* (2007), and I *Can Do Bad All by Myself* (2009) topped the box office during their opening weekends, outperforming other movies that were released at the same time. Tyler Perry's *Boo 2! A Madea Halloween* (2017) and *A Madea Family Funeral* (2018) continue the long-running hit franchise movie series.

Tyler Perry's success prompted John Singleton to speak out against the myth that Black movies do not make money: "Whatever anybody wants to feel and say about Tyler [Perry] movies, he's sustaining the audience. He's proving that you can make a picture that a wide African American audience will go see, and it will be very profitable. And that's what I'm proudest of that he's done because they can't say, Oh, these movies don't make money. There's no audience."[46] Popular with audiences, Perry's movies particularly draw the Black, female, Christian audiences that attended his plays on the theater "Chitlin Circuit" before following him to the silver screen—group similarly drawn to theaters during the pre-1960s race-movies era with the popularity of religious-genre films such as Spencer Williams's *The Blood of Jesus*.[47] The success of African American directors, such as Tyler Perry's repeated box-office triumphs, shows that dedicated patrons of Black images in theaters do exist.

In addition to support from Black audiences, Black movies also receive sizable crossover audiences composed of multiple racial groups. Besides Black audiences, non-Black audiences also desire stories about diverse racial groups. In particular, young audiences increasingly prefer movies with racially diverse casts to movies with homogeneous casts, suggesting that integrating Hollywood movies from the customary white-cast movies to movies with lead actors and casts who are African American would actually help rather than hinder box-office profits.[48] Even audiences thought that white-led films such as *Gods of Egypt* (2016) and *The Great Wall* (2016) should have been more diverse. Meanwhile, *Star Wars: The Force Awakens* (2015)—presenting more racial diversity in its cast than most films in the tent-pole franchise, with Lupita

Nyong'o and John Boyega starring alongside the white actors Harrison Ford, Mark Hamill, and Carrie Fisher, among others—eclipsed all other movies to become the all-time biggest grossing film in the domestic market, with an unprecedented $936 million at the box office. Citing such evidence, scholars and directors argue that myths about Black-cast movies are false and that African Americans' obstacles to Hollywood directing exist in spite of their movies generally having favorable responses from Black audiences as well as sizable crossover audiences of viewers of other races.[49]

In spite of the general rule of limited theatrical releases in foreign markets for Black-directed, Black-cast, and Black-star movies, some exceptions do occur. Black stars can make money overseas, as the Quentin Tarantino–directed *Django Unchained* proved; that film starred Jamie Foxx, Kerry Washington, and Samuel L. Jackson and defied preconceived notions that westerns and movies with Black heroes would not perform well compared to movies with white heroes. Richard confesses that *Django Unchained* is

> [the] highest-grossing Tarantino film of all time, 33% bigger than INGLOU-RIOUS BASTERDS. . . . [It also] performed to the same ratio as INGLOURIOUS (62% of worldwide gross coming from overseas) even with a genre and theme that would seem a lot less likely to do this (Western, African-American hero). DJANGO outgrossed INGLOURIOUS in every region, including Eastern Europe (by 47%), Western Europe (by 33%), Latin America (by 24%), Australia (by 24%), and Africa/Middle East (by 10%). TRUE GRIT, another big western-themed film [with an all-white cast], grossed $171 million for domestic, but international managed just $78 million (31% of the worldwide box office).[50]

Beyond *Django*'s success compared to other Tarantino films, its performance in western Europe beat out all other nonfranchise movies, only registering behind big blockbuster tent-pole movies such as *The Hobbit*, *Hunger Games*, *Iron Man*, and the animated sequel *Despicable Me 2*. The success of the Jamie Foxx–led movie debunks preconceived myths about the limited overseas profitability of Black-star vehicles. However, successful Black-star movies are overlooked as Hollywood decision-makers dogmatically stand by myths that failure for these movies is the norm.

The director Steve McQueen and the actor Chiwetel Ejiofor, both British and Black, headlined *12 Years a Slave*, the tale of a free Black man who is kidnapped and sold into slavery, to a showing of $56.7 million domestically and more than $131 million internationally, roughly a 30/70 split, on a $20 million production budget. However, Black directors and filmmakers insist that "companies sometimes do not support them with the sort of wide international release that is being lined up for *12 Years a Slave*."[51] Stuart Ford, a white British founder and former chief executive of the internationally acclaimed independent studio IM Global, declares, "Despite the perceived wisdom that African-American films don't travel, a great movie is a great movie, and great movies are at a premium right now."[52] Among other movies, McQueen's *12 Years* showed the path for the success of Black-directed, Black-cast movies in international markets. However, studios remain hesitant to invest in Black movies at a comparable level to their investment in white movies.

Ironically, studio executives even acknowledge the success of Black-cast movies, at least in private, behind closed doors. Meg, a studio executive, displays her exuberance for the box-office success of the Black-star movies *No Good Deed* and *The Equalizer*, writing in all caps (the Internet version of shouting), "BETWEN NO GOOD DEED HITTING IT BIG SEX TAPE ACTUALLY HITTING SOME DECENT NUMBERS EQUALIZER ACTUALLY BLOWING IT OUT OF THE WATER [*sic*]."[53] From various vantage points, *The Equalizer* was a successful movie. In an article titled "5 Reasons Why Denzel Washington's 'Equalizer' Exploded at the Box Office," the writer Todd Cunningham recalls, "It was the biggest opening for an R-rated movie ever in September and Washington's biggest since 'Safe House' debuted to more than $40 million in February of 2012."[54] The movie's performance generated career bests for Washington and Fuqua. *The Equalizer* was Fuqua's best opening in his directing career. In addition, the sequel to *The Equalizer* will be Washington's first sequel in his over-three-decade-long acting career.

Yet, despite ample evidence to the contrary, industry decision-makers repeatedly make claims that Black movies are unbankable. Black directors and stars are hardly commended for their successful movies. Notwithstanding support from various audiences, including Black communities, crossover audiences, and even foreign audiences, the model for disseminating Black-cast movies and Black-star films remains restrictive, as there is no effort by Hollywood executives to provide them with greater financial support. All in all, Black directors and actors find immense difficulty shaking the "unbankable" label of the Hollywood Jim Crow.

* * *

Under the Hollywood Jim Crow, Black movies and directors suffer a race penalty. Hollywood insiders label Black stories "unbankable" to suggest that they are not economically viable products and are not guaranteed or expected to make sizable returns at the box office. Hollywood insiders also allege that Black movies would not draw audiences from foreign markets that are key to increasing bottom-line profits. These racial logics craft limited spaces for Black creative talent. Behind the camera, Black directors are primarily assigned to movies with Black casts, themes, and characters—the very movies that Hollywood labels unbankable and perceives to be financially risky. Studios' target audiences for Black-cast movies is majority African American, which is revealed by the way the movies are promoted and advertised. Ad campaigns for Black-cast movies are targeted specifically to Black audiences and secondarily to Hispanic audiences. Subsequently, studio executives allege, in a circuitous manner, that Black-cast movies only perform well with Black audiences, which restricts Black movies and directors to limited paths.

Compared to films with white protagonists, casts, and directors, films with Black protagonists, casts, and directors receive inferior production values, such as small budgets, on the basis of the justification that investing more money into them is too great a financial risk for any sensible business to take. Hollywood insiders use such arguments that Black movies do not perform well at the box office to justify marginalization of Black directors. However, the same reasoning is not uniformly applied to white directors to exclude them from working on lucrative movies. Whereas under the Hollywood Jim Crow, Black directors and their films are labeled unbankable, white directors and their films evade such labels. White directors who previously helmed unsuccessful films are not restricted from directing big-budget pictures. Conversely, successful Black-cast movies and directors are often overlooked as exceptions to the rule of unbankability. Unlike white movies and directors, they are not rewarded with a considerable or consistent increase in production values for future projects. The association of Black movies with negative outcomes runs counter to the conventional principles governing market performance of cultural products in creative industries—that performance is unpredictable, "nobody knows" what products will succeed and fail, and "all hits are flukes." Essentially, the "unbankable" label turns these maxims upside down to say that "everybody knows" Black movies will underperform.

"Unbankable," thus, remains a racial code that is not used objectively but only as a justification for marginalization of Black directors and films. On the basis of the "unbankable" label, Hollywood is free to legally marginalize Black stories and directors. Blackness is devalued and linked to cultural and economic inferiority, and whiteness is valued and linked to cultural and economic superiority—corroborating the Jim Crow logic that assumes racial difference. Here, the marginalization is couched in economic and cultural logics and thus evades violating the norm of racial equality of the post-civil-rights era. In this new age of explicit racism, race is linked to economics and culture in a manner that is also palatable to neoliberal and neoconservative philosophies governed by the pursuit of profit. Racial hierarchies are maintained and reproduced in a mode that continues to privilege whites atop a racial system of cinematic production.

3

Directing on the Margins

The director Rick Famuyiwa is probably best known for his romance dramas *The Wood* (1999) and *Brown Sugar* (2002). *The Wood* became an instant classic among Black film enthusiasts. It starred Omar Epps (as Mike), Richard T. Jones (as Slim), and Taye Diggs (as Roland)—three friends dealing with one's cold feet on his wedding day, interspersed with flashbacks of their youth. In *Brown Sugar*, the hip hop label executive Dre (Taye Diggs) and the magazine editor Sidney (Sanaa Lathan) discover their unexplored love for hip hop and each other. Under Famuyiwa's direction, both films achieved great success at the box office. *The Wood* grossed $25 million at the domestic box office, more than four times its $6 million budget. A few years later, *Brown Sugar* grossed $27 million to eclipse its $8 million budget more than three times. Famuyiwa's most recent movie, *Dope* (2015), is about a geek whose life changes drastically upon receiving an invitation to an underground party in Los Angeles. An independent movie distributed by Open Road Films, *Dope* was made on a meager $700,000 budget yet grossed more than $17 million at the box office, nearly twenty-five times its production budget.

Despite Famuyiwa's proven track record of success, he expresses frustration with stagnant budgets from film studios. He recalls, "Even though I work in the Hollywood system, the budget levels I am at, the schedules I am given, the margins that I have to work with, still feel very much like independent cinema."[1] The Black-cinema scholar Mark Reid asserts that Black directors are relegated to small production budgets despite their films' high marketability, which he defines as the ratio of box-office gross to budget.[2] Illustrated by Famuyiwa's case, having a film perform three or four times its production budget, or more, is not necessarily enough for Black directors to secure work on more financially lucrative film projects.

Sociologists of race advance the theory of racialization to show how a racial order that governs the organization of society would also seep into social institutions, including media institutions.³ Due to racial inequality in the United States, workers in the U.S. film industry are likewise stratified by race. As a racialized popular-culture industry, the Hollywood film industry organizes workers and its occupational structures along racial lines in a fashion that privileges white workers and subordinates workers from marginalized racial groups. As a result, Black Americans are relegated, to a great extent, to subordinate positions of disadvantage in the film industry's labor market. Across employment sectors, racial minorities are known to occupy low ranking positions. This is also true within positions. The pervasive racial structure in society has implications for what places people occupy in the elite occupation of Hollywood film directing.

Film directors are a group of highly skilled, specialized labor. The film scholar Janet Wasko provides a concise summary of the director's role: "The director is in charge of production and is usually considered the 'primary creative force' in a film's manufacture. The director controls the action and dialogue in front of the camera and is therefore responsible for interpreting and expressing the intentions of the screenwriter and producer as set out in the screenplay."⁴ The director's position offers a significant amount of control over a cinematic production. While Black directors have gained increasing representation in Hollywood over the past decades, their opportunities remain limited by persistent experiences of racial inequality that are reminiscent of disparate treatment of African Americans in prior eras of U.S. history.

Today's placement of Black directors in Hollywood draws parallels with Jim Crow systems of racial hierarchy. During the Jim Crow era, racial groups were stratified, with whites having the best resources and privileges and Blacks having the worst resources and shouldering disadvantage in all aspects of social life—from education to public facilities to access to employment. Black directors fare the same in the Hollywood Jim Crow in that they are subject to subordinate positions with diminished resources in the film industry.

The language of framing Black casts and directors as an economic disadvantage is commonplace among Hollywood insiders, or people with decision-making power in the film industry. Hollywood insiders render Black directors and their movies unbankable, socially engineering the notion that they do not have the potential for big returns at the box office, especially among international audiences. In doing so, they use economic and cultural logics to normalize the idea of inferiority and superiority of movies on the basis of racial characteristics. Acting on these labels of racial inferiority and superiority, Hollywood insiders regulate who creates cinema at different levels of production. At first glance, the Jim Crow system within Hollywood might appear to make economic sense. But upon closer inspection, it is deeply rooted in racial biases that boldly reinforce behaviors that keep racial disparities alive in the production circuits of popular cinema.

This way of thinking, of propagating myths about cultural and economic inferiority of Black movies and directors, affects the integration of workers on the job. It contributes to Black directors' marginalization in the film industry. Under the Hollywood Jim Crow, most Black directors are unable to participate in all aspects of cinematic production. Instead, they are marginalized and face limitations working with major studios, receiving big production budgets, and having their movies widely released in international markets. Operating under a racial double standard that privileges whiteness, white directors of Black-cast movies face fewer restrictions compared to Black directors of Black-cast movies. Furthermore, Black female directors are doubly disadvantaged in Hollywood, with race and gender working against them in an industry that foremost privileges white men.

Small Budgets

"I am trying to stay away from this position of me 'returning to my roots.' As if my roots are that I'm only comfortable working on low budget, small films. That's not the case at all. I think if people looked at my body of work, they'd see a great breadth of work."[5] Spike Lee laments his ghettoization on small-budget movies. Without sufficient financing, a film concept would, at most, never make it to the big screen or, at the very least, never be realized in the way that it was imagined. A movie's production budget encompasses above-the-line costs for writers, actors, directors, producers, scripts, and stories. It also includes below-the-line costs, such as expenses for technical labor and equipment. Importantly, the budget can steer the direction of the movie and the scale of production.

Arranged by budget, most Hollywood films fall into one of three categories. At the top of the hierarchy are big-budget tent-pole blockbuster movies. These films record production budgets at or above $100 million, with roughly one-third of the budget spent on marketing and promoting the film. Along a second tier, middle-budget movies have average budgets of around $40 million, with only between 10 and 15 percent of the budget spent on advertising the film. On the low end of the spectrum are small-budget independent movies, which generally cost less than $10 million to make and have minuscule promotion budgets that only increase if the film performs well at the box office.[6] Of the three levels, Rick Famuyiwa and many other Black directors have been limited, on the whole, to the bottom rung.

Hollywood executives assert that assignment of projects and budgets is based on prior success—recent box-office performances—with the logic that prior successes predict future successes. Observing Famuyiwa's record, however, this explanation appears to be untrue for Hollywood's treatment of Black directors. Although a number of his movies performed well at the box office, their success did not lead Hollywood executives to conclude that he would have future successes. In fact, his success at the box office did not allow him to move up the ranks to direct a middle-budget or big-budget film. Instead, he has been constrained by small budgets throughout his career. Analyzing Black directors' participation on big-budget movies that are central to Hollywood production provides another way to measure their quality of representation and assess their level of centrality within the film industry. Racial disparities regarding who directs big-budget movies means that African Americans are less likely to access the advantages of directing high-profile films.

Rarely do Black directors work on studios' core cultural products: lucrative, big-budget movies. No matter their successes, most never work on a big-budget or even a middle-budget movie. Instead, they are more often hired for movies at a distance from the locus of Hollywood production. Rick Famuyiwa and Spike Lee, who describe restrictions on their movie budgets, are not the only directors, by far, to hold the sentiment that race influences the level of financing allocated to their movies. Numerous African Americans echo this notion of being relegated to small-budget movies. Indeed, few Black directors find work on film projects with big production budgets, demonstrating a limitation on the scale of movies that they are hired to direct.

The logic used to limit Black directors' and movies' production budgets is that an increase in spending would not make economic sense, as it allegedly would not lead to increases in profits. The media studies scholar Nicholas Garnham writes that "the function not just of creating a cultural repertoire matched to a given audience . . . but at the same time of matching the cost of production of that repertoire to the spending powers of that audience . . . is a vital function totally ignored by many cultural analysts."[7] Likewise, the justification for small budgets blends cultural and economic explanations that audiences for Black movies are smaller than audiences for white movies and, therefore, consumer spending power for Black movies is smaller than consumer spending power for white movies. However, this Hollywood-insider logic contradicts actual figures that demonstrate the opposite: that audiences prefer racially diverse movies to monoracial white casts and that Black-cast movies are quite bankable. Nevertheless, executives in the film industry use these myths to inform decisions about movie production, which puts Black directors and movies at a significant disadvantage and, simultaneously, privileges white movies and directors.

Small budgets are tied to movies with racial-minority stars and directors, movies that Hollywood insiders perceive to be "domestically oriented." The Hollywood insider Billy remarks,

> As discussed in this morning's meeting, I believe that too many medium budget pictures are still being made that are domestically oriented. This defies the fact that the marketplace is internationally/globally driven. If a picture is unlikely to work worldwide then it is significantly riskier compared to other product. . . . When [the studio] made Equalizer they had to know that Denzel opens pics domestically, however the international gross would be somewhat limited (hence the disparity in distribution expenses). In a day when 65%+ of a tent pole picture's theatrical gross can come from international I think a studio should only make product such as The Equalizer for the right price, and [the studio's] price was too high.[8]

Billy's statement illustrates the process by which Hollywood insiders place budget limitations on Black cinematic productions. They label movies with Black stars, casts, and directors as risky, adhering to strong convictions that they would have, at best, favorable domestic box-office returns but limited international success. The strong urging is that movies with Black stars and directors be made "for the right price," with small budgets. Billy is emphatic that even medium budgets are too high for Black-star vehicles. In contrast, movies with white casts and directors are not similarly constrained with small budgets and low performance expectations.

Film statistics reveal that Black directors' production budgets are significantly smaller than white directors' production budgets on movies distributed by Hollywood studios. Between 2000 and 2016, for more than thirteen hundred Hollywood movies, Black directors had the smallest average production budget of all racial groups. Latino/as had the biggest average production budget at $79.8 million. Guillermo del Toro led Latino/a directors with a $190 million budget for *Pacific Rim* (2013). The average production budget for Asian directors was $67.5 million. Next, the average production budget for white directors was $62.1 million. Fixed squarely at the bottom of the racial hierarchy, Black directors' average production budget was $37.4 million.[9]

Large racial disparities exist in directing big-budget movies. Asian directors of Hollywood movies regularly helmed big-budget movies. James Wan's $190 million *Furious 7* (2015), part of Universal's *Fast & Furious* franchise was the highest budgeted movie for an Asian director, followed by Justin Lin's $185 million *Star Trek Beyond* (2016). Lin also directed the $160 million *Fast & Furious 6* (2013). Paramount studios was a top distributor for movies directed by Asian men, including Lin's *Star Trek Beyond*, M. Night Shyamalan's $150 million *The Last Airbender* (2010), John Chu's $130 million *G.I. Joe: Retaliation* (2013), John Woo's $125 million *Mission: Impossible II* (2000) and $60 million *Paycheck* (2003), and Wayne Wang's $45 million *Last Holiday* (2006), which starred Queen Latifah as a woman who upon hearing she has a terminal illness sells off her possessions and travels abroad to enjoy life's precious moments. Meanwhile, few African Americans directed Hollywood films with budgets over $100 million. Between 2000 and 2016, the upper limit of production budgets for African Americans was $130 million, achieved by Tim Story for *Fantastic Four: Rise of the Silver Surfer* (2007). Antoine Fuqua's *King Arthur* (2004) cost an estimated $120 million. In contrast, white directors received much bigger production budgets, with over 230 white-directed films having production budgets over $100 million, more than 110 white-directed movies having budgets of $150 million or more, and more than 40 white-directed films with budgets above $200 million. Indeed, the upper limit for white directors was $300 million—a sizable $170 million above the upper limit for Black directors—for Gore Verbinski's *Pirates of the Caribbean: At World's End* (2007), the third film in the *Pirates of the Caribbean* movie franchise.

In 2017, F. Gary Gray became the first Black director to helm a mega-budget picture, directing the $250 million *The Fate of the Furious* (2017). The eighth installment of the hit *Fast & Furious* movie franchise, Gray's film made over $226 million at the domestic box office and more than $1 billion at the foreign box office. Though it is quite common for white men to direct movies with budgets of $200 million and larger, it is a rarity for Black directors to attain such commercially lucrative projects. The fact that the top-budgeted films for all directors are tent-pole franchise movies reveals that disparities in who directs lucrative franchise movies add greater dimensions to the complex puzzle of racial inequality in contemporary Hollywood.[10]

In the face of evidence to the contrary, studio executives deploy myths that Black-cast movies will underperform at the box office or will not draw sizable audiences in domestic or foreign markets to provide economic justifications for insufficiently financing Black movies. No matter their successes, due to the "unbankable" label, Black movies are never spoken of as reliably profitable. For these reasons, it becomes increasingly difficult for African American directors to get funding from Hollywood studios to make movies with multiple Black leads. The director John Singleton expressed this dilemma about securing financing: "If I aspire to make movies with mostly African Americans in them, it is harder to get studios to finance them. . . . For those kinds of movies, you have to find the money and go do them."[11] Often Black directors have to look outside Hollywood to finance projects. When they do receive financing from Hollywood studios, directors observe that their films are made within tight budgetary constraints, since Black-cast projects are perceived as unbankable beyond small-budget thresholds.

The production budget impacts the way directors initially conceptualize and ultimately create a film. Speaking about budget limitations, Neema Barnette, who directed *Woman Thou Art Loosed on the 7th Day* (2012), explains how a dearth of funding impacts production values, shooting schedules, marketing, and promotion: "Obviously the budget constraints affect the vision because you want the best. You want more days and more time to rehearse and all those things that you don't have."[12] Small budgets place limitations on directors. If the budget is too small, directors must scale back their expectations or, in dire circumstances, risk not making the movie at all.

Some specialized knowledge and skills are only attainable by working on big-budget movies. Directing big-budget pictures allows directors to gain experience that is unfathomable on small projects. For example, John Singleton describes his experience working on the Lionsgate film *Abduction* (2011): "We shot a huge sequence during the baseball game. That was the first time I ever done that, with almost 30,000 spectators there. So I had six, seven cameras . . . and [was] jumping from one side of the fence into the next with Taylor [Lautner] doing the action while trying to make sure people weren't taking pictures of us. Every day on the set there's at least five, six hundred girls way off that we're trying to hide out of the shot."[13] Directing big-budget movies gives directors the ability to work on elaborate sets with multiple cameras and to create scenes that are impossible with small budgets.

While Latino/a and Asian directors face underrepresentation in Hollywood relative to white directors, their production budgets reflect some measure of overcoming the barriers of hierarchical representation in the film industry, in their ability to access core, lucrative positions beyond the relegation to small budgets and marginalization outside lucrative positions that continuously plague Black directors. Chances to direct movies of tremendous proportions are hardly bestowed on Black directors, to the point that Hollywood executives set limits on their perceived capabilities. Underrepresentation on big-budget movies constrains opportunities for Black directors to develop their filmmaking craft. Meanwhile, it solidifies hierarchies of racial difference that have profound consequences for workers' careers.

Major Pains

The director Stella Meghie remarks, "Whether you're doing independent [films] or whether you're doing studio, it just depends on the story you're telling and who wants to put money behind it."[14] The process to make movies varies widely. Film concepts can originate within a major studio, director, writer, or producer. For directors to disseminate their movies, they can work with major studios, independents, or both throughout their careers. Films become associated with distributors at different stages. The point of origin determines whether ideas for movies are developed in-house (within studios) or out-of-house (outside studios). Films that are distributed in-house originate with studios and are developed and produced by a major studio. When studios develop and produce their own films, a green light from studio executives means a film project is set to move into preproduction. "Development hell" means a film project never receives production funds.

Other times, producers bring film packages to studios that can finance production and/or arrange distribution. Some independent studios or individuals make arrangements with major studios for development and distribution of their movies. For example, a distribution deal involves getting outside financing, while agreeing to use studio resources to distribute and market a film. In a negative pickup deal, studios arrange distribution for a movie without having provided production funds. With a first-look deal, a studio might provide a producer with overhead to supplement additional outside financing in order to secure an option for distributing a film. Some films attract distributors at festivals, which could facilitate their international distribution down the pipeline. Other collaborations involve the cost sharing of production between two distributors. Producers also might approach major studios only to negotiate rights to distribute movies in international markets only. In other cases, conglomerates pick up successful independent features for distribution by the conglomerates' indie subdivisions, also known as studio independents. In this way, major studios are often involved solely in the distribution side of independently produced films.

No matter the process, it is universally understood by scholars and directors alike that distribution is a critical stage for a film's success. Clearly representation among film distributors matters. The media studies scholar Nicholas Garnham writes that distribution is the "key locus of power and profit. It is access to distribution which is key to cultural plurality."[15] Janet Wasko notes that "distribution holds the key to power in Hollywood."[16] She explains that "distribution involves a number of different markets where revenues are gleaned for the lease or sale of motion pictures, as well as other related products."[17] As a distributor, a film company coordinates a movie's promotion to the general public and facilitates its release to theaters in exchange for collecting a portion of the film's box-office receipts.[18] For theatrical distribution, distributors arrange for the exhibition of films on a particular schedule and collect receipts and fees from exhibitors. Decades ago that meant literally distributing film reels from one movie house to the next. Today, however, this means transmitting digitized electronic prints from a central server to cinemas via DVD, satellite, or fiber-optic links.[19] In addition, distributors provide strategies and action plans for how, when, and where a film will be released to audiences. Often distributors conduct market research and develop strategies for advertising and promoting a movie.

Industry-level studies of Hollywood have separated film studios into categories based on their size and scope of production.[20] In particular, Thomas Schatz describes a three-tiered system. Atop the system and most central to film-industry operations are Hollywood's core institutions, the six major film companies: Paramount, Sony, 20th Century Fox, Universal, Disney, and Warner Brothers. In the middle of the three-tiered system, just outside this core group, are studio independents, which are owned by major conglomerates but operate independently to produce niche genre films on smaller budgets for more specialized markets. At the bottom of the hierarchy are independent film companies that usually deal with even smaller-budgeted films and are involved in a more limited market of territories.[21]

Several benefits accompany working outside Hollywood's core of major-studio, big-budget, blockbuster franchise movies. Apart from commercial success, movies aim to achieve other accolades—most notably critical acclaim. For example, although Spike Lee's *Bamboozled* (2000) obtained limited theater showings and consequently experienced limited commercial success at the box office, it was well received in critics' circles. Some directors even desire to work on small-budget art-house movies. The director of *Selma* (2014), Ava DuVernay, once passed on an offer to direct *Black Panther* (2018), the first Marvel Studios comic franchise movie starring a Black superhero. She describes her reasons for doing so:

> For me, it was a process of trying to figure out, are these people I want to go to bed with? Because it's really a marriage and for this it would be

three years. It'd be three years of not doing other things that are important to me. So it was a question of, is this important enough for me to
do? . . . What my name is on means something to me—these are my chil-
dren. This is my art. This is what will live on after I'm gone. So it's important to me that, that be true to who I was in this moment. And if there's too
much compromise, it really wasn't going to be an Ava DuVernay film.[22]

As DuVernay suggests, concerns that pit issues of artistic ownership
of one's films against commerce factor into career decisions, such that
some people opt out of major-studio movies to pursue other projects.

Although the indie circuit offers worthy avenues for further study,
movies distributed by Hollywood studios and fairly large independents
are key sites for the making of racial inequality within each stage of
cultural production, distribution, and consumption. At the distribution stage, which links production and consumption, an audience is
found or made for a cultural work. According to the communications
scholar Anamik Saha, racial inequality is made, reproduced, and made
sense of between production and consumption, at the site of cultural
distribution: "Through cultural distribution, culturally diverse arts are
recognised and made visible, but positioned in such a way that they cannot disrupt the core—a kind of *keeping at arm's length*."[23] The stage of
cultural distribution is where efforts to curb racial inequality are un-
dermined by keeping some movies from widespread audiences. Distribution in Hollywood is unequally allocated based on the racial makeup
of cultural content and imagined audience interests. Guided by the assumption that white films and directors are more marketable than Black
films and directors, directors' representation with large film distributors
varies. Unequal distribution gives unequal access to audiences and is
determined using racial considerations.

Corporations that control the film industry, major studios operate
as oligopolies in the way they protect, promote, and determine policies
for the industry. Compared to the majors, other production and distribution companies are significantly less influential in the film business.
Because major studios have the potential to offer directors advantages
that smaller distributors cannot, representation at different levels carries substantial weight. For example, concerning the representation
of writers in elite or core agencies compared to noncore agencies, the

sociologists William and Denise Bielby found that representation by a core agency provided writers with greater reputation, resources, authentication, and legitimacy.[24] Compared to noncore agencies, core agencies also played a more active role in the production process. Though a number of small companies and independents compete for market share in the film industry, major studios reap most of the rewards from film production through their control of distribution. The oligopoly of major distributors, now part of diversified global entertainment conglomerates, dominate the film business. They have the resources to attract the best creative talent and to develop the priciest movies.

Movies distributed by major studios are heavily promoted and publicized. Nationally, these firms have branch offices in key regional markets, thus allowing them to maintain extensive and continuous contact with theater chains across the country in order to coordinate strategic placement of their films among the schedule of release dates. In the domestic market, major film studios consistently release a large number of movies on an annual basis and command a significant share of box-office revenues, estimated between 80 and 90 percent of all films.[25] In foreign markets, major studios get their pictures viewed worldwide because of their international ownership ties and/or extensive global networks and alliances through distribution cartels and agreements with foreign entertainment organizations that provide infrastructure for overseas production and distribution. A critical advantage for film directors, major studios have access to distribution networks that contribute to a film's accessibility and, in many respects, success in the marketplace. On the other hand, other film-releasing companies are less strategically networked with exhibitors and generally have greater difficulty marketing, publicizing, and gaining large theatrical releases for their films.

The picture of underrepresentation of racial-minority film directors is incomplete without understanding their level of participation in different distribution channels. Given the benefits of belonging to core organizations, disproportionately limited access to core organizations, namely, major film studios, demonstrates further evidence of African Americans' marginalization in cinema distribution. Looking at hierarchies of representation for different distributors, it becomes evident that a uniformity of underrepresentation at all levels is not the norm. Though aggregate numbers suggest that Black directors are underrepresented across the film industry, in actuality, however, not all studios uniformly underrepresent Black directors. In fact, the racial composition of directors varies significantly by distributor. Examining individual distributors reveals patterns in racial representation. Due to the sheer size and volume of films of the six major studios, they distribute more movies directed by Black directors compared to other distributors. However, despite major studios having larger numbers of Black-directed films, they tend to distribute smaller proportions of Black-directed films compared to other distributors.

The Hollywood Jim Crow establishes a racial hierarchy that marginalizes Black directors and racial-minority directors in general. Both groups have less representation at major studios and are therefore further removed from key centers of cultural production. Tables 3.1 and 3.2 show racial representation in film directing for ten distribution arms: Disney / Buena Vista, Sony, Universal, Paramount, Warner Brothers, 20th Century Fox, Sony Screen Gems, Fox Searchlight, MGM, and Lionsgate. Black directors and other racial-minority directors are underrepresented at all major studios. For instance, between 2000 and 2016, Disney had only 2 percent Black directors and 7 percent directors of African, Latino/a, or Asian descent. Similarly, Warner Brothers had 4 percent Black directors and 6 percent racial-minority directors. Of all major studios, Paramount had the largest proportional representation of racial minorities, with 7 percent Black directors and 11 percent directors from all racial minority groups. Altogether, directors from all racial minority groups directed just 8 percent of movies distributed by major studios,

TABLE 3.1. Film Distribution Organizations and Racial Representation of Directors, 2000–2016, Major Distributors

Distributor (majors)	% Black (n)	% white (n)	% racial minority (n)	# of films
Buena Vista / Disney	2 (4)	93 (154)	7 (12)	166
Paramount	7 (13)	82 (144)	11 (19)	176
Sony	5 (9)	88 (162)	8 (14)	185
20th Century Fox	5 (13)	87 (207)	8 (19)	239
Universal	6 (14)	84 (213)	11 (27)	254
Warner Brothers	4 (10)	90 (245)	6 (16)	271

Source: Data compiled from www.boxofficemojo.com and www.imdb.com.

TABLE 3.2. Film Distribution Organizations and Racial Representation of Directors, 2000–2016, Independent / Studio Independent Distributors

Distributor (independents / studio independents)	% Black (*n*)	% white (*n*)	% racial minority (*n*)	# of films
Fox Searchlight	17 (17)	58 (59)	25 (25)	101
Lionsgate	14 (28)	67 (132)	18 (36)	196
MGM	13 (9)	70 (50)	17 (12)	71
Sony Screen Gems	13 (10)	70 (55)	18 (14)	70

Source: Data compiled from www.boxofficemojo.com and www.imdb.com.

and African Americans directed only 5 percent of movies distributed by major studios. While Latino/a directors are underrepresented across all distributors, Asian directors are near parity at Universal, comprising 4 percent of directors.

Compared to major studios, the independent distributors MGM and Lionsgate and the studio independents Fox Searchlight and Sony Screen Gems proportionally have much greater representation for Black and racial-minority directors. Each had representation of African Americans near parity with or greater than their proportion of the U.S. population. Fox Searchlight had 17 percent Black representation, compared to 20th Century Fox's 5 percent. Sony Screen Gems had 13 percent Black representation, compared to Sony's 5 percent. Clearly Hollywood studios more often distribute Black-directed movies with studio independents than via major studios. Besides studio independent distribution arms, other distributors unrelated to the majors, such as Lionsgate and MGM, also demonstrate better representation of African Americans and directors from marginalized groups. Still, racial minorities as a whole are underrepresented even at independents and studio independents. Fox Searchlight led all distributors with 25 percent of directors of African, Asian, or Latino/a descent. Even though numerical representation outside major film companies has improved considerably for racial minorities, their presence falls short of their 36 percent of the U.S. population.

Breaking down proportional representation by distributor, it becomes evident that outside major studios, African Americans have actually achieved parity in proportional representation within some distribution outlets. However, they still remain on the margins of major studios, the institutions that are most central to the Hollywood film industry's operations. Though Black directors as a group are underrepresented in the film industry, blanket generalizations about the totality of movie distributors exercising unequal practices against African Americans and directors from underrepresented groups do not fully explain the nuances of racial representation in the film industry. In actuality, the employment practices of only *some* film organizations, primarily major studios, reflect poor inclusion of African Americans, while Black directors find greater inclusion away from the industry's core institutions.

Having bigger budgets, greater exposure to audiences, and greater commercial success, directors for major studios' movies experience considerable advantages compared to directors whose films are primarily distributed outside majors. Another way racial inequality persists in Hollywood is that Black directors and directors from other racial-minority backgrounds are less able than white directors to tap into the resources of major studios, a disadvantage that fosters divergent career paths. Figure 3.1 shows racial differences in average production budgets between Black and white directors at major studios. For all distributors, white directors received bigger movie budgets than Black directors. Furthermore, the extent of racial inequality in production budgets varies by distributor. At 20th Century Fox, for example, the racial gap in average production budgets between Black and white directors was smallest, at just $6 million in favor of white directors. Paramount, Sony, and Universal had racial gaps

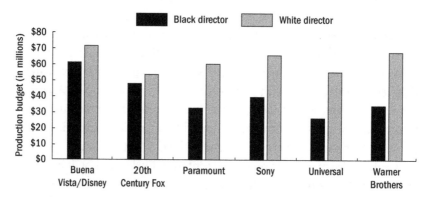

Figure 3.1. Average production budgets by race of director at Hollywood studios, 2000–2016. Data compiled from www.boxofficemojo.com.

in budgets close to $30 million, and Warner Brothers had a racial gap of $33 million. Overall, major studios have substantial racial disparities in production budgets. Hence, even at major studios, organizations that are thought to have the most economic resources for all directors, Black directors experience disadvantage, having smaller production budgets than white directors. The Hollywood Jim Crow produces a result of racial disparities in resources for Black and white directors on the grounds that white-directed movies are economically less risky and culturally more appealing to global audiences. The outcome is marginalization of racial-minority directors both outside and within major studios, further exacerbating racial disparities in society.

The movie producer Stephanie Allain explains, "If studios are willing to spend the money to build awareness for Black movie stars and directors, Black American film culture will travel. More money for studios and more opportunity for us. It's that simple."[26] She believes that so long as major studios put in the effort to support and promote Black cinema, it will succeed. However, with African Americans having only marginal inclusion in major studios and on lucrative film projects, racial inequality and hierarchy persist within the film industry, despite an influx of African Americans into the directing profession.

Although major studios are known to possess more extensive networks to facilitate a movie's promotion, distribution, and exhibition, disproportionate disadvantages for Black directors disallow them from fully accessing these benefits that are assumed always to accompany directing films for major studios. For Black directors, the advantages of directing at a major studio are somewhat dampened by the racial disadvantages they face. Racial disparities in film budgets illustrate that Black directors' gains from having films distributed by major studios are considerably less compared to the rewards that accompany white-directed Hollywood films. Even at major studios, the "unbankable" label that renders Black films and directors risky investments prohibits Black directors from accessing the upper echelons of the film-directing profession.

Black Casts, White Privilege

"Named directors of UK and Irish origin are few but they do of course add to the package, certainly for media attention if not for the public."[27]

Advising on market and production trends for the UK market, Bruce gives a nod to using white directors of UK and Irish origin for Hollywood movies, suggesting that they are useful for promoting and marketing movies to audiences. Hollywood movies are global cultural products that are increasingly produced and consumed around the world. The global expansion of the film industry also means a global workforce, which disadvantages U.S. racial minorities, who face underrepresentation and marginalization compared to white directors of Hollywood movies—both whites who are American and whites who are not. In an era of white supremacism around the globe and in Hollywood, whiteness is prioritized and valued over Americanness such that a white European director from Ireland or England is perceived by whites in Hollywood as having greater currency compared to American directors of African, Latino/a, Native, or Asian descent. Latino/a and Asian directors are especially underrepresented relative to their foreign-born counterparts, and African Americans and Latino/as are underrepresented also relative to their proportion of the U.S. population. Still more troubling, Native American directors are virtually nonexistent in Hollywood, meaning that images about Native Americans, for the most part, are created without their perspectives taken into consideration.

Privileging whiteness on a global scale means that white Americans, white Europeans, and white immigrants to the United States access advantages in the Hollywood-cinema labor market over Blacks, Asians, Latino/as, and Native people who are U.S. citizens. This privilege manifests itself in many ways, including when it comes to making decisions about Black-cast movies. Under the Hollywood Jim Crow, studio executives label Black movies and directors unbankable and consequently disadvantage movies with Black characters in the production process. Generally, Hollywood insiders assume that Black directors should only direct movies with a Black cast or a Black character in a major role. The exception is, however, when a movie has a big budget and is high concept: having an easily pitched premise, a seemingly broad appeal, and expectations of a successful performance at the box office. In the case of high-concept movies with named stars, studio executives usually select white directors over Black directors even if the cast is majority Black. For instance, in a discussion between Hollywood insiders about a potential *Harlem Globetrotter* movie that would feature African Americans in two of three lead roles—as the head coach and the star basketball player—a white director is the favored choice in discussions about possible directors, while an African American director is not under serious consideration.[28] Assigning Black directors to Black-cast movies is not always the norm for mainstream movies that are expected to have crossover appeal. White privilege in the film industry leads to white directors having access to work on lucrative Black-cast films.

With the exception of *Black Panther* (2018), none of the biggest budgeted movies starring Black casts have had Black directors. The white director Michael Bay directed *Bad Boys II* (2003), an action flick about two narcotics cops investigating the drug trade in Florida, which starred Will Smith and Martin Lawrence and was made on a $130 million budget. Another white director, Michael Mann, helmed the $107 million *Ali*, starring Will Smith as the heavyweight-champion boxer Muhammad Ali. Of the popular Eddie Murphy star vehicles—the $84 million *The Nutty Professor II: The Klumps* (2000) directed by Peter Segal, the $70 million *Dr. Do Little 2* (2001) directed by Steve Carr, and the $60 million *Norbit* (2007) directed by Brian Robbins—none had Black directors behind the camera. The Black-cast music film *Dreamgirls* (2006) featured Eddie Murphy alongside the top R&B vocal talents Beyoncé Knowles and Jennifer Hudson. *Dreamgirls*, too, was directed by a white director, Bill Condon.

Movies featuring Black casts appear to have different upper limits for budgets depending on if they are directed by Blacks or whites. Tables 3.3 and 3.4 compare top-budgeted Black-cast movies for Black directors and non-Black directors. A pattern of racial hierarchy is evident. Overall, Black directors' movies have smaller budgets than white directors' movies. Most Black-cast movies with big-name stars—such as Will Smith, Eddie Murphy, and Martin Lawrence—tend to have white directors. Movies with big-name stars are lucrative for directors because they generally attract large audiences and perform well at the box office. *Norbit* made more than $95 million, while *Dreamgirls* grossed more than $103 million, and *The Nutty Professor II* grossed more than $123 million at the domestic box office alone. The estimated total box-office gross, including international gross, for each movie was upward of $155 million. *Bad Boys II* was even more successful, grossing more than $138 million at the domestic box office and more than an estimated $273 million in total box-office gross. Black-directed Black-cast movies tend to have smaller budgets and less well-known casts compared to white-directed Black-cast movies. The assignment of directors to Black-cast movies shows a racial hierarchy in who directs movies with high and low production values.

Ultimately, Black directors and movies that do pass through the production, distribution, and exhibition pipelines receive low production values compared to white directors and movies. In making race distinctions between Blacks and whites, the Hollywood Jim Crow ghettoizes Black directors onto nonlucrative career tracks, with few directing big-budget movies. Rarely are Black directors hired to direct lucrative high-concept Hollywood movies that executives believe will be highly profitable. Jim Crow structures of racial hierarchy in the film industry enable white directors to occupy the most advantageous positions. Even on Black-cast movies, whites direct the most commercially lucrative movies. Film-industry decision-makers select white directors to oversee high-concept crossover movies that feature Black stars. Oscar-nominated movies such as *Hidden Figures* (2016), *The Help* (2011), *Dreamgirls* (2006), and *Ray* (2004) had white directors. Black directors' aspirations

TABLE 3.3. Top-Budgeted Black-Cast Movies by Black Directors, 2000–2016

Film	Year	Distributor	Budget ($, in millions)	Director
Littleman	2006	Sony Revolution	64	Keenen Ivory Wayans
Red Tails	2012	Fox	58	Anthony Hemingway
Miracle at St. Anna	2008	Buena Vista/ Disney	45	Spike Lee
Head of State	2003	DreamWorks	35	Chris Rock
Welcome Home Roscoe Jenkins	2008	Universal	35	Malcolm D. Lee
Barbershop 2: Back in the Business	2004	MGM	30	Kevin Rodney Sullivan
Coach Carter	2008	Paramount	30	Thomas Carter
Straight Outta Compton	2015	Universal	28	F. Gary Gray
Madea's Big Happy Family	2011	Lionsgate	25	Tyler Perry
A Madea Christmas	2014	Lionsgate	25	Tyler Perry

Source: Production budgets from Boxofficemojo.com and IMDb.com.

TABLE 3.4. Top-Budgeted Black-Cast Movies by Non-Black Directors, 2000–2016

Film	Year	Distributor	Budget ($, in millions)	Director
Bad Boys II	2003	Sony	130	Michael Bay
Ali	2001	Sony	107	Michael Mann
The Nutty Professor II: The Klumps	2000	Universal	84	Peter Segal
The Longest Yard	2005	Paramount	82	Peter Segal
Dreamgirls	2006	Paramount / DreamWorks	70	Bill Condon
Dr. Dolittle 2	2001	Fox	70	Steve Carr
Norbit	2007	Paramount / DreamWorks	60	Brian Robbins
Get Rich or Die Tryin'	2005	Paramount	40	Jim Sheridan
Ray	2004	Universal	40	Taylor Hackford

Source: Production budgets from Boxofficemojo.com and IMDb.com.

to work on high-profile big-budget projects, even to do so with Black casts, remain largely unmet. Indeed, they are more often encouraged to work on small-budget projects or on films outside Hollywood's core moneymakers.

Foreign Box-Office Barriers

Greg writes, "This refers to TROIS, an African American film first released in 2000 (according to IMDb). I don't recall the title being released in international, but perhaps you could confirm. I would have thought that any re-issue potential would be for US only." In a matter-of-fact tone, Matthew replies, "Definitely no re-release for international."[29] Generally a foreign release is not considered for a Black-cast, Black-directed movie. Widely, Hollywood executives believe that such movies are unbankable at the international box office. Marginalization of Black directors is so customary that decisions about not releasing Black-cast movies in foreign contexts are often expedient and irreversible. For instance, when Hollywood insiders Greg and Matthew discuss the rerelease of the erotic romance thriller *Trois* (2000), starring Kenya Moore and directed by Will Packer, they quickly dismiss the idea of giving it an international release without much consideration of Moore's popularity and high visibility on Bravo's *Real Housewives of Atlanta* and Packer's acclaim with *About Last Night* and *Ride Along*. Despite *Trois*'s success, including revenues from theatrical, DVD, and cable-television markets, the verdict is negative for potential international release. White-cast erotic romance thrillers such as the popular adaptation *Fifty Shades of Grey* (2015) see ample exposure in international markets. In contrast, Black-cast films are firmly denied foreign-market distribution, leaving the international market, to a great degree, for whites only.

After screening the movie *Dear White People* (2014), Justin Simien's feature film about the perspectives of Black college students at the fictional predominantly white campus of Winchester University, the Hollywood insider Francis writes, "We have talked to the producers about possibly working with one of the indies (e.g., Roadside Attractions) to do a small release, but talks haven't gone anywhere. The picture is quite high concept (it picks up on recent headlines as a group of white college students throw a "come as an African-American party") but the picture isn't well-executed, so it feels like a small release if anything."[30] Despite his assessment that the movie has a high-concept premise, Francis imagines it having a small release—which is typical for the way Hollywood insiders arrange limited distribution for movies with Black casts and themes. Subsequently, limited distribution particularly in foreign markets becomes the grounds for racial bias in employment.

Since as early as the 1920s, the U.S. film industry has made efforts to market movies to global audiences. But during the 1980s, the deregulation and privatization of media operations marked a key moment for Hollywood's expansion into global markets. During this globalization period, transnational entertainment conglomerates exported cinema abroad, making entertainment the second-largest export from the United States (next to aerospace).[31] Recently, the focus on blockbuster movies and sequels and their exportation to foreign markets has increasingly shaped the outlook of studio executives' decision-making about film production and distribution.

The turn to foreign markets also arises at a time when Black-cast movies are achieving undeniable success domestically. Over the years, films by and about racial minorities have made increasing profits in domestic markets as films by and about whites have seen decreasing profits in domestic markets. Concurrently, there is a shift in the framing and measurement of success in the film industry. Success is now bifurcated into domestic- and foreign-market outcomes. Movies that perform well domestically only are perceived to be limited, narrow in potential, and risky. On the other hand, other (white) movies are thought to have potential to perform well globally and are perceived to be better risks. In no small twist of irony, as Black movies attain success in the domestic market, the domestic market ceases to hold importance and maintain its value in the minds of Hollywood insiders. The film scholar Donald Bogle theorizes that while the guise of racial stereotypes in Hollywood's on-screen images might change, the presentation of stereotypes remains.[32] Likewise, behind the camera, Black directors continue to be marginalized but in a different manner than when they faced total exclusion from participation. The current prevailing guise for inequality is the foreign-market box-office standard for success.

The definition of success in Hollywood is socially constructed, in this case, to support the premise that movies with white casts and directors are the most valued at the cinematic box office. The standard for success becomes the mirror image of white movies, especially the patterns of white tent-pole franchise movies, while other models of success are ignored. The foreign-market threshold for success that zooms in on foreign box-office returns is arbitrary and biased in favor of the performance of white movies, directors, actors, and narratives, while positioning racial minorities as culturally insufficient and not meeting the standard. The current preoccupation with the foreign market effectively silences movies that either are not distributed internationally or do not adhere to the artificial standard of disproportionate gross overseas, no matter the success that the movie finds domestically. On the basis of a foreign-market focus, a movie can be profitable domestically but still be assessed as inferior to another movie that was less successful but saw greater foreign-market gross.

The entertainment critic Michael Cieply, like others in Hollywood, labels success in the domestic box office problematic. He writes, "More usual, even for awards-caliber films, is the experience of *The Help*, a 2011 release that focused on the travails of black maids in the Jim Crow–era South. It was an enormous hit, with worldwide ticket sales of almost $216.7 million, but about 80 percent of that came from domestic markets."[33] Although *The Help* grossed more than eight times its budget worldwide and more than six times its budget in the domestic market, regardless some critics proclaimed that the movie's performance was disappointing, relying too heavily on a biased view that foreign-market performance is the only standard for success.

The norm in Hollywood to evaluate a film by its foreign-market performance prevails. Black-directed movies face insurmountable box-office barriers at the stage of foreign-market distribution. Hollywood insiders view Black-cast movies, which Black directors so often direct, as a liability in foreign markets. Advising coworkers on market trends, the Hollywood insider Arnold writes that Black-cast movies are not worth pursuing in the UK market: "The downsides remain the African American movies, sport centric and really dumb comedy with a cultural American skew."[34] Singling out Black-cast movies as a liability gives validity to a racial production and distribution culture that legally discriminates against Black directors and movies, in the name of steering clear of financial risk and pursuing the highest profits.

Black directors believe their movies are marginalized in the way of small distribution and small budgets despite successful box-office runs. The director of *Best Man Holiday*, Malcolm D. Lee, says, "I'm tired of the dismissive, marginalized way that movies starring African-American actors who don't happen to be Will Smith or Denzel Washington or Kevin Hart [are talked about when they] perform well at the box office. Tyler Perry makes a movie and it's number one almost every time. *Think Like a Man* was number one two weeks in a row. People talk about [*Best Man Holiday*] over-performing, but I feel like we got under-estimated."[35] Directors commonly express dissatisfaction with the way their successful movies are framed as having "overperformed" an imagined low bar set by studios, so that they can feign surprise at the box-office receipts. However, Black-cast and Black-directed movies have been grossing well for decades.

Similarly, Ava DuVernay expresses that successful Black-cast movies and directors are often overlooked: "It's hard for Black filmmakers who have been in the business for a long time to think: 'This is It.' You would hope Hollywood would take each of these kind of renaissances as precedent-setting, like this is a foundational year and next year we will build on it. But it never happens. Black films never set precedent. We always have to start over."[36] With a persistent message of Black films' inferiority underlying the institutional logics of Hollywood, no matter the actual box-office performance, every success is viewed as having overperformed and overcome low expectations, though no quantity of phenomenal performances elicits high expectations for Black-cast or Black-directed movies. Marginalization is a key aspect of the Hollywood Jim Crow that constantly undermines Black directors' career trajectories.

The assumption that Black movies will perform poorly and that a hit is unexpected fuels the narrative to restrict Black movies from getting big budgets and distribution overseas—where many white movies find most of their profits. The foreign market is reserved almost exclusively for white movies and directors, though, in no small irony, the global majority is composed of a racially diverse mix of mostly African, Asian, Latino/a, and Native peoples. Even so, Hollywood insiders contend that white movies play best to these internationally varied audiences and vehemently refuse to regularly and widely distribute movies with U.S. racial minorities in the forefront.

Besides the technical advantages of directing big-budget movies, there are also economic advantages. Since profits are highly correlated with production budgets, underrepresentation on big-budget projects prevents Black directors from achieving huge amounts of commercial success at the box office. Commercial success is thought to provide movies and directors with positive rewards and has a favorable impact on a director's ability to work on future film projects. Large viewership for directors presumably leads to greater credibility with studio executives. Tim Story agrees that his many successful films have enabled him to direct more movies: "The biggest thing that [commercial success at the box office] does is that it lets me make more movies. . . . Everyone loves when [his or her] movie is successful or seen by the widest audience, but it does allow [me] to do more films; and at the end of the day, that's what I'm in this for. . . . It allows me to stick around a little longer."[37] Without a doubt, the racial gap in production budgets impacts commercial success. The Black/white racial gap in domestic box-office performance mirrors the gap in production budgets. For Hollywood movies theatrically released between 2000 and 2016, white-directed movies grossed an average of $78 million at the domestic box office, compared to Black-directed movies' average of $52 million, a difference of $26 million.

The very foundation of the Hollywood Jim Crow is that studio executives label Black directors and movies inferior commercial investments. At the foreign box-office level, this means that studio executives have little faith that Black-directed movies will perform well overseas. Consequently, the racial disadvantages that Black directors encounter extend to the foreign market, where their films receive little to no marketing, promotion, and distribution. Although it appears that no amount of success will convince Hollywood studio executives to regularly promote Black-directed movies overseas, the foreign box office has long become the saving grace of many white-directed movies. Foreign markets routinely provide a cushion for movies with white directors and casts. Darnell Hunt and colleagues illustrate convincingly, in their *2014 Hollywood Diversity Report*, that movies with diverse casts draw higher ratings and box-office receipts than films with homogeneous casts that lack diversity. In spite of everything, movies directed by white men that cast white male stars in commercial genres tend to receive the broadest distribution in both domestic and foreign markets.[38]

In fact, it is not uncommon that a white-directed, white-cast film finds little popularity in the United States but performs well abroad due to intense marketing and promotion strategies. One example of this phenomenon is Darren Aronofsky's action drama *Noah* (2014). Released by Paramount, *Noah*'s $93 million return in the domestic market fell short of its $125 million budget, despite playing at a peak of thirty-five hundred screens nationwide. Domestically, however, the film grossed less than three-fourths of its initial budget. But the foreign box office saved *Noah* from complete failure. Its estimated foreign-market gross topped $200 million, effectively recovering from its domestic flop.

Likewise, the success of the white American director Joseph Kosinski's *Oblivion* (2013) was only conceivable because of Universal's insistence that the film get widespread international distribution. Similar to *Noah*, *Oblivion* underperformed at the domestic box office, grossing $89 million while failing to recover its $120 million budget. Yet the production was resurrected from the red when it grossed $200 million in foreign markets.

Numerous white movies perform extremely poorly domestically and are only saved by their foreign-market releases. *Battleship* (2012), adapted from the eponymous board game and directed by the white

American Peter Berg, took in $66 million domestically on a $209 million budget. It was rescued by the foreign-market box office, where it grossed $237 million. The sci-fi/adventure movie *John Carter* (2012), directed by the white American Andrew Stanton, made only $73 million at the domestic box office on a hefty $250 million budget. A wide foreign-market release enabled it to recoup its budget, with $211 million at the box office in international markets. *Battleship* and *John Carter* are pertinent examples of the waning interest for white movies in the domestic market and the increasing reliance on the foreign market to keep white movies afloat.

White movies are regularly excused from their underperformances at the U.S. box office. Hollywood insiders dogmatically maintain that any film with a white cast has potential for success in a global marketplace. Thus, the many white movies that perform poorly at the U.S. box office are excused on the alleged grounds of their potential. These examples are far from anomalies. Myriad other white-directed and white-cast movies have been rescued from failure by heavy promotion and consumption in foreign markets. Meanwhile, the ghettoization of Black movies in domestic markets undermines their potential for success in overseas territories.

The difference between having and not having foreign-market distribution is vital in understanding a director's ability to attain the highest levels of commercial success at the box office. For Hollywood studios today, foreign-market revenues are significantly larger than domestic-market revenues. Even in 2003, foreign-market revenues outpaced domestic box-office revenues by more than $6 billion.[39] On the whole, American films capture a large share of Europe's continental box office. They also maintain a stronghold of dominating box-office receipts in Asia. Studios' dependence on foreign ticket sales is so immense that the current production models of big-budget movies would be unsustainable without foreign-market expansion. Because there is exceedingly more revenue to be earned in markets abroad compared to domestic markets, Hollywood directors whose movies are distributed in foreign markets stand to gain more than directors whose movies are rarely distributed overseas.

Under the Hollywood Jim Crow, in which Hollywood insiders actively create and maintain racial disparities among movies and directors, Black directors are unable to benefit from Hollywood's expansive global reach. Studio executives claim that Black-cast and Black-directed movies will not attract markets outside the African diaspora. Even by this argument, not distributing Black-cast movies overseas essentially ignores African audiences in Europe and in the Americas. Hence, the institutional practice of limiting Black movies and directors in foreign-market distribution commonly denies Black-directed movies distribution overseas and instead ghettoizes them in domestic markets, yet another example of racial disadvantage under the Hollywood Jim Crow. This disadvantage further extends to other U.S. racial minority groups that are underrepresented as directors of films with foreign-market distribution. Virtually nonexistent in foreign markets, Black directors are marginalized in a way that is detrimental to their success and longevity in the film industry, only further cementing their unequal treatment.

An Endangered Underclass

"There are almost no Black women in film. You can go to whole movies and not see one Black woman," writes Chris Rock. "I go to the movies almost every week, and I can go a month and not see a Black woman having an actual speaking part in a movie. That's the truth."[40] Rock's keen observation about Black female actors rings even truer for Black female directors, who are virtually invisible behind the camera of Hollywood motion pictures. In 1989, Euzhan Palcy's *A Dry White Season* became the first national theatrically released movie by a Black woman. Julie Dash's independent film *Daughters of the Dust* (1992) was the first theatrically released movie by an American-born Black woman. Shortly thereafter, Leslie Harris, with *Just Another Girl on the I.R.T.*, distributed by New Line Cinema in 1993, ushered in an era when Black women's movies received mainstream theatrical showings. The following year, Darnell Martin's *I Like It like That* (1994) became the first Black-female-directed movie with a major studio release, with Columbia Pictures. Even while Black men have made some gains in film directing, it remains difficult for Black women to break into Hollywood.

Though many Black women write and direct their own movies, it is rare that they are employed as directors for hire for Hollywood productions. Among the top-six-hundred-grossing movies between 2007 and 2013, for example, only two movies were directed by Black women.[41]

From a scholarly standpoint, very little is known about Black women's representation in Hollywood directing. Most reports focus on race or gender diversity in Hollywood, obscuring the experiences of women from underrepresented racial groups. Even while Black directors, as a whole, face discrimination and marginalization in Hollywood, the impact of the Hollywood Jim Crow is gendered such that Black women are further marginalized. It is commonplace in professional occupations in the United States that race and gender inequality combine to influence hiring decisions and job promotion in a way that doubly disadvantages Black women. In the same way, Black women face a double disadvantage and near exclusion from Hollywood cinematic production circles. Indeed, the Hollywood Jim Crow renders movies by and about Black women unbankable and supposes they would be of little interest to domestic and international audiences, such that their presence in the film industry resembles that of a permanent underclass, with little opportunity to break into movie directing, much less forge successful careers.

Over the first decade of the twenty-first century, Black female directors were behind the camera of only about one mainstream-distributed film per year. Unlike white men or to a much lesser extent white women or Black men, in any given year, Black women were not guaranteed to make a movie that obtained a national release in theaters. Whereas Black men and white women are underrepresented and marginalized, Black women as double minorities face even greater disadvantages in film directing, so much that they are endangered and teetering on the brink of nonexistence. Thus far, Black women constitute less than 1 percent of directors of contemporary Hollywood movies, and no Black woman has sustained a successful career primarily through directing Hollywood movies.

Sanaa Hamri, Gina Prince-Bythewood, and Kasi Lemmons are some of the more commercially successful Black female directors, each having directed at least three movies with large theatrical showings. However, their only-sporadic presence means that they cannot sustain careers solely directing feature films and can only engage in directing Hollywood movies as a part-time activity. Even while more films with Black casts and themes are featured in theaters, few films with national releases and sufficient marketing and promotion are helmed by Black female directors. With an inconsistent presence from year to year, they are threatened with nonexistence in the mainstream film industry.

Figure 3.2. Ava DuVernay at the Ultimate Disney Fan
Event, Anaheim Convention Center. Photo by
Disney / Image Group LA, July 15, 2017.

Black women are also vastly underrepresented as directors of big-
budget movies, whereas men of all races and white women direct more
expensive pictures. Estimated at just over $100 million, Ava DuVernay's
Wrinkle in Time (2018), about a girl, her brother, and her friend ventur-
ing into space to find her missing father, who is a scientist, is the biggest
budgeted movie directed by a Black woman. Based on the novel by Mad-
eleine L'Engle, the multiracial-cast *Wrinkle in Time* stars Oprah Winfrey,
Gugu Mbatha-Raw, the South Asian actor Mindy Kaling, and the white
actors Reese Witherspoon and Chris Pine. The second biggest budget
for a Black-female directed film is only $50 million for Angela Robin-
son's *Herbie Fully Loaded* (2005), about a young white woman training

to become a NASCAR competitor. At any rate, these numbers trail behind the biggest budget movies directed by white women. For example, Patty Jenkins's action/adventure flick *Wonder Woman* (2017) was made on a $149 million budget.

Even the most successful Black female directors who helm multiple films for Hollywood studios face limited production budgets. Sanaa Hamri's *The Sisterhood of the Traveling Pants 2* (2008) was made for $27 million. The white-cast movie with one Latina star, America Ferrera, follows four college freshmen whose lives take on divergent paths, though they keep in touch while sharing a pair of jeans. Gina Prince-Bythewood's *Love and Basketball* (2000), a romance drama in which two childhood friends move through adulthood sharing a love for basketball, and *The Secret Life of Bees* (2008), a southern drama about family and beekeeping, were made for $20 million and $11 million, respectively. Kasi Lemmons's *The Caveman's Valentine* (2001), a crime/music drama about a cave-dwelling man who vies to bring to justice the murderer of a homeless boy, and *Black Nativity* (2013), a music drama about a teenager who spends the Christmas holiday with estranged relatives in New York City, were made for $13.5 million and $17.5 million, respectively.

Some Black-female-directed movies reach a mainstream market or get international exposure, but many Black-female-directed movies that are theatrically released face scarce resources and do not receive enough studio support to sustain long theatrical runs. Moreover, few Black-female-directed movies get international exposure. Rather than theatrical distribution, Black women's movies tend to travel through other venues: such as DVD distribution, broadcast and cable television, film festivals, and online releases—though nontheatrical distribution routes tend to garner smaller audience viewership and receive less attention from critics.[42]

Movies by and about Black women are scarce on the big screen. DuVernay believes that white leadership in Hollywood is not interested in movies told from a Black female perspective: "I'm interested in films about the interior lives of Black women, which I cannot find a studio that's interested in that kind of story. . . . [They're] not interested in that type of story from a Black woman's gaze, maybe interested in it from a white man's gaze."[43] A rare exception to Black women's cinematic underrepresentation in lead roles in front of and behind the camera is the movie *Everything, Everything* (2017). Stella Meghie, who was born in Canada to Jamaican parents, directed the teenage romantic comedy, which stars Amandla Stenberg as Maddy, a girl who has spent most of her life indoors fearing she has a life-threatening condition that would make her gravely ill if she ventured outdoors, and Anika None Rose as her overprotective mother. The writer, Britain Danielle, uses the hashtag #BlackGirlMagic to describe the film, which she feels empowers Black women and girls by having them occupy key roles. In addition, the movie was adapted from a book written by a Black woman, Nicola Yoon. While it is quite typical to witness movies written by, directed by, and starring white men in theaters, a film with Black female creative talent across these roles continues to be an anomaly in the mainstream film industry. The racial logics of Hollywood insiders constrain the production of movies by and about Black talent, labeling them unbankable to the extent that Black female stories are marginalized to the brink of invisibility.

Film and television scholars agree that African Americans represent themselves best on-screen and that movies by Black people are the best means for seeing the complexity of Black cultures on-screen.[44] Often Black women's movies center around narratives about Black women, telling stories about ordinary women, who may be ignored in mainstream media. At times, their movies engage in a "revisionist" cinema to serve as a corrective to misrepresentations of Black women in cinema.[45] In making movies, Black women shift power dynamics to construct "self-definitions" of their own images.[46] Sometimes functioning as tools of ideological resistance, their "constructed knowledge" serves to replace controlling images that perpetuate racist and sexist ideologies with empowering and multidimensional characters. The agency of self-definition is lost when Black women are vastly underrepresented on Hollywood feature films and are not structurally integrated into the film industry. An integral component of tackling the Hollywood Jim Crow includes ensuring that Black women gain work in cinema production, while dismantling the barriers that impede their progress.

* * *

The racial organization of the film industry, making race into economic assets and liabilities, has direct consequences for film directors.

By presuming that Black movies are inferior commercial vehicles and labeling Black unbankable, Hollywood gives Black movies and directors inferior status, initiating organizational practices of marginalization of African American creative personnel. So long as Black movies, directors, actors, and writers are labeled unbankable, studio executives are free to discriminate against Black films and the people who direct them.

Everyday institutional racial practices in the film industry circumscribe the parameters of inclusion for Black directors. Untiringly, Hollywood insiders make use of the "unbankable" code to justify the grounds for marginalization and underrepresentation of Black directors at the film industry's core institutions (major studios) and on the film industry's core cultural products (big-budget films). Racial gaps in production budgets give white directors more financial resources to make movies compared to Black directors. Even on Black-cast movies, white directors tend to receive bigger budgets for their films, while Black directors generally work on Black-cast movies with small budgets. In foreign markets, Black directors face great barriers to gaining distribution for their movies, exacerbating the racial gap in Hollywood. White directors, on the other hand, regularly make the lion's share of their profits in overseas markets, keeping afloat movies that would otherwise drown at the domestic box office. Overall, these employment disparities create racial hierarchies that relegate Black directors to the margins of the film industry and obstruct their full integration into Hollywood, despite increases in their proportional representation.

Advocating for and even achieving gains in proportional representation alone would not necessarily lead to making inroads at major studios or in the production of core cultural products in the film industry. Therefore, efforts toward gaining full participation and attaining equal rights to produce popular cinema should focus not only on increased presence but also on a better quality of representation that includes gaining more opportunities to work for major studios and on a variety of projects, especially on big-budget films, which tend to receive the widest theatrical releases and the greatest financial returns at the box office. Deracializing Hollywood would require efforts to dismantle institutional practices that relegate Black directors to lower rungs of film production and to increase representation of Black directors, as well as directors from other underrepresented racial groups, in areas that are central to the film industry.

Moreover, Black women face unique obstacles in establishing careers as directors in Hollywood. With Black women constituting less than 1 percent of contemporary Hollywood directors, they are practically an endangered species in the mainstream film industry. Efforts to employ Black female directors and enable them to work in lucrative areas would move toward greater equality for all.

4

Making Genre Ghettos

One Hollywood insider, Harry, acknowledges that "thrillers for a predominantly African American audience are rare."[1] He finds it extremely difficult to find comparable movies for the thriller *No Good Deed*, starring Idris Elba and Taraji P. Henson. Harry utters what film directors and scholars have long suspected: that African Americans working in Hollywood have limited genre opportunities for projects.

The director Mario Van Peebles recalls how Hollywood studios have restrained his directing opportunities to a limited number of genres: "After *New Jack City*, I went around pitching another type of story, a Black family drama. But they kept wanting to put the family in the 'hood or on crack. 'Hey,' they'd say, 'the movies that make money are killer or shoot-em-up movies. Whatever makes money.'"[2] Similarly, Lee Daniels agrees that Hollywood executives have constrained Black movies and directors to a narrow range of genres. Daniels remarks, "I think that safe is always better from a studio perspective and safe equals comedy and safe equals action in regards to [Black] people. . . . If you are real and honest and making a true story, it is hard to penetrate white America."[3] Both directors suggest that Hollywood executives are eager to fund Black movies with comedy, action, or violence but are reluctant to finance films without these elements.

Joined together by narratives, images, themes, and symbols, genre films evoke shared meanings among audiences. Throughout history, Black directors have demonstrated considerable aptitude across a multitude of genres—from the commonplace family, documentary, and music genres to the less familiar urban and pastoral hero films.[4] In recent decades, horror, Black women's films, Black middle-class films, ghetto/'hood cinema, and "buppy love" romantic comedies have emerged as popular contemporary genres.[5] As Black directors continue their quest for greater integration into incrementally influential positions of control within the major spheres of Hollywood film production, genre remains a primary area of contention.

Through the process of typecasting, Hollywood decision-makers stereotype creative talent into a few narrow roles, limiting them to small segments of work.[6] The film scholar Ed Guerrero argues that the film industry sets genre traps for Black directors, clustering their work into "genre ghettos" such as comedy and action with one-dimensional stories and formulaic narratives.[7] The director Carl Franklin's career substantiates this notion of genre trappings. Before moving into television directing, Franklin spent much of his feature-filmmaking career directing crime dramas: *One False Move* (1992), *Devil in a Blue Dress* (1995), *High Crimes* (2002), and *Out of Time* (2003). In Hollywood, genre is an important category for understanding how film directors face unequal employment.

The Hollywood Jim Crow creates racial hierarchies of who can direct which movies. Under the Hollywood Jim Crow, Black directors and directors from racial-minority backgrounds are branded as unbankable; Hollywood insiders claim that their movies are risky investments. As a consequence, Hollywood decision-makers position white directors on lucrative movies in commercial genres. They defend their hiring choices using economic and cultural logics—that white directors and movies are preferred by international audiences and, therefore, are better financial investments. Notwithstanding racially biased marketing campaigns and the arbitrary focus on foreign box-office performance over the domestic box office, Hollywood insiders use these justifications to stratify opportunities and outcomes by race.

In Jim Crow systems, racial segregation locates whites in the most desirable locations and Blacks in undesirable places—for example, in the most impoverished and economically disadvantaged neighborhoods. The Hollywood Jim Crow reveals a parallel racial division of labor. The places where racial minorities are least represented, on blockbuster franchise movies in lucrative genres, are key sites where racial inequality is solidified.

While white directors occupy the most commercially lucrative genres, the places where Black directors find representation tend to be in marginal areas rather than more lucrative genres. Black directors in Hollywood are most overrepresented in the music genre, which is familiarly associated with performance and innate, physical talent through song and dance. Furthermore, in the music genre, Black directors are located in the ghettos of cinema production, in both a literal and figurative sense. Figuratively, the music genre is the "ghetto" of film genres, recording the smallest average production budgets. Meanwhile, many music-genre films are quite literally situated in the ghetto, carrying dominant, stereotypical themes of inner-city violence, despair, and gangster life. Directed by F. Gary Gray, *Straight Outta Compton* (2015) tells the story of the rap group NWA, including portrayals of Dr. Dre, Eazy-E, Ice Cube, DJ Yella, and MC Ren. The group came out of the Compton neighborhood in Los Angeles, California, and its music and lyrics echo tales of life's struggles in the neighborhood and encounters with excessive policing. Music-genre films locate Black directors in a niche that is both performance oriented and also viscerally reminiscent of disadvantaged lives.

At the other extreme, African Americans are routinely underrepresented as directors of economically lucrative blockbuster franchise films and science-fiction movies. A dearth of African Americans directing sci-fi movies is a marked disadvantage on the grounds of symbolic and material concerns. Symbolically, Black underrepresentation in the science-fiction genre operates in dialogue with racialized ideological discourses that stereotype African Americans outside intellectual cultures. Materially, sci-fi films record the largest production budgets, theatrical releases, and box-office grosses of all genres. Therefore, Black directors are also underrepresented in the most financially lucrative sector of directing. Because many serial films (e.g. *Batman*, *Superman*, *James Bond*, and *Iron Man*) often involve major sci-fi themes, it is also rare that African Americans direct lucrative franchise movies. Instead, racial politics that label Black movies and directors unbankable steer Black directors away from the sci-fi genre and thereby from top film franchises.

Securing jobs in film-directing positions on Hollywood studios' marquee cultural products signifies a vital barometer for Black employment opportunities and outcomes in prominent positions in cinematic production. What results is an incomplete integration into Hollywood that impedes Black directors from penetrating the core of the motion-picture industry and disallows them from attaining the highest levels of commercial success in film directing.

Music-Genre Ghettos

Hip hop musicians such as Master P, Queen Latifah, and Ice Cube have used their successful music careers to enter the film industry and establish thriving film-production companies.[8] A similar pattern arises with Black directors who gain access to film directing through the music genre. This is so much the case that the music genre is the only genre in which African Americans are overrepresented, compared to their proportion of the general U.S. population, directing many movies with major themes of music and dance. While overrepresentation in any area within the film industry might on the surface appear to be a positive outcome for Black directors, overrepresentation in the music genre does come with its disadvantages. Typecasting Black directors into the music genre can limit their career progression into more lucrative genres. In addition, compared to other genres such as sports, comedy, romance, science fiction, action, drama, and thriller, the music genre records the smallest average production budgets. In this way, the music genre is a metaphorical "genre ghetto" in Hollywood. According the U.S. Census, ghetto tracts are defined by their high concentrations of poverty within a given area. By this view, the music genre can be characterized as the most "impoverished" genre, with the lowest production values of all genres.

If big budgets, commercial success, and exposure in theaters are desirable for film directors, African Americans' ghettoization in the music genre stands as a serious impediment to their likelihood of achieving successful careers. A more dismal outlook, however, is the possibility that music-genre films have the smallest average budgets, opening-weekend grosses, domestic box-office grosses, and theatrical releases *because* more African Americans direct these movies. The "unbankable" label suggests that white Hollywood insiders devalue Black movies and directors and, hence, steer them away from big budgets. In that case, rather than expecting that integrating Black directors into more genres will fix the problem, whatever genre in which African Americans are concentrated would be expected to have the lowest production values.

Besides placement in a figurative genre ghetto of small budgets and small box-office grosses, music-genre films also locate Black directors in literal genre ghettos—on movies in which crime, drugs, violence, and urban ghetto life are prominent themes. In *Idlewild* (2006), *Turn It Up* (2000), *State Property 2* (2005), *Notorious* (2009), and *ATL* (2006), gangsters, crime, and drugs are common themes. In *State Property 2*, for example, gangsters battle for control over Philadelphia. Similarly, in

Idlewild, gangsters vie to take over a Michigan nightclub owned by the speakeasy performer Rooster (Big Boi); meanwhile, Rooster's piano-playing partner, Percival Jenkins (Andre Benjamin), helps ward off the gangsters. Set in Brooklyn, *Turn It Up* follows Diamond (Pras Michel), who hopes that music, rap, and a studio contract will forge his way out of a tumultuous inner-city life.

A contemporary subgenre of the Black music film, African American dance movies also incorporate themes of life in urban communities. Generally, these movies follow the exploits of young, poor, disadvantaged African American men in their teens and early twenties who rely on dance for upward mobility and a way out of a tough inner-city life. For these characters, dance represents a tangible means to achieve success—characterized by wealth, socioeconomic mobility, and/or respect. In *Dance Flick* (2009), for instance, Thomas Uncles (Damon Wayans Jr.) is a street dancer from the "wrong side of the tracks" who quickly realizes that dance might help him realize his dreams despite his unlucky social status.

Breaking the pattern of male protagonists, *Save the Last Dance* (2001) and *Honey* (2003) feature female protagonists. Hailing from New York's East Harlem, Honey (Jessica Alba), in the eponymous film, aspires to become a successful music-video choreographer. A hip hop dance instructor at a local youth center, Honey encourages young kids to stay out of trouble and off the streets by attending her dance lessons. In *Save the Last Dance*, Sara (Julia Stiles) is a white student who is forced to move to a predominantly Black neighborhood in inner-city Chicago to live with her father after her mother passes away. Sara is one of only a few white students in her school, and her goal is to attend a top dance school and become a ballerina, a path that will allow her to escape her current inner-city neighborhood.

The story lines of many music-genre films feature a recurring narrative that dance, or more broadly performance, is a way for poor Black youth to overcome disadvantaged positions in ghetto communities. This narrative is similar to one that channels thousands of poor Blacks into professional sports and entertainment industries, purporting those paths to be more viable than other options, such as educational attainment or entrepreneurship, for African Americans' success and socioeconomic mobility. The recurring appearance of ghetto themes in music-genre films perpetuates controlling images of African Americans. Meanwhile, overrepresentation in the genre with the lowest production values raises questions about the kinds of career trajectories Black directors can achieve and how racial hierarchies, which stratify Blacks and whites in a similar manner to Jim Crow, obstruct their advancement.

Progress or Place?

Despite overwhelming links to ghetto stereotypes, Black directors' overrepresentation in the music genre is not to be wholly condemned. To some extent, it perhaps should be celebrated as the one place in the film industry where integration, both historically and at present, has manifested itself most prominently. Since the late 1920s, music-genre films have marked the most significant entrée into Hollywood for Black actors; African American musical and dance acts enabled talking pictures to become viable commercial products for Hollywood studios.[9] During this period, a growing demand for Black-cast music-genre films emerged, especially among upwardly mobile white audiences, a trend that mirrors today's voracious consumption of Black hip hop and gangsta rap music and movies among suburban white teenagers.[10]

Furthermore, African Americans witnessed some of their earliest progress toward integration and recognition within the music genre. The only Black person to win any Academy Award during the 1970s was Isaac Hayes, who won Best Original Song for "Theme for Shaft," featured in the movie *Shaft* (1971). Between 1983 and 1990, African Americans added another eight top industry honors in sound and music categories. Irene Cara's "Flashdance . . . What a Feeling" in *Flashdance* (1983), Stevie Wonder's "I Just Called to Say I Love You" in *The Woman in Red* (1984), and Lionel Richie's "Say You, Say Me" in *White Nights* (1985) each won Best Original Song. Best Original Score went to Prince for *Purple Rain* (1984) and Herbie Hancock for *Round Midnight* (1986). Meanwhile, Best Sound / Sound Mixing accolades were awarded to Willie D. Burton for *Bird* (1988) and Russell Williams II for *Glory* (1989) and *Dances with Wolves* (1990).[11] The dawn of the twenty-first century saw continued honors for Black music-genre films. Best Original Song went to Juicy J, Frayser Boy, and DJ Paul's "It's Hard Out Here for a Pimp" in *Hustle & Flow* (2005), while Best Sound Mixing went to Willie D. Burton for

Dreamgirls (2006).[12] The rhythm-and-blues singer John Legend and the rapper Common won Best Original Song for "Glory" in *Selma* (2014). Furthermore, the actors Jamie Foxx in *Ray* (2004) and Jennifer Hudson in *Dreamgirls* (2006) won Best Actor and Best Supporting Actress, respectively, for their performances in music-genre films. Together, the history of Black-cast musicals and Academy Award honors illustrate a long tradition of Black success in film with regard to musical talent, indeed more recognition than African Americans have achieved in movie directing, producing, editing, and cinematography combined.

Beyond awards programs, music-genre films are of historical importance for American culture. They offer the opportunity to celebrate great American musicians. Hollywood movies have commemorated the musical and performance talents of James Brown, Nina Simone, Tupac Shakur, Notorious B.I.G., Ray Charles, and many others. The music genre is also popular with television programs that highlight African American dance, music, and hip hop cultures. Some popular music-genre television shows include the hip hop mogul Sean "P. Diddy" Combs's *Making the Band* (2000–2009), the choreographer Laurieann Gibson's *Born to Dance* (2011–), the gospel competition show *Sunday Best* (2007–), the DJ competition show *Master of the Mix* (2010–2013), the reality-television drama *Love and Hip-Hop* (2010–), the elite youth majorette-competition reality show *Bring It!* (2014–), and the hip hop network drama *Empire* (2015–).

In part, Black directors' disproportionate work on music-genre movies could result from a matter of choice. For some directors, placement on music-genre movies reflects past experiences. Directors such as DJ Pooh, F. Gary Gray, and Sanaa Hamri began their careers in music before embarking on feature-film directing. Before DJ Pooh directed the comedies *3 Strikes* (2000) and *The Wash* (2001), he was a record producer for Tupac Shakur, Dr. Dre, LL Cool J, and Snoop Dogg. Similarly, Sanaa Hamri directed videos for Mariah Carey, Nicki Minaj, Christina Aguilera, and Prince before she directed motion pictures such as the teen drama *Sisterhood of the Traveling Pants 2* (2008) and the romantic comedies *Something New* (2006) and *Just Wright* (2010). F. Gary Gray's career trajectory presents yet another example of transitioning into Hollywood film directing after music-video directing. Between 2000 and 2003, Gray directed music videos and music-video documentaries for artists such as Outkast, Ice Cube, R. Kelly, and Babyface. Following his music-video stint, he became a successful Hollywood director, working on movies such as the action/crime thriller *The Italian Job* (2003), the action/crime drama *A Man Apart* (2003), the music/crime comedy *Be Cool* (2005), the crime/drama thriller *Law Abiding Citizen* (2009), and the hip hop / biography drama *Straight Outta Compton* (2015). The $28 million *Straight Outta Compton* was a huge hit, grossing $161 million at the domestic box office and an estimated $40 million in overseas markets. For these directors, music-genre movies follow quite logically from their previous experiences. The historical importance of the music genre for African Americans in cinema, and for Black directors in their past careers, could account for why African Americans are so overrepresented in this area of film directing.

While the prevalence of Black directors in the music genre could be reflective of functional processes, racial progress, or an ideal fit between skill set and Hollywood job openings, it could also be a source of conflict and a reaffirmation of racial practices that circumscribe a limited place for Black directors in the film industry. The issue that lingers unanswered is whether African Americans are overrepresented in the music genre because performance is viewed as the most socially acceptable position for Black people in a white-dominated film industry. In U.S. society, African Americans have long held and achieved success in positions as musicians, comedians, and entertainers. African Americans working in areas associated with musicality are less likely to upset the status quo that contains Black people in entertainment-oriented roles. In the music genre, the singing, dancing, rapping, and the like emerge from the individual rather than from the theatrics of nondiegetic special effects. Therefore, although many Hollywood movies intend to draw audiences through spectacles of performance, the argument could be made that music-genre movies are the most performance oriented of all genres.

Despite the various positive aspects of African Americans in music, ultimately, overpopulating Black directors in the music genre further ghettoizes them into limited directorial projects that center on stereotypic subjects. Typecasting in music can limit directors' careers. The Hollywood Jim Crow segregates Black directors on narrow paths and forecloses other opportunities. Not having the opportunity to showcase their technical skills on a variety of projects, the full spectrum of representation is closed off to directing in more lucrative genres.

Missing Faces of Science Fiction

For many film patrons, the movie *Black Panther* (2018) resurrects the memory of the Black superhero genre that once dominated the silver screen during the 1970s Blaxploitation era. In the movie, Chadwick Boseman, who played the Major League Baseball Hall of Famer Jackie Robinson in the film 42, stars as T'Challa, the Black Panther and Prince of Wakanda who is poised to become king after his father's untimely death. Boseman's role is a rarity in Hollywood for Black actors, who are seldom featured as superheroes. Black underrepresentation behind the camera of science-fiction action/adventure films is also pronounced. Hence, throughout the preproduction process, the discussion of who would play the title role in the adaptation of the Marvel comic drew much less interest than conversations surrounding who would direct the film. The unlikely convergence of a Black superhero movie, the sci-fi genre, and a dearth of Black directors in Hollywood raises questions about African Americans' presence behind the camera of lucrative sci-fi movies that are critical to understanding their place in the contemporary Hollywood directing hierarchy.

Science-fiction movies are characterized by portrayals of fantastical plots, narratives, and characters rooted in far-off worlds: past, present, and future. Underlying themes of sci-fi media tackle contemporary social, political, moral, religious, technological, and environmental issues. Sci-fi filmmakers propose philosophical conjectures about the world, human existence, and the future.[13] By far, the most visible face of any African American talent in the Hollywood science-fiction genre is Will Smith. Smith and his manager, James Lassiter, explain that Smith's success in the genre was strategically calculated. As they recall, they charted his path to becoming a huge global movie star by analyzing the top-grossing movies of all time. Lassiter explains, "[We] said, OK, what are the patterns? We realized that 10 out of 10 had special effects. Nine out of 10 had special effects with creatures. Eight out of 10 had special effects with creatures and a love story."[14] Their observations of top-grossing movies summarize their clever strategy to pursue hits in the sci-fi genre.

Few African Americans have been able to make inroads into the genre, but Smith has done so as a major star and producer. In *I Am Legend* (2007), Smith embodied the role of a scientist who attempts to engineer a cure for a debilitating virus in order to save humankind. Occupying dual roles, Smith was a producer and lead star of the futuristic tale of robots and criminality *I, Robot* (2004) and the renegade-superhero movie *Hancock* (2008). Smith also starred in and produced *After Earth* (2013), in which a father and son (Will Smith and Jaden Smith) face being stranded on earth one thousand years after humans abandoned the planet. Smith's double threat as a global box-office draw and cofounder of the production company Overbrook Entertainment, the conduit through which several of his star vehicles are produced, enables him unfettered entrée into this area that is generally closed off to African American producers and directors.

Unfortunately, Will Smith is almost unique. Besides Smith, there is a vast marginalization of African Americans on the production side of Hollywood sci-fi films. Between 2000 and 2016, whites directed more than 155 sci-fi movies, compared to 7 for Asian directors, 5 for Latino/a directors, and 3 for Black directors. While whites directed 91 percent of sci-fi movies, African Americans directed only 2 percent of sci-fi movies. In contemporary Hollywood movies, Black directors are nearly absent in both the sci-fi genre and the related fantasy genre, which regularly features supernatural and magical elements. The odds of directing a sci-fi film distributed by a Hollywood studio are noticeably slim for Black Americans.

Indeed, few Black directors have broken into the genre. Some exceptions include Paul Hunter's MGM fantasy film *Bulletproof Monk* (2003), which follows a mysterious Tibetan monk's relationship with a young street kid in their attempt to protect an ancient scroll from enemies. Tim Story's comic-book-based *Fantastic Four* (2005) and *Fantastic Four: Rise of the Silver Surfer* (2007), both distributed by 20th Century Fox, chronicle the adventures of a group of astronauts with superpowers. In Olatunde Osunsanmi's Universal film *The Fourth Kind* (2009), supernatural happenings occur when extraterrestrials descend on a small Alaskan town. Soon after *The Fourth Kind* debuted, Albert Hughes and Allen Hughes directed the postapocalyptic Warner Brothers movie *The Book of Eli* (2010), about the journey of one man (Denzel Washington) to protect secrets that will save humankind. In large part, these films represent the small group of Black-directed Hollywood films that are categorized within the sci-fi (and the related fantasy) genre. Collectively, Hollywood sci-fi films are almost exclusively white futuristic fantasies.

Black directors' underrepresentation on sci-fi movies is of great consequence to their foothold in the industry. They lose standing in a genre that not only is financially lucrative but also reaches large audiences. Between 2000 and 2016, the average budget for Hollywood sci-fi movies was just over $100 million. Of all movie genres, sci fi films are the high est grossing. Because of sci-fi's immense popularity and box-office success, it is a particularly lucrative genre for Hollywood directors' careers. Coupled with underrepresentation in directing sci-fi films, the fact that many sci-fi films are also part of serial Hollywood blockbuster movie franchises multiplies African Americans' magnitude of marginalization in the film industry.

No doubt, the dearth of Black directors in the sci-fi genre also impacts the characters, themes, and narratives present in Hollywood sci-fi movies. Studies on racial representations in genre classics such as *Star Trek* and *Planet of the Apes* as well as research on race in sci-fi cinema across multiple films reveal patterns of underrepresentation of African Americans in sci-fi cinema.[15] Rarely are Black characters envisioned in popular sci-fi films. Casts in sci-fi/fantasy blockbusters tend to be mostly white, while roles for African Americans, as well as characters representing other underrepresented racial groups, are typically underwritten.[16] Even the presence of some characters—such as Laurence Fishburne as the legendary computer hacker Morpheus in *The Matrix Trilogy* (1999, 2003)—is accompanied with restrictions on Black cultural expressions. Few self-consciously Black characters exist in sci-fi films, though some notable exceptions surface in independent movies. For instance, *Space Is the Place* (1974) features a jazz space prophet, Sun-Ra, who endeavors to save the Black race from its power struggles on planet Earth. In *The Brother from Another Planet* (1984), outer-space bounty hunters chase a mute alien (Joe Morton) through the streets of New York City's Harlem. The sci-fi action movie *Sleight* (2017), directed by J. D. Dillard, was an independent hit, grossing nearly $4 million at the domestic box office on a meager $250,000 production budget. *Sleight* features a street magician and engineering guru, Bo (Jacob Latimore), who turns to selling drugs to support his sister when his parents pass away.[17] Unlike these independent films, most mainstream movies avoid placing characters rooted in a Black experience in their narratives. Rather, although on-screen Black representation in sci-fi has increased dramatically, these characters rarely convey expressions of Black political sensibilities, history, cultural identity, or subjectivity; nor do they expound on notions of past, present, future, or imagined Blackness.[18]

Regarding the presentation of racial themes, sci-fi blockbuster movies also tend to be problematic. Irrespective of cast, sci-fi and fantasy blockbuster franchise films, by and large, propagate fantasies of white patriarchy and conservatively depict a nostalgic white masculinity that is unchallenged by race, class, or gender hierarchies.[19] To date, the film scholar Adilifu Nama's study of African Americans' (mostly on-screen) representation in sci-fi films from the 1950s through the current moment presents the most extensive treatment of Black representation in sci-fi cinema. Nama stresses that sci-fi films embody symbolic discourses and ideological messages concerning what people should desire, fear, or believe about race. Commonly, mainstream sci-fi movies either (1) ignore race completely by repressing race in the subtext, (2) privilege class over race, or (3) present a colorblind future. In other cases, there is ambiguity among cultural producers concerning whether sci-fi characters can be interpreted as racial or nonracial.[20] In the event that the subject of race is implicitly broached in sci-fi movies, problematic themes of Black racial stigma, fear of racial assimilation, racial contamination, and othered Black bodies materialize.

Hollywood's racial logic of assumptions of unbankability for Black films and directors has real effects on the careers of film-industry workers. African Americans' marginalization behind the camera of sci-fi films means that they have little control over the articulation of characters on-screen and the ideological framing of race within sci-fi narratives. The dearth of Black directors of Hollywood sci-fi cinema also demarcates limited parameters for African Americans' careers in the film-directing profession.

Sci-Fi Gatekeepers

Tyler Perry has yet to release a sci-fi film in theaters, though he voices a willingness to direct one. Although Perry is best known for his Madea comedies and dramas, he expresses having flexibility in multiple genres. Calling himself a "big sci-fi guy," Perry once stated that he was working on a sci-fi script.[21] In one interview, Perry quips, "I'm open to everything. I'm just as comfortable with *Star Trek* as I am with *Precious* as I am with *Boyz N the Hood* as I am with *Madea*. I'm all over the place. It's like my musical taste is from Jazz to Rap and Rock and Country. It's everything."[22] Notably, Tyler Perry has achieved more consistent economic success at the box office than have the majority of directors, regardless of race. In addition, he has written, produced, and directed several successful television shows, adding to his versatility. Yet, despite his affinity for a variety of genres, his directing career has been limited to few genres, predominantly comedy and romance, and no big-budget movies. Perhaps as a consolation prize, Perry played an admiral in *Star Trek* (2009), but as a director, Perry's career has been effectively contained to working in few, narrow genres.

As film-industry statistics show, few Black directors find work in the science-fiction genre. What is left to understand is whether this under-representation is a matter or choice or a result of structural impediments

Figure 4.1. "She's Back," billboard ad for Tyler Perry's *Madea's Class Reunion* at 1101 New York Avenue, NW, Washington DC. Photo by Elvert Barnes Photography, September 12, 2004.

to breaking into the genre. Black directors' marginalization on sci-fi and blockbuster franchise films could result from the intentional and/or unintentional acts of white gatekeepers. It is possible that unconscious or subconscious bias could be at play if decision-makers are unaware and unintentionally marginalizing Black Americans away from directing lucrative sci-fi franchise films. Assignments to films could also be based on informal, closed social networks that give preference to directors whom studio executives know and trust and with whom they have existing social ties. The director Tim Story discusses how the use of social networks for hiring decisions excludes potential directors: "In my business you find the reasons for 'no' are ridiculous. Sometimes they have nothing to do with you. They have to do with somebody was promised something years ago and it just so happens they have to look at a few people, so they can say 'hey, we looked at a few people.' But that job was already given to a certain person beforehand."[23] Historically, African Americans have been excluded from these networks in which many business relationships and connections are developed and exploited.[24]

Black Americans' marginalization probably occurs by deliberate design rather than by casual error. From an economic standpoint, studio executives assert that because Hollywood is a profit-driven industry, studios make movies for audiences without much regard for equality, much less the personal tastes of creative personnel.[25] Though whites are no longer the proportional majority at the box office, studio executives privilege the desires of white audiences. First, Hollywood insiders imagine white and international audiences to be the targets of big-budget movies.[26] Second, Hollywood insiders suggest that these audiences prefer white movies and directors over Black movies and directors and that these audiences would not patronize Black work outside stereotypical genres.[27] A Jim Crow system is rooted in assumptions of racial superiority and inferiority. In this case, Hollywood insiders use cultural and economic logics to back their assumptions of racial superiority and inferiority of cultural products. Studio executives offer unflinching support for white directors, whom they more often choose to direct sci-fi films, which primarily feature majority-white casts, themes, and stories.

Besides financial motivations, Hollywood insiders could have ideological reasons for Black directors' underrepresentation in sci-fi works, with white producers acting as gatekeepers who prevent African

Americans from entering scientific domains—erecting the same institutional boundaries that exist in occupations and educational attainment within fields of science. In addition, the airing of media programs involves making decisions about the framing of value systems and positions on social issues.[28] Studio executives could feel that Black directors would disrupt or dismantle ideologies that are perpetuated in the most popular franchise films and genres. With so much at stake in the influence that Hollywood movies exert in shaping popular national and global discourses around substantial topics, it is possible that Black directors' inclusion into popular franchise films would undermine movies' underlying ideological support of a white-dominated power structure.

Furthermore, marginalization of African Americans in directing franchise films could occur to maintain the status quo of employment hierarchies in a white-male-dominated film industry. If African Americans completed successive profitable projects on the scale of Hollywood blockbuster franchise movies, by virtue of their success, they could not be easily denied access to big budgets on future projects; rather, they would be entitled to subsequent projects of similar magnitude. With time, if an increasing number of African Americans directed blockbuster franchise films, the privilege and economic benefits attached to directing lucrative movies would be shared across racial groups, thereby upending the existing racial hierarchy of the Hollywood Jim Crow.

Commenting on African Americans' underrepresentation in popular sci-fi literature, the African American literature scholar Gregory Rutledge theorizes that Black underrepresentation in sci-fi genres could operate due to personal choice (1) if socioeconomic inequality or race struggles (rather than sci-fi narratives) dominate Black intellectual work—in the case that African Americans due to their aggregate socioeconomic disadvantage have little time or creative distance to develop speculative fiction—or (2) if sci-fi narratives contradict the spiritual traditions of African Americans, the majority of whom maintain strong ties to religious faiths.[29] Directors, however, debunk the myth that their absence from helming sci-fi films is a product of choice. Usually directors are not the originators of the source material for Hollywood sci-fi movies, as most major-studio sci-fi films are developed and produced in-house, so their time available to develop speculative fiction is not an obstacle to directing a studio-developed project. From Black directors' perspectives, their absence in the sci-fi genre is hardly reflective of a lack of interest. In fact, directors communicate a desire to direct sci-fi films. For example, Reginald Hudlin expresses the desire to direct a sci-fi film: "For me, I sort of looked at George Lucas' career. He did the teen comedy *American Graffiti* and went on to do *Star Wars*. I always wanted to do the same thing. I figured I'd do *House Party* and then do my version of *Star Wars*. I had a big sci-fi project, several of them, that I kept trying to get off the ground and wasn't successful at getting those off the ground. It hit this glass ceiling in Hollywood."[30] Hudlin's testimonial gives credence to the notion that white gatekeepers, rather than Black directors' personal aspirations, are greater actors in the underrepresentation of African Americans in the sci-fi film genre.

Unable to fully participate in the full spectrum of Hollywood directing, Black Americans are instead marginalized and located away from profitable sci-fi movies, impeding their ability to reach the upper echelons of commercial success in an industry that generously rewards box-office hits. Ultimately, the Jim Crow–like segregation of Black directors away from profitable sci-fi movies amounts to a racialization of film genres in Hollywood. Racial politics predetermine a location for Black Americans that is outside the central cultural products of media institutions. In effect, this marginalization prevents them from attaining the highest levels of economic achievement in the film industry. Directing a sci-fi film, therefore, becomes a structural barrier for Black directors who, despite their experience, are unable to penetrate the lucrative genre.

Closed Doors for Tent-Pole Franchise Movies

"Studios need tent pole franchises to create huge profit, a few successful tent poles a year can make a slate. From 2000–2014 franchises are . . . the least risky pictures. . . . Trying to create tent pole franchises should be a thought on every picture produced. It isn't always possible, here it was and [the studio] took a safe direction which in this case is not likely to create a true tent pole franchise."[31] Here the Hollywood insider Billy discusses how studios depend on franchise movies. Tent-pole movies are expected to be big hits that support the entire structure of the film studio through their generation of huge profit—hence the imagery of a central pole supporting the structure of a tent. But Billy is negative about Black directors and casts, even ones with high popularity, headlining franchise movies. He does not believe they can "create a true tent pole franchise." This way of thinking by Hollywood insiders restricts Black Americans and other racial minorities from attaining lucrative jobs in commercial genres. The vast majority of these roles go to white directors and actors.

The science-fiction genre holds significance beyond itself, interacting with tent-pole blockbuster franchise movies in a way that calcifies obstacles for African Americans' advancement to prestigious directing positions. Blockbuster movies are profitable, high-concept films with commercial stories, recognizable stars, and story lines that are easily pitched in a few sentences.[32] In the late 1970s, the sci-fi genre merged with the emerging action/adventure, big-budget-blockbuster franchise model to create a special-effects-driven action/adventure brand of sci-fi films. The hybrid genre gained popularity following the successes of *Star Wars: Episode IV—A New Hope* (1977) and *Star Trek: The Motion Picture* (1979).[33] With the emergence of the blockbuster model of huge investments and big returns came the creation of stratified levels of films. The sci-fi genre simultaneously adopted the blockbuster strategy of investing a large amount of money into a creative production with the goal of yielding even larger profits through high-volume sales.[34] Studio executives approached the film business with the logic that most movies fail, few succeed, and one huge success outweighs many losses. In turn, they drastically altered their film production and finance strategies to support preestablished material with built-in audiences.

This shift to the blockbuster model resulted in a dramatic upswing in production costs and substantial promotional support of only a few films (and consequently only a few directors).[35] Moreover, the shift to the blockbuster model created a stark hierarchy between a few lucrative film-directing opportunities and many less profitable positions. Marginalization in small-budget productions largely precludes directing the most lucrative big-budget films: tent-pole blockbuster franchise movies—serial films that are major productions for Hollywood studios and allow directors to gain experience, popularity, success, and reputation. Perhaps unsurprisingly, racial hierarchies aligned to determine which directors did and did not receive lucrative opportunities.

Billy explains, "Event pictures, when successful, throw off huge profit. So studios build their slates around event pictures—and ideally pictures that have a large inherent upside (which many of [the studio's] extra bets don't have). Event pictures are huge cash cows when they hit and more important they lead to franchises. Aiming for home runs with a fall back of a double seems like a solid strategy to me."[36] Billy discusses the importance of potential blockbuster movies—"event pictures" that yield huge profits when successful. Such pictures can be "huge cash cows" around which studios build their slate of movies. Surprise hit movies, such as *The Fast and the Furious, Paranormal Activity, and Scary Movie*, can become franchise movie series that bring profits to studios for years to come. At the same time, this Hollywood insider suggests that lucrative movies with big budgets should not be made with Black stars or casts. He believes that they do not have the potential for huge profits, that they are risky and do not "have a large inherent upside." Racial politics is embedded into who directs and stars in tent-pole blockbuster franchise movies. Racial minorities, and in particular African Americans, feel the brunt of racial hierarchy in film directing, characterized by their lack of access to central positions.

In addition to the underrepresentation of Black directors in the sci-fi genre, they also face marginalization in directing Hollywood franchise movies. Tables 4.1 and 4.2 list top-grossing franchise films released to theaters between 2000 and 2016 for Black and non-Black directors. Of all Black directors, Tim Story directed the largest number of franchise movies, including the popular *Fantastic Four* and *Ride Along* series and the Black-cast romantic comedy *Think Like a Man* series. Tyler Perry created his own franchise films with the popular Madea character played by Perry dressed up as a woman. Malcolm D. Lee also directed a number of franchise movies with his work on *Scary Movie 5* (2013), *Best Man Holiday* (2013), *and Barbershop: The Next Cut* (2016). African Americans' representation on franchise movies, however, is largely race bound, structured by racial hierarchies that place them on the least profitable franchise films.

Although Black directors are present on franchise movies, they find the greatest underrepresentation on the most highly marketed and lucrative franchise films. It took eighteen films before the Marvel Comic Cinematic Universe added a Black director, Ryan Coogler, to its slate of franchise-film directors, for *Black Panther* (2018). Other franchise series still fail to be racially inclusive of Black directors behind the camera. Popular series such as *Harry Potter, The Lord of the Rings, Star Wars, Batman,* and *Superman* lack racial inclusivity in the directing position.

Directing franchise films helps directors achieve commercial success and attain large production budgets. F. Gary Gray's *The Fate of the Furious* (2017) and Ryan Coogler's *Black Panther* (2018) each grossed more than $1 billion worldwide, more commercial success at the box office than either director had with any of his previous movies. Even while directing less profitable and smaller-budgeted franchise movies compared to white directors, Black directors have found the most commercial success with franchise movies. Compared to Black-directed movies that are not part of franchises, Black-directed franchise movies boast bigger budgets, larger theatrical releases, and better box-office performances. Between 2000 and 2016, seven out of the top-eight highest grossing Black-directed films in the domestic market were franchise movies: Tim Story's *Fantastic Four* (2005), *Fantastic Four: Rise of the Silver Surfer* (2007), and the action/crime comedy *Ride Along* (2014), Keenen Ivory Wayans's horror spoof *Scary Movie* (2000), John Singleton's action/crime thriller *2 Fast 2 Furious* (2003), Ryan Coogler's sports drama *Creed* (2015), and Antoine Fuqua's action/crime thriller *The Equalizer* (2014). The only top-performing nonfranchise movie was F. Gary Gray's top-grossing music drama *Straight Outta Compton* (2015). It is also not by coincidence that the best performing film at the box office between 2000 and 2016 that was directed by a Black woman—Angela Robinson's *Herbie Fully Loaded* (2005), about a white female NASCAR competitor (played by Lindsay Lohan)—is also part of a franchise movie series.

The success of blockbuster movies has spurred the operational model that currently governs the film-production culture at Hollywood studios. Blockbuster films and movie franchises have become the marquee products of the American film industry, commanding top performances at the global box office. Adaptations from previous works, such as comic books, novels, television shows, board games, video games, and previous films, serve as source material for many new movies. Increasingly, Hollywood movies are recycled materials. Accordingly, the journalist Simon Reynolds notes that the first decade of the twenty-first century was "dominated by the re- prefix: *revivals, reissues, remakes,*

TABLE 4.1. Black-Directed Franchise Movies, 2000–2016

Film	Year	Distributor	Budget ($, in millions)
Scary Movie	2000	Miramax	19
Shaft	2000	Paramount	46
Scary Movie 2	2001	Miramax	45
Barbershop	2002	MGM	12
Honey	2003	Universal	18
2 Fast 2 Furious	2003	Universal	76
Barbershop 2: Back in the Business	2004	MGM	30
Taxi	2004	20th Century Fox	25
Diary of a Mad Black Woman	2005	Lionsgate	6
Fantastic Four	2005	20th Century Fox	100
Herbie: Fully Loaded	2005	Buena Vista	50
Fantastic Four: Rise of the Silver Surfer	2007	20th Century Fox	130
The Sisterhood of the Traveling Pants 2	2008	Warner Brothers	27
I Can Do Bad All by Myself	2009	Lionsgate	13
Madea Goes to Jail	2009	Lionsgate	18
Madea's Big Happy Family	2011	Lionsgate	25
Madea's Witness Protection	2012	Lionsgate	20
Think Like a Man	2012	Sony Screen Gems	12
Best Man Holiday	2013	Universal	17
Scary Movie 5	2013	Weinstein/Dimension	29
A Madea Christmas	2014	Lionsgate	25
The Equalizer	2014	Sony	55
Ride Along	2014	Universal	25
Think Like a Man Too	2014	Sony Screen Gems	24
Creed	2015	Warner Brothers (New Line)	35
Barbershop: The Next Cut	2016	Warner Brothers (New Line)	20
Boo! A Madea Halloween	2016	Lionsgate	20
Ride Along 2	2016	Universal	40

Source: Box-office estimates and production budgets from Boxofficemojo.com and IMDb.com.
Note: Includes movies distributed by Sony, Universal, 20th Century Fox, Paramount, Buena Vista, Warner Brothers, Miramax, MGM, Focus, Lionsgate, New Line, Fox Searchlight, Sony Screen Gems, and Weinstein/Dimension. Box-office numbers above $1 million are rounded to the nearest million.

Domestic gross ($, in millions)	Foreign gross ($, in millions)	# of theaters	Director
157	121.0	2,912	Keenen Ivory Wayans
70	0.4	2,433	John Singleton
71	70.0	3,220	Keenen Ivory Wayans
76	1.3	2,176	Kevin Rodney Sullivan
30	32.0	1,972	Bille Woodruff
127	109.0	3,408	John Singleton
65	0.9	2,711	Kevin Rodney Sullivan
37	32.0	3,001	Tim Story
51	0.2	1,703	Darren Grant
155	112.0	3,619	Tim Story
66	78.0	3,521	Angela Robinson
132	157.0	3,963	Tim Story
44	0.3	2,714	Sanaa Hamri
52	N/A	2,255	Tyler Perry
91	N/A	2,203	Tyler Perry
53	0.8	2,288	Tyler Perry
66	1.0	2,161	Tyler Perry
92	5.0	2,052	Tim Story
71	2.0	2,041	Malcolm D. Lee
32	46.0	3,402	Malcolm D. Lee
53	0.9	2,194	Tyler Perry
102	91.0	3,236	Antoine Fuqua
135	20.0	2,867	Tim Story
65	5.0	2,225	Tim Story
110	64.0	3,502	Ryan Coogler
54	1.0	2,676	Malcolm D. Lee
74	2.0	2,299	Tyler Perry
91	33.0	3,192	Tim Story

TABLE 4.2. Top-Grossing Hollywood Franchise Movies, 2000–2016

Film	Year	Distributor	Budget ($, in millions)	Domestic gross ($, in millions)	Foreign gross ($, in millions)	# of theaters	Director
Avatar	2009	20th Century Fox	237	750	2,028	3,461	James Cameron
Harry Potter and the Deathly Hallows Part 2	2011	Warner Brothers	125	381	1,342	4,375	David Yates
Transformers: Dark of the Moon	2011	Paramount/ DreamWorks	195	352	771	4,088	Michael Bay
Marvel's The Avengers	2012	Buena Vista	220	623	896	4,349	Joss Whedon
Iron Man 3	2013	Buena Vista	200	409	806	4,253	Shane Black
Avengers: Age of Ultron	2015	Buena Vista	250	459	946	4,276	Joss Whedon
Furious 7	2015	Universal	190	353	1,163	4,022	James Wan
Jurassic World	2015	Universal	150	652	1,019	4,291	Colin Trevorrow
Star Wars: The Force Awakens	2015	Buena Vista	245	937	1,132	4,134	J. J. Abrams
Captain America: Civil War	2016	Buena Vista	250	408	745	4,226	Anthony Russo, Joe Russo

Source: Box-office estimates and production budgets from Boxofficemojo.com and IMdB.com.

re-enactments."[37] Trade publications also discuss this trend and its over-kill with audiences. In 2014, an article in *The Atlantic* was titled "The Reason Why Hollywood Makes So Many Boring Superhero Movies."[38] Years later, the sentiment remained. A 2017 *Variety* article was titled "How Too Many Aging Franchises Wrecked the Summer Box Office."[39]

Despite an onset of franchise-movie fatigue, tent-pole blockbuster franchise films continue to play an integral role in Hollywood film production. Studios are reliant on franchise films for huge profits, and these films command the biggest budgets and theatrical releases. Directing tent-pole features enables directors more latitude and credibility on future film projects. Yet even though Hollywood franchise movies allow directors to demonstrate their abilities to direct commercially viable films, Hollywood's racial logics and practices foreclose myriad opportunities for Black directors on lucrative tent-pole franchise films.

Unlike Black directors, white directors—even those inexperienced in film directing or unsuccessful at the box office—experience no such marginalization. The white American filmmaker McG began his feature-film career directing the Hollywood action/comedy franchise movies *Charlie's Angels* (2000) and *Charlie's Angels: Full Throttle* (2003), with $93 million and $120 million production budgets, respectively. Later in his career, McG helmed the Warner Brothers sci-fi/action flick *Terminator Salvation* (2009), a $200 million production that grossed over $370 million at the worldwide box office.

Likewise, Joss Whedon, also a white American, wrote and directed his first feature, the sci-fi/adventure film *Serenity* (2005), distributed by Warner Brothers, on a $39 million budget and grossed a paltry $25 million at the domestic box office. His film *Much Ado about Nothing* (2012) was even less successful, making just over $4 million in domestic markets. Indeed, Whedon's only commercially successful features are his sci-fi/action Marvel comic-book adaptations *The Avengers* (2012) and *Avengers: Age of Ultron* (2015); the former was made on a $220 million production budget and grossed more than an estimated $1.5 billion worldwide, while the latter was made on a $350 million budget and grossed more than $1.3 billion worldwide.

Studio executives regularly cite uncertainty about how a director would handle a project of a large magnitude or a big-budget movie as reasons for exclusion of Black directors from movie projects. However, a bevy of white directors who have not directed big-budget movies or had huge success in cinema gain access to directing tent-pole franchise movies. Obviously, the hiring of white directors is not guided by this logic of risk aversion. Quite the opposite of Black directors, white directors are given a special dispensation to produce films despite their inexperience in cinema or their box-office flops. Numerous other directors' trajectories point to a racial disparity in who directs which franchise films. The racial politics of the film industry inform everyday practices that routinely put African Americans at a significant disadvantage.

Following the success of franchise movies, directors are often given more latitude to direct other projects. After directing the Warner Brothers tent-pole franchise movies *Batman Begins* (2005), *The Dark Knight* (2008), and *The Dark Knight Rises* (2012), each with between $150 million and $185 million budgets, Christopher Nolan, a white British director, was given a $160 million budget for his sci-fi/action film *Inception* (2012), also distributed by Warner Brothers. Subsequently, Nolan was granted a $165 million budget for his sci-fi/adventure film *Interstellar* (2014), distributed by Paramount, about a team of outer-space explorers attempting to save the human race. Similarly, Peter Jackson, a white director from New Zealand, started off on small indie projects but nonetheless directed the fantasy/adventure *The Lord of the Rings* trilogy: *The Lord of the Rings: The Fellowship of the Ring* (2001), *The Lord of the Rings: The Two Towers* (2002), and *The Lord of the Rings: The Return of The King* (2003), which were each distributed by New Line Cinema and made on $94 million production budgets. Following the success of *The Lord of the Rings* films, Jackson's budgets for future films increased incrementally; he directed a reboot of the classic ape movie *King Kong* (2005) on a $207 million budget for Universal, while his fantasy/adventure *The Hobbit* films—*The Hobbit: An Unexpected Journey* (2012), *The Hobbit: Desolation of Smaug* (2013), and *The Hobbit: The Battle of the Five Armies* (2014), all distributed by Warner Brothers—had production budgets of between an estimated $200 million and $250 million.

Multiple lucrative pathways are open to white directors, both Americans and non-Americans. However, directing positions in the sci-fi genre and on tent-pole franchise films, though incredibly lucrative, remain largely closed off to Black directors. The Hollywood Jim Crow, which is mired in racial bias, segregates Black directors to work primarily on projects outside Hollywood's most commercially lucrative genre, a marginalization that profoundly shapes their future possibilities as movie directors.

* * *

The genres in which Black directors are most and least represented and the characteristics of those genres reflect the racialized, hierarchical nature of the Hollywood Jim Crow. Examining the relationship between race and film genre, a racial division of labor emerges, with Black directors overrepresented in the music genre and underrepresented in the science-fiction genre. In Hollywood, music-genre films have the smallest average production budgets. For Black directors, music films also commonly carry dominant themes of ghetto life. Materially, that Blacks are overrepresented in the music genre with the smallest average production budgets demonstrates that they occupy a subordinate place, a metaphorical ghetto, in the white-dominated film industry. Meanwhile, sci-fi genre movies have average production budgets of more than $100 million. Black directors are largely denied access to this financially lucrative film genre and the commercial success that comes with it.

Genre segregation presents material and symbolic barriers for the complete inclusion of African Americans in contemporary media institutions and in U.S. society. The underrepresentation of Black directors in the science-fiction genre and their overrepresentation on music films operates in dialogue with racialized ideological discourses about the place of African Americans in U.S. society—stereotyping them out of intellectual cultures and into performance cultures. Ideologically, the location of Black directors in the music genre stereotypically suggests that performance cultures are perhaps the most acceptable place for African Americans in the film industry. Quite problematically, sci-fi cinema confronts America's social problems, including racial issues, from the unilateral perspective of one racial group, whites. Genre segregation has implications for the kinds of stories that appear about African Americans in Hollywood films and the types of narratives that are excluded. The fact that Black directors are virtually nonexistent on science-fiction and blockbuster franchise films has implications for the presence of Black American narratives in a white-dominated popular-culture industry. Their underrepresentation means that Black philosophical renderings of the future, for instance, are seldom found in mainstream media. Marginalized outside sci-fi domains, African Americans are stripped of the ability to philosophize and disseminate their worldviews to mass audiences via mainstream cinema. Black Americans' inclusion in all genres of media production is important to instill racially diverse voices in mass-distributed popular-culture stories.

In addition to the ideological significance of genre segregation of Black directors, it has material implications for sustaining gainful careers in the film industry. Hollywood insiders suggest that Black movies and films are unbankable at the global box office, and presumably for this reason, rarely do Hollywood studios produce sci-fi movies with Black directors or casts attached. Underrepresentation in sci-fi movies thwarts Black directors' ability to establish successful careers in the most lucrative film genre. Because there is considerable overlap between the sci-fi genre and franchise films, marginalization in the directing of sci-fi films also disadvantages African Americans' participation in the most profitable Hollywood movie franchises. Black directors are routinely underrepresented on tent-pole franchise movies, the fulcrum of Hollywood-studio operations. Racial politics that results in Black directors' underrepresentation on sci-fi and blockbuster franchise films not only situates them away from an area that some people would argue is characterized as thought driven and intellectual minded but also prevents them from accessing high-paying jobs in the motion-picture industry, symbolizing their incomplete integration into the film industry. But due to the lucrative nature of these movies, African Americans remain largely excluded from the genre. With the Hollywood Jim Crow, establishment and legitimization of racial hierarchies sorts directors onto disparate career tracks. As a result, genre segregation further impedes Black directors' ability to attain the highest levels of economic success in the Hollywood film industry.

5

Manufacturing Racial Stigma

During the development of the romantic comedy *Hitch*, Columbia executives were opposed to a Black love interest alongside Will Smith; they wanted the movie to evade the perception of being a "Black film." Hollywood executives and insiders propel the myth that Black movies have diminished chances of success, particularly at the foreign box office, compared to white movies. They place an undue focus on success at the foreign box office and devalue movies such as those with Black casts and directors that perform exceedingly well domestically but are deliberately limited in their international exposure. The argument goes that international audiences prefer movies with white casts and directors, and so white movies are the best economic investments and the least risky cultural products. This argument forms the basis of the Hollywood Jim Crow—that the racially biased assumptions of Hollywood institutions and workers lead to everyday, routine practices that create and legitimize racial hierarchies. Under a Jim Crow system, first, there is an assumption of Black, and other nonwhite, inferiority. Next, the premise of racial difference serves to justify marginalization and segregation that advantage whites and disadvantage Blacks and other racial minorities. In Hollywood, cultural and economic logics are used to give whites the most lucrative film projects with big budgets in commercial genres—often fast-tracking their careers. This chapter reveals yet another impact of the Hollywood Jim Crow: the manufacturing of racial stigma.

The assumption that movies with Black casts will be unsuccessful carries weight for people who direct those movies. Invariably, Black movies carry the burden of an invisible disclaimer that reads, *Warning: this Black film is doomed to fail! Proceed with caution!* Hollywood's labeling Black movies and directors "unbankable" or unprofitable at the box office has far-reaching effects. From decreasing production budgets to shaping casting decisions, the "unbankable" label erects racial barriers for actors and directors. The larger concept of Blackness is also under assault. Hollywood's economic and cultural logics that determine Black films and directors to be unbankable metastasize into a larger stigma that shrouds Blackness. Black casts are framed as a problem that needs to be resolved. Directors counter the racial stigma by invoking language that stresses the universality and humanity of their movies and characters. Still, Hollywood executives and producers urge Black directors to work on movies with white casts or stars if they are to see increasing production values. The result is that the Hollywood Jim Crow not only creates racial hierarchies, reminiscent of prior stratified systems of racial division in the United States, but also manufactures an environment where experienced Black directors hone their skills on movies without Black casts. This reinforces a self-fulfilling prophecy, with talented Black directors working to make box-office hit movies with white (or multiracial) casts, while focusing less on improving the merits and qualities of Black-cast movies. Conceivably, this pattern undermines the underlying expectation of representational politics— namely, that advocating for Black directors would contribute to greater visibility of Black images.

The Black Problem

There is a striking similarity between the characterization of films with Black characters and themes as "problems" and the "Negro problem" of yesteryear. In *The Souls of Black Folk*, the pioneering sociologist W. E. B. Du Bois poses the question, "How does it feel to be a problem?"[1] With this inquiry, echoed in his article "The Study of Negro Problems," he critiques how the white American majority conceived of African Americans, then "Negroes," as a social problem.[2] Such a characterization shifts the burden of solving racial inequality from white American society to Black American individuals. If the Black person is the problem, in the way Du Bois explains that the dominant white society interprets Black people's plight, then the Black person must change in order to no longer be the problem. More than a century after Du Bois's writings, the problem of race that Hollywood manufactures in the twenty-first century resembles this earlier framework of a "Negro problem." Refashioning the stigma that Black Americans face in the larger U.S. society, Hollywood likewise brands Blackness as problematic.

Jim Crow systems define the meaning and significance of race in a way that fosters the stigmatization of Blackness. Manufacturing a stain of Blackness, the stigma attaches negative connotations to Black identities, social experiences, and milieus. The legal scholar Michelle Alexander's "New Jim Crow" of mass incarceration, for example, stigmatizes Blackness by normalizing the association of African Americans with criminality and deviance.[3] A similar racial stigma emerges from the Hollywood Jim Crow, which gives Blackness a pariah status. Blackness is negatively defined as marginal, particular, and specific, not universal. Organizational practices of Hollywood studios make Blackness into a stigma—a race that should be avoided at all costs if directors intend to progress along the hierarchy of movies to direct big-budget pictures.

In this way, Hollywood resurrects and refashions the age-old notion of a "Negro problem," one that fails to recognize how the structure of racialized organizations within a racial society gives rise to inequalities between Black and white directors. Instead, Hollywood insiders create a Black stigma that makes racial inequality into an individual problem that directors, actors, and writers must overcome and not a structural problem that the industry as a whole should correct. As an individual problem, the solution for racial inequality, then, is that Blackness—and not the unequal racial structure of Hollywood that manufactures stigma around racial difference—must be reconfigured.

The framework of a "Negro problem" does not acknowledge underlying organizational practices within Hollywood that label Black movies risky and inferior investments prior to their production or theatrical release. Nor does the framework of a "Negro problem" recognize the impending discrimination and segregation behind the camera that acts on those assumptions of unbankability to disadvantage Black directors—with small budgets, restricted genres, and limited prospects—often in spite of their achievements at the box office. Under the rhetoric of a "Negro problem," the entire system of inequality that distributes unequal opportunity to directors on the basis of race is rendered invisible. With deliberate disregard for systemic racism, the framework of a "Negro problem" ignores all problems with organizational and institutional structures and, rather, assigns all racial disparities to individual deficiencies—to a Black stigma.

Instead of Hollywood's race problem being an industry-wide quandary resulting from biased organizational practices, innate Blackness is its own undoing. In effect, Hollywood assigns Blackness pariah status, as something that is in need of fixing or should be avoided at all costs. If the assumption is an economic and cultural argument that Black movies and directors are unbankable, the obvious resolution is that Black movies and directors should become less Black. Therefore, the only way to integrate Black cultural products so that they become bankable is to get rid of their Blackness. As a consequence, Black characters and themes in movies become problems that need to be surmounted. Black directors who helm many of these movies unfairly assume the burden of remedying Hollywood's race problem.

Black directors do not enter on a level playing field with white directors but, rather, have to make up for the stigma of Blackness. The burden of proof, that a film is not too Black to receive a large production budget, falls on the directors. With this newly introduced burden, directors attempt to brand themselves and their careers in ways that overcome the stigma of Blackness. They constantly strategize to market their movies in ways that mitigate this seemingly unavoidable racial stigma.

One way they attempt to evade the stigma is to deemphasize Blackness. The director of *Girls Trip* (2017), *Barbershop: The Next Cut* (2016), *The Best Man Holiday* (2013), and *Scary Movie 5* (2013), among other movies, Malcolm D. Lee, remarks, "I'm a black filmmaker and I fully acknowledge that I tell stories with African-American actors and characters. But they are all very universal. It's not just a movie for African-American audiences. It's a movie for everyone."[4] In order for directors to prove that their films are beyond Blackness, they employ strategies to explain how their narratives and characters are "human" and "universal."

Besides influencing how directors talk about their movies, the Black stigma also impacts the presentation of Black culture and themes in movies. In an industry where Blackness is stigmatized, African Americans, sometimes reluctantly, direct films with fewer Black themes or characters, in exchange for increasing budgets, commercial success, and career advancement. Often the most commercially successful Black directors are denied opportunities to work with big budgets unless they direct films without Black themes, casts, and cultural references. Ultimately, the Black-culture stigma causes an evasion of Blackness in Hollywood.

Though Black culture is present in some forms, it is, by and large, absent symbolically. When Blackness is stigmatized and branded as something to be avoided or downplayed in Hollywood executives' economic models, Blackness in movies is also rendered problematic in a way that undermines its unadulterated realization in American popular movies. Still today, W. E. B. Du Bois's conceptualization of the "Negro problem" persists within the quotidian language and practices of major U.S. institutions and within the nation's hallmark film industry.

Being Human and Universal

Backed against the wall of Black stigma, directors are often tasked with defending their movies in ways that emphasize their universal appeal. In one instance, Tyler Perry feels compelled to explain that his movie characters embody the behaviors and characteristics of human beings and not stereotypes: "If you try to eliminate and eradicate a group of people and make them nonexistent because you are embarrassed by them or you are by that part of us and our culture and history, and you want to say just because Obama is in office, these people don't exist anymore, well that's not true. We're all human. We're all still here. We all have these experiences. These are not stereotypes; these are real people."[5] Without a doubt, it would be odd to hear a white filmmaker declare, *We're all human. We have these experiences. These are real people*, in defense of white movie characters. Hollywood insiders manufacture a stigma around Blackness that creates an ever-present burden for African Americans to justify the universal appeal of their movies and characters as representative of humanity, not just exemplars of stereotypes or caricatures.

Throughout U.S. history, the fight for Black humanity has assumed a literal struggle. During the 1787 U.S. Constitutional Convention, for example, white Americans from both northern and southern states, when determining a state's population or legislative representation, agreed to count each enslaved African as *three-fifths of a person*, a decision known as the Three-Fifths Compromise. Through the use of law, white Americans devalued Black humanity below personhood and tasked African Americans with the burden of overturning the law in order to have their humanity recognized. Even after the abolition of the Three-Fifths

Compromise, after full humanity was symbolically granted to African Americans under the law, this humanity was not extended in practice. Du Bois reflects, "No recent convention of Socialists has dared to face fairly the Negro problem and make a straightforward declaration that they regard Negroes as men in the same sense that other persons are."[6] No matter the legal and social norms, white Americans were reluctant to recognize the humanity of Black folk.

Today the stigma of Blackness in Hollywood draws its roots from this historical refusal to accept the humanity of African Americans, a recalcitrance that is now deeply entrenched with the normalization of whiteness within the mainstream film industry. Movies by and about Black people, or people from racial minority groups, are not honored with the same production values as movies by and about white people. Hollywood manufactures a Black stigma in which Blackness is perceived as a negative and constraining characteristic of a film. Blackness is framed as a problem in need of fixing. Meanwhile, whiteness is rendered invisible, unproblematic, and normal. The sociologist Eduardo Bonilla-Silva discusses how the white mainstream media use language that normalizes whiteness and problematizes Blackness via a concept he calls "racial grammar."[7] In the mainstream media, stories about whites are deemed "universal," meaning they would interest all people, whereas stories about African Americans or other nonwhite racial groups are presumed to interest only people from those groups, thereby normalizing whiteness and problematizing portrayals of nonwhites. Likewise, Hollywood operates through a racial grammar of sorts.

Even press reports conform to the biased language of racial grammar. For example, in an article about Steve McQueen's *12 Years a Slave*, the writer Michael Cieply acknowledges that the movie was very successful at the foreign box office, but Cieply quickly expresses doubt regarding the possibility of success for other Black-cast movies. "With few exceptions, Black stars and filmmakers—when they tell a specifically African-American story—have found it difficult to penetrate international markets, a significant handicap. . . . Like westerns and baseball films, movies about the experience of black Americans may be seen as too remote by audiences in countries that have little cultural connection to the subject matter."[8] Cieply explicitly opines that Black American stories are specific to their communities and distant from other global cultures; in the same breath, he implies that white American stories are general, universal, and transferrable across international cultural lines. His viewpoint reinforces the racialized economic and cultural logics that Hollywood insiders incessantly reiterate—the very logics that disadvantage Black movies and directors and, on the other hand, advantage white movies and directors in the film industry's marketplace.

The overwhelming stigma of Blackness in Hollywood compels Black directors to brand their films and characters as human and universal, to explain how their movies would defy the laws of racial grammar and why people outside Black communities (namely, white Americans) would understand and empathize with their movie characters' experiences and emotions. To counter the "Black film" label that is often accompanied by the disadvantages of small theatrical releases and small budgets, Black directors have emphasized, on several occasions, that their movies are universal and speak to all audiences. Directors employ the strategy of calling their films "universal" to undermine the underlying assumption that Black films are particular to Black communities. Russ Parr stresses about his independent romantic comedy 35 and Ticking (2011), "This is a film that has universal appeal because everyone has the same issues, whether one is Black or white."[9] It might seem peculiar if, in a press interview, a white director addresses his film's universality; however, this declaration is commonplace among directors from racial minority groups, whose movies Hollywood presumes will attract only narrow, racially homogeneous audiences. Post-civil-rights America is practically witnessing a mirror image of the Du Boisian era with regard to discussions of Black humanity. A prevailing mantra of the Hollywood Jim Crow, and broadly of the dominant racial order, is that a Black stigma subjects African Americans to a burden of proof to validate their existence. For Black directors to prove their appeal to mass audiences is, essentially, a call to prove their humanity.

In some cases, the quest to prove Black humanity or universality comes at the expense of engaging in deeper conversations about Black communities. When Lee Daniels was asked whether his movie The Butler provides new insights for the Black community, he responded, "This is a movie about loving your family, loving your father, loving your son. At the heart of it, it's a father-son story [about] how they learn to love each other. To me, it's universal. It goes beyond the African American experience."[10] Rather than Daniels discussing how his film speaks to Black folk, he evades the prompt and speaks only of *The Butler*'s universality. His response could be read as an attempt to avoid racial grammar that marks movies about Black people as particular and not universal. One can imagine that a white director would never be asked whether his or her movie provides new insights for the white community. Perhaps Daniels recognized these politics of racial grammar and the questions that would be asked of a Black, Latino/a, Asian, or Native American director but never to a white American director. In light of these double standards of racial grammar and the limitations that accompany films labeled "Black" and stigmatized as particular, his response is quite reasonable and understandable. By speaking of stories about people and families and not just about *Black* people and *Black* families, he highlights the universality of Black narratives and also dodges the narrow stigma of a Black film.

Still, what opportunities are missed when Black directors are reluctant to discuss how their films relate to Black communities? Are there not messages in *The Butler* and in other movies that are pertinent *only* to Black communities? As Du Bois theorizes African Americans' dual identity as Black and American, their *double consciousness*, structures their experiences and cultural identities in ways that differ from the experiences of most white Americans.[11] Unlike whites, African Americans are affected daily by racial oppression, experiencing the brute forces of racism, racial discrimination, and racial prejudice. Questions about films' relations to Black communities go unaddressed if every inquiry is presumed to be a question that attacks Black humanity and perpetuates a Black stigma. To some degree, the racial stigma undermines directors' ability to communicate directly to Black people through mainstream media—to be sure, one important, if not the primary, objective of attaining Black representation—for fear of negative consequences.

When "Black" is marked as a racial stigma that should be avoided at all costs, directors attempt to circumvent the stigma by explaining how their movies will reach broad audiences. Branding their movies beyond Blackness, directors pitch how their movies will appeal to viewers outside an imagined narrow group of Black audiences. David E. Talbert recalls about his romantic comedy *Baggage Claim* (2013), "Once we had [Patton], we knew that the landscape of actors opened up to us immediately. Paula is a woman, who in her last couple of films was opposite Tom Cruise and Denzel Washington with *Mission Impossible: Ghost-Protocol* and *2 Guns*, respectively. The landscape opened up because these were her last leading men and so we knew we could approach a Djimon Hounsou, a Taye Diggs, and it wouldn't feel like a small Black movie. It would feel like a mainstream movie and that's to Paula Patton's credit."[12] The racial stigma even shapes the way Black workers in Hollywood think about Black-cast movies. As Talbert implies, even Djimon Hounsou and Taye Diggs might be hesitant to accept roles in Black-cast movies, for fear that they are stigmatized as small, not mainstream, and unprofitable. Talbert feels that his movie can transcend the limitations facing Black movies by casting Paula Patton, who is light complexioned and biracial with a white mother and a Black father, as the leading actor. Along with Patton's multiracial status, Talbert believes her prior visibility on predominantly white-cast movies such as *Mission Impossible: Ghost Protocol* (2011) with Denzel Washington and the white actor Tom Cruise would help brand his movie beyond Blackness. The lead actor's race and prior roles in non-Black movies help in crafting an argument to evade the racial stigma.

It would be quite unlikely for a white director to feel compelled to defend how his or her white film would reach broad audiences or how the white characters developed in it are human. Yet, for Black directors, such discussions are daily rituals. Racial practices of the Hollywood Jim Crow that establish racial hierarchies among directors and movies facilitate the normalization of whiteness and the stigmatization of Blackness. Black-cast movies are associated with unbankability, the expectation of poor box-office performance—especially among foreign audiences. These economic and cultural logics are the justification for why Hollywood insiders make movies with Black casts for small production budgets compared to the amount they spend on movies with white casts. Holding a pariah status, Black directors labor to brand their films beyond Blackness. Maintaining that their films and movie characters are human and universal, they resurrect centuries-long discussions of Black humanity. These conversations demonstrate just how much racial hierarchies have endured in the United States, and in Hollywood, and how they affect everyday workers even in the face of symbolic milestones of racial progress.

"Do Our Movies"

John Singleton distinguishes between Hollywood movies and his own movies: "I can do action pictures with a lot of different people in them, and I can go back and do my core stuff."[13] Making a similar distinction, Reginald Hudlin stresses the unique challenges African Americans face as they progress through the ranks of Hollywood directing: "When I look at my peers, like Spike Lee and John Singleton, we all reached that same point where we had great success doing personal films and then all of a sudden Hollywood said: 'Now we want you to do our movies.' We still

Figure 5.1. John Singleton at a Canadian entertainment cultural showcase presented by TD, Black Artists' Network in Dialogue, Clement Virgo Productions, and Canadian Film Centre. Photo by George Pimentel, February 13, 2013.

wanted to do what we wanted to do, but 'if you want to work, you'll do our movies.' We each hit this point of frustration that none of us could figure how to work around."[14]

Both Singleton and Hudlin distinguish between "personal films" and Hollywood movies. For them, getting work and sustaining a directing career largely implies doing Hollywood movies. Seldom do Hollywood executives give a Black director a big budget to make a movie with a Black cast or theme. Perhaps at some point, directors realize that their continued success and likelihood of securing future work in Hollywood, especially work with big budgets and for major studios, depend on their concentrating on fewer "personal" (read: Black) films and more mainstream Hollywood (read: white or at the very least multiracial) movies. In exchange for integration into Hollywood, directing films with bigger budgets and in more commercial genres, Black directors are pressured to abandon the types of films on which many of them built their careers, films with Black casts and themes, and instead pursue films without Black casts, themes, or cultural experiences.

The idea of "doing Hollywood movies," of Black people, more or less, shedding Blackness for mainstream success, is embodied in the phenomenon of the crossover star, a concept first used to describe screen actors who appeal to multiracial audiences. In crossing over to mainstream movies, actors seemingly "transcend race" by drawing viewership from multiracial audiences, and especially large white audiences, in addition to attracting audiences from their racial group.[15] The actors Sidney Poitier, Richard Pryor, Eddie Murphy, Whoopie Goldberg, and Will Smith, to name a few, found success as crossover stars, most notably in the genre of biracial buddy films, where they are featured in starring roles alongside a (usually) white lead.[16] Like actors, directors also experience pressures to transcend race through directing crossover films that Hollywood decision-makers believe will attract multiracial audiences.[17]

With Black labeled inferior and relegated to low production values under the Hollywood Jim Crow, directors feel pressure to move away from Black-cast films to further their careers, whereas white directors who make white-cast films rarely feel the impetus to stray from that format. As Black Hollywood directors progress in their careers, they commonly either include more white characters in their films or direct predominantly white- or multiracial-cast films.

Tyler Perry's *Madea's Witness Protection* (2012), *A Madea Christmas* (2013), and *Single Mom's Club* (2014), unlike his earlier films, each feature mixed-race casts with white characters in more prominent roles. In *Witness Protection*, as part of the safety program, Madea (Tyler Perry) is temporarily relocated to the home of George and Kate Needleman (the white actors Eugene Levy and Denise Richards). Set in a small, rural southern town, *A Madea Christmas* depicts an interracial relationship between Lacey (Tika Sumpter) and Connor (the white actor Eric Lively). Similarly featuring a multiracial cast, *Single Mom's Club* follows a support group for struggling moms: May (Nia Long), Lytia (Cocoa Brown), Esperanza (the Colombian actor Zulay Henao), Hillary (the white actor Amy Stuart), and Jan (the white actor Wendi McLendon-Covey). Concerning the intrusion of white characters into Black films, the media studies scholar Monica White Ndounou emphasizes that "in the case of nonwhite narratives, a white point of entry becomes an economic necessity if filmmakers want to secure studio financing or distribution. . . . While the white point of entry is problematic for many black narratives and filmmakers exploring black subject matter, it has been used strategically and subversively onscreen and off. . . . The white point of entry can negatively influence African American storytelling by promoting superficial racial reconciliation narratives."[18] Possibly the inclusion of white actors as major characters could serve as leverage to negotiate bigger production budgets or to convince white studio executives that a film would appeal to larger audiences, but with certainty, this change does not come without shifts in the movie's narrative and messages.

On top of increasing the number of white characters in Black films, directors are urged to direct films in which Black themes, casts, and culture are not central, if they desire to receive big budgets and substantial financial support from major Hollywood studios. To date, the biggest budget that Spike Lee has received for a film was for *Inside Man* (2006), a crossover bank-heist movie starring Denzel Washington alongside the white actors Clive Owen and Jodie Foster. The film is also Lee's biggest box-office hit, grossing more than $88 million at the domestic box office and an estimated $184 million worldwide, on a $45 million production budget. Yet despite the film's commercial success, the familiar Spike Lee themes of poignant commentary on race, Black culture, and community life are notably absent. Generally, films with prevailing markers of

Black characters and culture do not receive widespread marketing and promotion from Hollywood. In exchange for steep upswings in marketing, promotion, and production budgets, Black directors are expected to direct "their movies"—*Hollywood* movies.

Typically, directors who experience the greatest mainstream success—those who primarily direct films that have relatively big budgets, are distributed by major studios, and generate the greatest profits at the box office—are most at risk of having Black themes, culture, and content removed or absent from their films. A "Black Hollywood director's oeuvre" predetermines the kinds of films that African Americans who desire to work on big-budget or major-studio projects can make. Black directors generally start out on "personal," small-budget auteur films, usually Black-cast movies, on which they have immense creative control over elements of production. For commercially successful directors, however, their oeuvre changes to include crossover films with multiracial casts, movies that can diminish hints of their individual styles. Some observers might say that this shift in aesthetics holds true of all directors who work in Hollywood, but the racial stigma positions Black directors in a unique predicament in which part of the commitment to becoming a Hollywood director involves evading Blackness.

As an example, John Singleton's filmography reveals elements of the Black Hollywood director's oeuvre. Set in South Central Los Angeles, Singleton's first film, *Boyz N the Hood* (1991), follows three friends who attempt to escape a vicious cycle and avoid situations such as gun violence and incarceration to which young Black residents in urban neighborhoods are particularly vulnerable. Furious Styles (Laurence Fishburne) hopes to instill in his son, Tre (Cuba Gooding Jr.), values of hard work and self-respect in order to avoid the pitfalls of a stereotypical Black urban youth upbringing. Like Tre, Ricky Baker (Morris Chestnut) seeks a way out of the inner city, via a college football scholarship. In contrast, Ricky's half brother Doughboy (Ice Cube) more easily succumbs to precarious lifestyles. Debuting just two years after *Boyz N the Hood*, Singleton's $14 million romantic drama *Poetic Justice* (1993) centers on a young poet and hairdresser, Justice (Janet Jackson), and a mail carrier, Lucky (Tupac Shakur), who form a bond based on their intimate and tragic experiences with violence in America. Continuing familiar themes of social problems facing youth, *Higher Learning* (1995) captures an incendiary brew of racial tensions, prejudice, and misunderstandings on the fictional college campus of Columbus University. Singleton's first films, popularly known as the "Hood Trilogy," focus on social problems such as violence, crime, and poverty that plague residents of low-income urban communities.

Immediately following the Hood Trilogy, Singleton's next movies—*Rosewood* (1997), *Shaft* (2000), and *Baby Boy* (2001)—also center on racial themes. Featuring a predominantly Black cast, the $16 million *Baby Boy* shares the most similarity in setting and characters to Singleton's previous films. An auteur crime drama written and directed by Singleton, *Baby Boy* follows Joseph "Jody" Summers (Tyrese Gibson), an unemployed man who struggles to do right by his family, including the mother of his son, Yvette (Taraji P. Henson). Unlike Singleton's previous films, *Rosewood* and *Shaft* feature white characters in leading roles; predictably, they also drew bigger budgets, at $25 million and $46 million, respectively. Written by Gregory Poirier, the historical action movie *Rosewood* dramatizes a 1920s racist lynch-mob attack on an African American community in Florida that ensues after a white woman falsely accuses a Black man of rape. The protagonists, Mann (Ving Rhames) and the white storeowner Jon Wright (Jon Voight), help persecuted African Americans escape Rosewood, a town already marred by intense anti-Black prejudice. Written by Richard Price, John Singleton, and Shane Salerno, the action/crime thriller *Shaft* follows the New York police detective John Shaft (Samuel L. Jackson), the nephew of the original 1970s *Shaft* detective, who suspects that the son of a real estate tycoon, Walter Wade Jr. (the white actor Christian Bale), has committed a racially motivated murder.

As Singleton gained more experience in Hollywood, not only did his films depart from Black themes, but they also featured majority-white or multiracial casts. Derek Haas and Michael Brandt are the writers of Singleton's biggest budgeted film, the $76 million blockbuster franchise movie *2 Fast 2 Furious* (2003), in which a white man and former Los Angeles Police Department cop Brian O'Conner (Paul Walker) enlists his childhood friend Roman Pearce (Tyrese Gibson) to help bring down Verone (Cole Hauser), a white drug lord from Miami. Posing undercover, the U.S. Customs Service agent Monica Fuentes (the Cuban actor Eva Mendes) joins them in the investigation. Also featuring a multiracial cast, the $45 million action/crime drama *Four Brothers* (2005) follows a racially diverse group of adopted brothers—Angel (Tyrese Gibson), Jeremiah (Andre Benjamin), Bobby (the white actor Mark Wahlberg), and Jack (the white actor Garret Hedlund)—who unite in Detroit to avenge their mother's death. Singleton's $35 million action thriller *Abduction* (2011) follows a white man named Nathan (Taylor Lautner) who tries to uncover the truth about his life when he finds his baby picture on a website for missing or abducted children, only to later become the target of an international, high-tech manhunt.

For Black directors, crossover success presents a mixed bag. While many directors desire support from organizations such as Hollywood studios that possess the institutional resources to sustain directing careers, the great caveat to crossover success is that crossover movies largely deny African Americans the opportunity to direct movies that showcase Black casts, cultures, or identities. Singleton's filmography illustrates the trend that African Americans who direct more economically lucrative Hollywood movies with increasing budgets for major studios face barriers to directing films with Black themes, narratives, and casts.

Scholars have taken up the issue of why the Black Hollywood director's oeuvre changes from Black movies to multiracial- and white-cast films. The African American studies scholar Wahneema Lubiano argues that it is uncommon for films to receive big production budgets if they oppose dominant Hollywood forms, styles, narratives, characters, and casts. Lubiano states that, for this reason, films that do have large monetary investments would likely not remain subversive to the status quo: "If a production has to return a profit in the millions of dollars, the likelihood of that production's remaining oppositional or subversive with regard to race might well be in inverse proportion to the extent the film relies on the support of a large (of whatever races), politically uncritical audience to turn a profit."[19] She reasons that mainstream movies would naturally need to be stripped of their subversive content, including content about race, in order to be easily digested and accepted by a vast number of (white) consumers.[20] Lubiano makes the case that an increase in the number of Black directors in Hollywood would not necessarily increase the number of movies wherein unadulterated Black themes play a prominent role.

A central paradox of directorial representation in Hollywood is that if Black directors are to advance beyond a partial integration that keeps them underrepresented at major studios and on big-budget, tent-pole franchise movies—to achieve a full integration—the current order forces them to make racial compromises in sacrificing Black casts, images, and themes. As studio directors for hire, Black Americans face immense pressure to do Hollywood movies. Because Hollywood is implicitly associated with whiteness, Black directors are strongly advised to deemphasize Blackness if they are to work on major-studio films or on big-budget projects. In pursuit of illustrious Hollywood directing careers, the most accomplished Black directors working on lucrative projects, in no small twist of irony, largely make movies devoid of Black themes and casts. As many successful Black directors become more engrossed in their careers and hone their directing talents, they are corralled into focusing their energies on movies with white or multiracial casts. Consequently, less attention is devoted to narratives that focus on Black culture and life. Especially absent are films with high production values that tell Black-centered stories. In deemphasizing Blackness, the norms of whiteness in Hollywood film themes, content, and casting remain unchallenged.

Incomplete Integration

Stuart Hall, in his seminal essay, posits, "What Is This 'Black' in Black Popular Culture?" Hall urges readers to question the kind of Black representation that is present (and absent) on-screen,[21] especially considering a popular-culture industry that stigmatizes Blackness. Grasping the impact of integration on Black culture includes assessing the overall impact of what representations are present or absent.

The comedian, actor, and director Chris Rock asserts that audiences do not receive a full range of Blackness through Hollywood representations and that some versions of Blackness are deliberately and calculatingly missing. Rock asks, "How many Black men have you met working in Hollywood? They don't really have Black men. A Black man with bass in his voice and maybe a little hint of facial hair? Not going to happen. It is what it is. I'm a guy who's accepted it all."[22] Rock contends that absent images of Black masculinity, such as those marked by deep voices and facial hair, are filtered through Hollywood's co-optation machine. Possibly due to their direct threat to corporate media's white racial frame of white hegemonic patriarchy,[23] images of Black masculinity are among the first to be culled from the Black director's cultural tool kit. From a broader outlook, Rock's comment points to a cultural politics at play, wherein Black directors have to make concessions in exchange for directing big-budget Hollywood movies. To a large extent, integration into Hollywood has the effect of negating the potency of Black culture and identity in movies directed by some of the most talented filmmakers, diminishing the ideological power of Black cinematic culture and world views. Despite gains in numerical representation, representation in the form of Blackness remains elusive in the most financially lucrative areas of Hollywood cinematic production, where Blackness remains symbolically excluded. With a prevailing racial stigma, the messages, narratives, and themes of big-budget films in commercial genres remain depleted of Blackness.

Perhaps most critical is that Hollywood's stigmatization of Blackness has a detrimental effect on the underdevelopment of Black cinema. If successful Black directors are channeled onto movies with white or multiracial casts, then what does integration mean for Black representation in Hollywood? Previous scholarship has taken up the debate of whether integration into white institutions could simultaneously result in the preservation of Blackness. On the face of it, integration into white America and the presentation of authentic Black cultures appear to be incompatible, competing goals.

Prior scholars have theorized that positive gains in integration would lead to negative outcomes for the conservation of Black culture. A staunch opponent of the integration movement, the scholar Harold Cruse, writes that integration and assimilation would result in the loss of everything Black.[24] Other critics point to a loss in the substance of Blackness. The sociologist Patricia Hill Collins argues that Blackness would be present on the surface but would lack a deeper cultural meaning: "being physically Black so that racial integration can be seen, but not culturally Black, for example, display any of the behaviors of an assumed authentic Blackness."[25] By this logic, African American representations might be physically present in high-concept popular movies but absent in any substantive form.

Manufacturing a stigma of Blackness affects directors, audiences, and cinematic messages. At one extreme, the film and ethnic studies scholar Jared Sexton writes that Black directors only provide the appearance of control, but Hollywood productions maintain their conventional culture, political agendas, narratives, plots, film forms, characterizations, and structures.[26] The popular-culture critic Leah Aldridge argues that there is an attempt to decontextualize and depoliticize ideological politics in the branding of Blackness in commercial culture.[27] The film scholar Ed Guerrero calls this phenomenon the *Black cinema paradox*: "The studio system is quite adept at containing insurgent impulses of *difference*, usually by excluding or ignoring them, but also in times of economic insecurity or shifting cultural relations by the more pervasive strategy of co-opting resistant images and narratives into the vast metamorphosing body of its cinematic hegemony. Thus a Black director may make the most popular film ever or successfully work a very lucrative genre only to find that the studio system has co-opted the form of blackness while emptying it of its emancipatory content and cultural impact."[28] As a containment strategy, depoliticizing Blackness serves to counteract subversive messages, such that less insurgent material arises from the studio system's production pipelines.

These theories present ideas for how integration might work in a practical sense. Arcing from Black-cast auteur films to white- and multiracial-cast Hollywood films, the Black director's oeuvre gradually decenters Blackness in a way that complicates directors' impetus as racial representatives. At the upper echelons of film production of big-budget movies in commercial genres, the visibility of African Americans in film directing takes precedence over the presence of Black cultures, casts, and themes. Regarding the burden of deemphasizing Blackness and the complementary idea of "transcending one's race," the film scholar Lorrie Palmer writes, "The persistence of this phrase [transcending race] across multiple media discourses makes me wonder if these writers believe (or think America believes) that . . . race is something that needs to be transcended."[29] The irony here is that in post-civil-rights America, integration into Hollywood and the industry's acceptance of African Americans appear to be predicated on compromising Blackness.

In stigmatizing Blackness, the Hollywood Jim Crow conditions directors to market their films and steer their careers toward paths that deemphasize Black culture, themes, and narratives—as a precondition for better production values, if they are to advance through the film industry's ranks. Hollywood's manufactured Black stigma renders Blackness something that needs to be eradicated. Paradoxically for Black directors, the very acceptance of crossing over as a valid strategy for career progression only adds further validity to the notion that Blackness is an inferior economic investment. Black directors' crossover films might appear to be more commercially successful and more technically polished compared to their Black-cast films, when in actuality, the former benefit from advantages of better production values (bigger budgets for casting, production, marketing, and promotion) and from the director being further along in his or her career (older, presumably wiser, and more experienced). While Hollywood studios do exert a preference for crossover and white-cast movies, they do so within the bounds of plausible legitimacy under the auspices of greater expected financial returns, making it difficult for Black directors to make indictments against racially discriminatory organizational practices.

The Hollywood Jim Crow erects a racial stigma on Black culture that by and large prevents Black movies with high production values from being realized. Essentially, it disenfranchises African Americans in their quest to be fully represented in mainstream, big-budget popular movies. Hollywood's attempt to undermine Black representation behind the camera is not always successful. Yet all too often, Black Hollywood directors lack the latitude to exercise their artistic choices. When directors achieve box-office success and look to integrate further into Hollywood, they are steered away from creating Black films. While they are hired to direct movies with white or multiracial casts, they are less likely to direct films with Black characters for mainstream audiences. Although African Americans are present behind the camera in Hollywood, they are denied full license to put forth their artistic expressions of themselves and their communities at all levels of cinematic production. Working in Hollywood, they are unable to inscribe their true reflections of Black identities or their perceptions of society via big-budget films with Black casts and themes. By design, Black directors face persistent barriers in expressing and disseminating their politics, ideologies, and worldviews, thereby diminishing their power to exert profound influence on others through mainstream cinema. The dearth of desired visions of Blackness in mainstream cinema leads to the symbolic exclusion of Blackness in Hollywood and limits African Americans' ability to impact the canon of mainstream American films. Genuine Black cultural identities are overlooked when Black representation manifests itself only in the forms and manners that reflect white studio executives' desires.

Furthermore, a Black stigma affects audiences. The argument that Hollywood insiders present to justify diminishing Blackness is, on the surface, about economic and cultural considerations, to accomplish bottom-line needs of attracting global audiences. On the contrary, when African Americans direct films with fewer Black characters and themes, they likely alienate otherwise-captive audiences. With $16 million at the domestic box office, Tyler Perry's multiracial-cast movie *The Single Mom's Club* (2014) recorded his smallest box-office gross, whereas Perry's films with majority-Black casts were considerably better attended. Steering directors away from movies with Black casts and themes, the Hollywood Jim Crow demonstrates blatant disrespect for Black audiences. During an interview, John Singleton condemned Hollywood's lack of investment in Black-cast movies and audiences: "Hollywood doesn't really care about Black people—it's like George Bush. I'm saying the Kanye West quote. Hollywood really doesn't care about the Black audience. They want the Black audience to go see action films and alien movies and romantic comedies with no Black people in them."[30] In the end, the racial stigma in Hollywood leaves audiences' desires to watch megabudget films with Black themes and characters almost always unfulfilled.

* * *

Under the Hollywood Jim Crow, Blackness reemerges as a social problem in the same way that American society constructed the Negro as a problem at the turn of the twentieth century, as articulated by the pioneering sociologist W. E. B. Du Bois. With Black films deemed unbankable and less profitable than white films, Hollywood executives manufacture a racial stigma to brand Blackness problematic and to manufacture validity for denying movies with Black casts, themes, or directors big budgets and high production values. Beneath the surface, the cultural and economic logics—of attracting audiences and meeting the bottom line—that Hollywood insiders use to stigmatize Blackness have racial undertones that denote a lower position within a hierarchical system of popular-culture production.

Hollywood's racial stigma is an impediment to the realization and celebration of Black culture on-screen. To avoid stigmatization and disadvantage, directors defend Black-cast movies as being human and universal. In doing so, they attempt to show how Black-cast movies appeal to everyone and not just a small segment of national audiences. When directors work on financially lucrative films distributed by major studios, they experience obstacles to bringing Black cultural images to the screen. As African Americans climb the ranks in Hollywood, they face limitations on the kinds of movies they can make and are likewise advised not to pursue films with Black content. If they desire to make more financially lucrative films with big budgets or for major studios, they are urged to make movies with white or multiracial casts. As a direct consequence, an absence of Black culture is pronounced at the upper echelon of Hollywood films—those movies with big budgets and major studio distribution. These most financially lucrative Hollywood productions commonly exclude films with Black themes or casts. Even the latest diverse-ensemble blockbusters such as *Star Trek* and *Star Wars* have racially diverse characters but are lacking in substance of different cultures. Truly the only exception to this general rule is the mega-hit *Black Panther* (2018), the Marvel comic book adaptation about a powerful, technologically sophisticated royal family in a futuristic African nation.

The importance of expressing one's desired images and disseminating those creative visions to mainstream audiences cannot be understated. Though currently Black cultures are largely symbolically excluded from Hollywood's most commercially lucrative spheres, collective efforts to revive mainstream Black cinema give hope that Black visions and cultures will one day be wholly reinscribed into national narratives.

6

Remaking Cinema

Signs of racial progress abound in twenty-first-century Hollywood. Directors have achieved symbolic advances such as recognition at the Oscars in Best Picture wins for Steve McQueen's *12 Years a Slave* (2012) and Barry Jenkins's *Moonlight* (2016). The director's chair is also more racially diverse than in prior decades. These promising strides give the appearance of a liberal Hollywood that grants full access to African Americans and to other underrepresented racial groups. Even in the face of a staunch appearance of liberalism, incomplete racial integration of the film industry problematizes the notion of Hollywood and the United States as racially inclusive, liberal spaces. Contemporary Hollywood studios, though no longer exclusionary of African Americans, remain unequal institutions for Black directors. Despite a fifty-year history of being behind the camera of Hollywood movies, Black directors have neither attained full proportional representation in the film industry nor received adequate support for their movies across all genres and scales of production. Rather, they are obstructed from attaining full participation via the Hollywood Jim Crow that uses economic and cultural rationales to uphold racial hierarchies of privilege and disadvantage among groups.

Relations among groups in the United States have long been consumed by systems of racial hierarchy. For centuries, different racial orders—slavery, Jim Crow segregation, and mass incarceration—have prevailed, with each successive era maintaining a caste-like social system. Each regime was bound together by a similar racial skeleton, the Jim Crow frame, in which whites assumed privileged standpoints and accrued benefits, while Blacks at the bottom of the social ladder suffered disadvantage. Because the dominant racial regime trickles down to institutions by virtue of existing within a racial society, it is reasonable to suspect that Hollywood film studios would also absorb some form of racial hierarchy into their organizational practices and structures.

Understanding prominent processes of inequality in prior racial regimes provides greater insight into Hollywood's race problem.

In Jim Crow regimes, Black Americans and other disadvantaged groups are assumed inferior, marginalized, segregated, and stigmatized by law or custom. Likewise, film-industry protocol permits legal disadvantages against Black Americans in an explicit fashion, ushering in an era in which differential treatment by race is no longer taboo but can be justified using economic and cultural logics. Racial marginalization in Hollywood is accomplished by often-overt racial codes to label Black directors and their movies economically unbankable and culturally undesirable to global audiences. Once Black directors and their films are deemed unprofitable, studio executives are free to channel them on disadvantaged tracks on the supposedly nondiscriminatory grounds of meeting the studio's bottom line. Hollywood insiders, the gatekeepers who control decisions about the popular-movie production process, socially construct a negative stigma around Blackness and then marginalize and segregate Black directors and their movies along the periphery of the film industry in areas of least privilege and power.

The treatment of Black directors provides a lens to investigate how Hollywood makes racialized others of racial-minority workers. Through completely legal practices, Black directors are denied equality of opportunity and outcomes in the film industry. Under the Hollywood Jim Crow, Black directors can achieve only an incomplete integration, one that is characterized by underrepresentation in the film industry's core of major studios, big-budget films, and tent-pole blockbuster franchise movies. Circumstances are particularly dire for Black women and other women from underrepresented racial groups. The Hollywood Jim Crow prevents Black women from being regular fixtures in the production of popular cinema, as their work is considered to be even less bankable, and they are sparsely represented behind the camera.

Black directors' efforts are so whittled by ghettoization and discrimination that even the presence of a Black director behind the camera of a big-budget Hollywood movie in a commercial genre does not necessarily mean that genuine representations of Black culture will materialize on-screen. The motive of the Hollywood co-optation machine is to filter out any glaring subversion of the status quo during production and postproduction. Black directors are encouraged to make certain films and discouraged from pursuing other projects through lack of or minimal funding so much that we can hardly assume that what movies ultimately emerge on-screen are the movies that directors ideally envisioned. The result is the symbolic exclusion of Black culture, a Black presence in name and face but generally less palpable in ideology, culture, and narrative.

In spite of the Hollywood Jim Crow, there remains hope that popular cinema in the United States can become more racially inclusive. Remaking cinema means enacting proactive strategies for change in order to make American cinematic production, distribution, and exhibition more racially inclusive. Implementation strategies for improvement happen at the structural level with changes in social systems and within the very organization of cinematic production both in Hollywood and in independent film. Change also happens at the micro-level in the way individuals think about movies. Decisions about movies reflect studio executives' and Hollywood insiders' mentality. One might suggest that reform can occur if Hollywood insiders' and executives' mentality alters to accept the value and potential of all movies. However, changing philosophies and ideologies might prove to be a difficult task, since racism has some rationality.[1] The mentality that Black movies are unbankable serves the purpose of promoting white films, disseminating favorable story lines about whites, boosting the stature of white directors and actors, and keeping white directors and actors gainfully employed (both on-screen and off-screen). Whether in Hollywood or outside it, efforts to achieve equality or establish new-age institutions will make strides toward racial inclusion in cinema.

The Uphill Climb

In the face of vocal challenges, Hollywood's race problem persists with such force that it appears to be insurmountable. A primary reason why Hollywood's race problem remains difficult to overcome is because few racial minorities work in positions of authority in Hollywood; they remain ostracized from central positions of power, where inequality could be most effectively tackled. Power in the film industry is almost exclusively white dominated. To this point, the 2015 *Media Diversity*

Report revealed that 96 percent of television-studio CEOs and 94 percent of film-studio CEOs were white.[2] For the most part, white studio executives hold full authority to hire and fire cast and crew, to allocate movie production budgets, and to establish and enforce organizational practices. Currently, minorities' promotion and advancement opportunities are tied to the subjective opinions and decisions of white Hollywood leaders. Single-handedly, white studio executives have unchallenged authority to pigeonhole directors to limited genres or small budgets or not to hire them at all. The American studies scholar Eithne Quinn observes that a "central power-brokering role of white practitioners [is] to reinforce or disrupt the industry's social relations of race and, in turn, its racial regimes of filmic representation."[3] With near-absolute power in the film industry, white Hollywood insiders' decisions going forward can either uphold or subvert the Hollywood Jim Crow.

The director Spike Lee highlights this racial imbalance in executive positions in Hollywood studios:

> Look, take away the big stars—Will Smith and Denzel—and look at the people who have a green light vote. Where are the people of color? That's what it comes down to. How many people, when they have those meetings and vote on what movies get made, how many people of color are in those meetings? That's not to say that's the only way to get a film made, but you're talking about Hollywood specifically here. And if you want to get a film made, it has to get green lit. And I want someone to tell me: Who is a person of color who has a green light vote in this industry today? . . . I'm talking about the people sitting in the room who have read the script—looking at the full package, who's in it, how much is it going to cost, how much is it going to make. The people who have that vote, there are no people of color who have that.[4]

As Spike Lee observes, there is certainly a dearth of racial minorities in positions to make decisions about Hollywood movies. Lee also comments that "it's easier to be the president of the United States as a Black person than to be the head of a studio. . . . That's mind-boggling. It shouldn't be that way." Confirming his proclamation, to date, no Black American has ever held the highest position as studio head of a major film or television studio.[5]

Moreover, racial-minority representation in decision-making positions at talent agencies is virtually nonexistent. Talent agencies often package deals and present directors, actors, writers, and other creative talent for studio movies. Without holding any critical power in studios or talent agencies, especially the power to green-light films and to assemble talent on projects, Black Americans and other racial minorities lack the authoritative ability to curb the organizational practices that sediment racial inequity.

Not only do Black Americans have virtually no control over decision-making at Hollywood studios, but they also have no control over theatrical distribution of films, the process of getting films to mass audiences in theaters. Directors rely on film distributors to advertise films and to facilitate the release of films to theaters. Who controls the distribution process ultimately decides what films get released to mass audiences via theaters. In the United States, the vast majority of distribution companies and theater chains are white owned. Of all Hollywood movies, white men have financed nearly 100 percent of them in some capacity and have exerted a similar exclusive dominance over theatrical distribution.[6] Because circulation of films remains mostly out of the control of Black Americans, they find distribution to be a significant, if not the greatest, impediment to their success in the film industry.

Money plays a huge role in the lack of control that Black directors have over the production of movies for mass audiences. The director Christopher Scott Cherot gives his take on how limited control over financial aspects of filmmaking affects production: "Whoever controls the money is the boss. When you control the money you're the boss of your product. If you're a director for hire, you don't control that production, that's a collaborative effort. You work in conjunction with the men around you. Hopefully everyone's on the same page and you make a great movie. In most cases that happens, sometimes it doesn't, but that's the bottom line."[7] The ethnic studies scholar Jesse Rhines attributes Hollywood's maintenance of power over directors to their financial control; the combination of Black films with white money suggests that whites continue to control the production, regardless of who is the film director.[8] Without control over film finances, Black directors are at the mercy of white decision-makers to produce and distribute movies. The inequalities that Black directors face are especially hard

Figure 6.1. Opened in 1935, the Carver Theater in downtown Birmingham, Alabama was the preeminent venue for Black audiences to watch first-run movies during the era of Jim Crow segregation. Photo by David Brossard, March 26, 2016.

to overcome due to their lack of control over decision-making about films and over the film-distribution process.

While some African Americans maintain careers as repeat directors, many find a lack of sustained work in Hollywood. Most Hollywood workers, regardless of race, have spells of unemployment accompanied by periods of intense work. In 2002, for instance, only 33 percent of the total entertainment industry workforce derived full-time income solely from working in the entertainment industry. Since most directors, and Black directors especially, do not have the luxury of directing feature films for a full-time career, increasingly they find work in other areas, such as television directing. For example, after directing *Drumline* (2000), *Mr. 3000* (2004), and *Paid in Full* (2002), Charles Stone III directed multiple television shows, including the ABC family drama *Lincoln Heights* (2006–).

In addition, Stone directed the hugely successful VH1 television movie *Crazy Sexy Cool: The TLC Story* (2013). With four and a half million viewers tuning into the premiere, *Crazy Sexy Cool* became cable television's top-rated original movie of the year and VH1's highest rated original movie in the network's history. Moreover, the Fox music drama *Empire* (2015–) has several Black directors: for example, Sanaa Hamri, Lee Daniels, Kevin Bray, Debbie Allen, Rob Hardy, Dee Rees, Anthony Hemingway, John Singleton, and Mario Van Peebles. More Black women also find representation behind the camera on television, such as Shonda Rhimes (*Grey's Anatomy, Private Practice, Scandal, How to Get Away with Murder*), Mara Brock Akil (*The Game, Being Mary Jane*), and Ava DuVernay (*Queen Sugar*) bringing several popular television shows to broadcast and cable networks. Justin Simien adapted his film *Dear White People* (2014) into a popular series streaming on Netflix. Other avenues for creative production allow directors to work while still fighting for inclusion in Hollywood.

The Jim Crow frame has developed over centuries, and therefore much effort is required to overcome its multiple dimensions of social control. Overcoming the Hollywood Jim Crow appears to be an uphill battle for Black directors, though it is one worth fighting in order to achieve full equality in the production of popular cinema. At this juncture, a fork in the road emerges. It becomes imperative for Black cinema directors, producers, writers, and audiences to assess whether, in fact, integration into Hollywood is worth pursuing or whether they foresee the film industry perpetually creating an unequal playing field for Black professionals. This knowledge would inform a progressive strategy moving forward, either to address the idea of continuing efforts to integrate into Hollywood or to labor toward a separate cinema.

At this crossroads, one fork represents the mission to alleviate inequality from within, which involves exerting continued pressure on Hollywood studios to broaden their workforces and on the Academy of Motion Picture Arts and Sciences to radically diversify its membership in order to more closely resemble the changing racial demographics of the U.S. population. Taking into account the reality that Black professionals are perhaps quite weary from the fatigue that inevitably settles in after an incessant struggle with the status quo, the other path highlights forging a separate channel for cinema production apart from the discriminatory establishment. On the one hand, if Blacks' integration into Hollywood is increasingly being realized, a strategy of improving their presence in the marquee film industry is practical. On the other hand, if the project of Black integration is inherently flawed, efforts to charter a new industry would better ensure that Black movies reach the silver screen.

Hollywood Reformation

The task of surmounting racial inequality in Hollywood is difficult, since racism has rationality for members of a society who benefit from the oppression of others. Although those at the bottom of the order develop views and practices to challenge the racial status quo, those at the top of the order develop views and practices to support the racial status quo.[9] Challenging racial inequality in Hollywood, Black Americans and racially oppressed groups will undoubtedly face contention from whites who benefit from the existing power structure. Eithne Quinn, for example, describes white ethnics' opposition to an integrated film-industry workforce after federal intervention:

> Since early 1969, [Daniel Patrick] Moynihan had been briefing [President Richard] Nixon on the growing fractures in the black-Jewish civil rights alliance. As calls by African Americans and their federal allies for proportional representation in employment gained steam, they started to sound alarm bells for some Jewish Americans when it affected sectors in which Jews were well-represented. As Nancy MacLean details, the budding neoconservatives were already framing the issue in zero-sum terms: more Black representation meant less Jewish representation. Along with higher education recruitment and academe, the good jobs in the film industry into which African Americans sought entry were occupations in which Jewish Americans had long enjoyed a strong presence.[10]

Whites in Hollywood view workplace integration as a zero-sum game, in which they stand to lose positions of privilege if racial minorities gain footing in the film industry.

The enormity of repression and opposition to equality in cinematic production, however, does not mean that integration into Hollywood holds no value and is not a worthwhile pursuit. In fact, some observers believe that social change in Hollywood is imperative for the industry's self-survival. Spike Lee declares that it is in studio executives' best interest to take the voices of racial minorities in America seriously and to consider their perspectives when they make decisions about which movies to green-light: "The U.S. Census has said white Americans are going to be a minority in this country by 2040. I just think it's good business sense to plan for that! The country is changing, and some people just don't want to understand that. I don't know how you can't take that into account. The smart people are going to take that number into account of how they do business."[11] As Lee contends, perhaps the nation's changing demographics alone are reason enough to consider diversifying the industry's creative talent, if only for the self-interested goal of satisfying the bottom line that is financial gain, both for major studios and for the film industry as a whole.

Increasing partnerships with studios and Black cinema producers would also provide more inclusivity for marginalized filmmakers. As an example, Devon Franklin left his job as senior vice president of production for Columbia Tristar Pictures to start his own company, Franklin Entertainment, securing production deals with studios to produce faith-based, religious-themed, inspirational commercial content. Similar to Tyler Perry's model for working with a large independent in Lionsgate and Franklin's case working with major studios, other filmmakers can adopt partnerships with Hollywood studios that are beneficial to all parties.

Vying for integration into Hollywood, directors seek full participation, outlined by equal opportunities and outcomes. But it is becoming ever apparent that even successful Black directors have not achieved equal standing or opportunity to direct films, especially the kinds of films they desire to direct. Possessing few resources, having little to no opportunity to fully realize their creativity, and lacking central control of the production of popular cinema, Black Americans are disenfranchised within Hollywood. Unequal access to the production of popular cinema denies them complete and unfettered citizenship; it denies them the inalienable civic rights inherent to truly belonging to a nation. Advocating for greater participation in the production of popular culture within Hollywood includes increases in representation, as well as a better quality of representation: improvements in production budgets, theatrical releases domestically and abroad, and control over film content. Full integration of Black Americans into Hollywood would facilitate increased employment and a greater realization of citizenship, as well as fostering egalitarian race relations in the United States generally.

Black Cinema Collective

The prominent scholar Cornel West points out the irony of Black Americans working within Hollywood, in his concept of the double bind, which highlights that "while linking their activities to the fundamental, structural overhaul of these institutions, [they] often remain financially dependent on them."[12] In addition to racial projects in which directors partner with Hollywood studios, racial projects outside Hollywood could prove to be effective in reversing the inequalities set by the Hollywood Jim Crow. Accordingly, the cultural theorist Stuart Hall suggests an alternative strategy to access media production and representation, one that engages in projects that use difference as a basis for producing culture and articulating a cultural politics that ultimately reshapes balances in power.[13] Hall advocates contesting popular hegemony by imagining possibilities outside capitalist constraints of major corporations. The likelihood that a path to true creative freedom in the production of popular cinema will emerge for marginalized racial groups is decidedly marked by the alacrity with which they can work together to forge their own filmmaking machines, outside dominant, hegemonic institutions.

Challenging the organization of the film industry or improving the position of a few directors might prove to be a futile exercise if the regressive Hollywood Jim Crow system itself does not change. While it remains important to continue to make inroads in Hollywood, it is also vital not to rely on a single vehicle for change. It is especially risky to rest all hope on altering a path over which Black Americans have little control. Significant effort must be made toward thrusting Black culture into the national and international limelight, not merely via the organizations that constitute Hollywood but also through institutions owned and operated by Black Americans themselves. Hence, there is a need to establish, maintain, and promote a Black cinema collective separate from the Hollywood film industry.

Hollywood studios are the primary vessels for white-cast movies. Studio executives decide on the number of movies they will release each year, as well as the genres, themes, and ideologies that emanate from the narratives. Alongside this carefully orchestrated mainstream lies a white independent cinema. On the whim of technicality, one might suggest that a Black mainstream of Hollywood films does exist. However, this alleged mainstream is wrought with budget restrictions, genre constraints, distribution limitations, editing-room co-optation, and disputed final cuts. Time and again, testimonies from Black audiences and directors confirm that the films Hollywood studios green-light fall short of realizing their unadulterated desires and visions. In their place are Black-directed films that succumb to the interests and mores of white studio executives, narratives that white Hollywood businesspeople believe are viable profit-making vehicles. Currently, Black Hollywood movies are more reflective of white Hollywood studio executives' goals and desires than of Black directors' ambitions, such that observers rarely point to these films as the epitome of Black filmmaking.

Because current Black mainstream movies are developed within white institutions that put parameters on their creativity, independent movies become the central canon, where genuine representations of Black culture are located. However, low production values, shoestring budgets, and guerilla financing methods hinder the consistency in quality of indie films.

Prior efforts to produce a separate cinema were short-lived or fell short of an organized, comprehensive Black cinema-production network. During cinema's early years, Oscar Micheaux and other pioneers thrived in an independent Black cinema industry that produced movies for Black audiences. However, in the same way that integration brought about the demise of many Black schools and newspapers, Black filmmakers' quest for inclusion into Hollywood diverted attention from investing continued energies into a separate cinema.[14]

Since the demise of the segregation-era Black film industry, there have been meaningful efforts to revive Black film collaboratives on a large scale. In the contemporary post-2000 era, both Tyler Perry and Ava DuVernay have employed innovative methods to reinvigorate Black film. Perry created Tyler Perry Studios, a production company headquartered in southwestern Atlanta, for the purposes of producing original film and television programs independently. Perry also created the 34th Street Films Studio in Los Angeles, California, with the aim of helping African Americans produce movies and secure distribution deals. Through this studio and Perry's relationship with Lionsgate, the first-time director Tina Gordon Chism, who penned screenplays for the hit movies *ATL* (2006) and *Drumline* (2002), directed the romantic comedy *We the Peebles* (2013) about a man (Craig Robinson) who crashes the family reunion of his girlfriend (Kerry Washington) to propose to her.

DuVernay, a publicist turned filmmaker, similarly helped independent Black-directed films secure distribution through her company, the African American Film Festival Releasing Movement (AFFRM). The now-defunct AFFRM strategically linked independent filmmakers to theatrical and multiplatform distribution. The company helped several independent films gain modest theatrical releases, including two of Du-Vernay's own films. Her narrative-feature-film debut, *I Will Follow* (2010), tells the story of a grieving woman (Salli Richardson-Whitfield) trying to move forward after the death of her aunt (Beverly Todd). DuVernay's second feature film is the social-issue prison drama *Middle of Nowhere* (2012). Part of her motivation for organizing AFFRM was that studios do a poor job of showcasing the perspectives of African Americans and especially narratives about Black women. DuVernay says, "No one's going to put out that film about a Black woman's intimate thoughts and feelings. There was no precedence for a studio scenario or corporate structure that would pay to make sure you all saw that."[15] DuVernay revamped AFFRM with a new organization, Array, which lists on its website, "We are an independent film distribution and resource collective comprised of arts advocacy organizations, maverick volunteers and rebel member donors worldwide. Our work is dedicated to the amplification of independent films by people of color and women filmmakers globally. Varied voices and images in cinema: Array now!"[16] Unlike the initial AFFRM project, Array broadens its borders beyond exclusively serving African Americans and includes the promotion and distribution of films by African Americans, other racial minorities, and women filmmakers.

Although Tyler Perry and Ava DuVernay have successfully ushered films into theaters, their efforts fall short of a Black film collective. DuVernay's AFFRM and Array support movies only at the tail end of the production process, with distribution and exhibition, but offer little assistance through the production and preproduction stages. Now absorbed into Tyler Perry Studios, Perry's 34th Street Films was better at developing filmmakers' work from the beginning through the end stages. But neither endeavor preemptively articulates a collective consciousness regarding the types of movies that should be made and the subject matter that should be addressed.

What is needed and sorely lacking among Black filmmaking is a *Black cinema collective*. A bold effort toward resurrecting a modern, minority-oriented cinema, a Black cinema collective is the formation of a structured system of production, distribution, and exhibition that is owned, organized, and operated by African Americans. A Black cinema collective would require African Americans to take meaningful action to ensure a fixed place in mainstream cinema production and in the occupation of film directing. Altering the methods guiding the current filmmaking and delivery process is a move toward developing Black cinema in the hopes of alleviating the social problem of Black marginalization in cinematic production.

Movies are a medium through which cultures can showcase their ideologies, desires, fears, insecurities, eccentricities, greatest accomplishments, and proudest moments. Rather than contain narratives, a Black cinema collective would ensure that Black philosophies are developed, dramatized, realized, and preserved on-screen. A Black film collective would need to build its identity and decide what kinds of stories African Americans want to tell (whether documentaries, dramas, action, sci-fi, or otherwise), how many of these films to release every year, and who should direct them—and then actually get them made, via Black owned and operated institutions.

Ideally, a Black cinema collective would (1) define what ideals, visions, and narratives should be depicted for mass audiences; (2) foster the development of directors and their films throughout the production process; (3) feature forgotten or invisible works of African Americans, including Black films of varied genres and also adaptations of Black writers—content rarely produced yet desired by audiences; and (4) see those films through the distribution and exhibition phases, whether through cooperation with the existing distribution and theater system in Hollywood or through creating an alternate means of reaching audiences.

Currently, independent Black cinema is not at all a formalized system but rather an assortment of individual projects by emerging or established directors, producers, writers, and filmmakers. The projects are small in scale and shaped by random events rather than molded by organized, regular occurrences. As a whole, Black filmmaking efforts lack any large-scale forethought, planning, or future outlook. No meticulously designed production slate of movies emerging from central institutions exists, only one-off productions by individuals. Black directors and talent are neglected in big-budget movies and in the sci-fi genre, yet there is no communal effort to pool resources and funds to make movies that fill these gaping holes in representation. Similarly, there is no attempt to make annual films in particular genres or on specific topics that are of importance to Black communities. Lacking organized systems of film production, no African American institutions are poised to become the bearers of landmark movies. The lack of institutionalization of cinematic production exemplifies why directors seldom have opportunities to undertake groundbreaking movie projects of grand scale outside Hollywood. Instead, their sole option has been resorting to wait for a green-light from Hollywood, in the manner of Kafka's parable "Before the Law," if they are to direct any movie of epic proportions.

A sustained effort to design and orchestrate a Black cinematic production system is sorely lacking. Energies devoted toward producing Black independent cinema should rather move toward organizing and becoming the primary industry for the distribution and exhibition of Black movies. Several directors articulate that the solution to having Black themes and narratives in theaters likely does not reside in Hollywood. The director Reginald Hudlin discusses the importance of institution building to realize the possibility of a variety of Black films coming to theaters:

> The only way we're going to have meaningful success is to not just focus on individual success, but building an institution. We are not going to do it if we're begging for a break. At the end of the day, people tell the stories that they want to tell. Yes, Black films are profitable in business, but studios are making fewer Black films than ever. When you go from 25 films a year to 12, it gets a little tight. What's going to get made, is not only commercial films, but commercial films that those executives have deep relationships with and those may or may not be our stories.[17]

With studios trimming their production slates, the likelihood that Black movies will be made in Hollywood decreases. Hudlin reiterates the notion that the stories Black directors desire to tell would likely differ from those stories that white studio executives typically support. Therefore, building an institution for the production, distribution, and exhibition of Black cinema is a way to ensure that those stories desired by directors and audiences find their path to the mainstream.

Chris Rock notes that better-quality filmmaking can emerge outside Hollywood. He quips, "The best [Black movies] are made outside of the studio system because they're not made with that many white people—maybe one or two, but not a whole system of white people."[18] Releasing Black directors and movies from the grips of the Hollywood system, according to Rock, is the best formula for extracting the most interesting nuances of Black cultures for cinema. Nevertheless, the purpose of a Black film collective is not to wholly exclude people of any given race. Even Oscar Micheaux, during the era of race movies, used camera operators and crew from various racial groups.[19] The important distinction between a Black cinema collective and Hollywood, however, is that the former would put forth Black visions that are neither corrupted nor co-opted.

The key intervention is ownership and control over the movie production and distribution process. Control over the content and message of movies is a necessary component for Black film production, especially to overcome Blacks' symbolic exclusion from the mainstream of big-budget movies. Spike Lee explains that with the ability to self-finance one's own films, an artist can make the movies he or she wants to make, as he did with *Red Hook Summer*: "I financed it myself, so we had to do it for a price. I just went to the bank, made some draws and wrote some checks! It was very hard, but we [Lee and his cowriter, James McBride] made the movie we wanted to make."[20] Tyler Perry also discusses the definitive power of ownership and leverage in the film production process: "I have the ownership and the leverage, so I do what I want to do. There's nobody that tells me what to do. There's nobody that gives me notes or makes me make any changes. So the stories that I'm telling are of my experience."[21] With ownership, Black directors can labor to curb unemployment rates by hiring African Americans to work as cast and crew. Exerting more control over the distribution of movies, they can also strategize to create avenues for greater overseas distribution. Without economic power and control over the film production process, too often Black directors' goals and messages are compromised to fulfill the wishes of white Hollywood executives.

In a Black cinema collective, financing would be pooled from African Americans, so as to preserve the integrity of movies and to decenter Hollywood studios from being the go-to institutions to make big-budget movies. Collectively investing in a minority-oriented film industry would give directors more resources to make movies outside Hollywood studios. Grassroots community organizing in the form of guerrilla filmmaking has worked in the past for movie financing. Recently, filmmakers have used crowd-funding sources such as Kickstarter to raise money for both short films and feature-length movies. In pursuing a Black cinema collective, because funding might be limited, directors might also be required to expand their creative capacities to challenge traditional ways of thinking about filmmaking, which can lead to developing new forms, genres, and techniques that are unique to these directors' conditions.

Additionally, the use of the internet and emerging digital technologies can help solve issues with access to cinematic production. Digital distribution possibilities are the future. Prior to online innovations with movies, the music industry provided an example of how the internet facilitated a deluge of cultural production and consumption in the face of exclusion from traditional media outlets. With politically charged rap music under threat of extinction in mainstream media, due in part to changes in media ownership concentration, African Americans in hip hop navigated to the internet to find new spaces for political expression; the internet gave hip hop producers a new location to gain leverage over major music companies and to contest their control and authority over financial and legal arrangements that formerly legitimated their dominance.[22] Major music organizations once limited Black music producers to a few genres. The online marketplace opened more direct lines of access to artists and a broader range of genres for production. Blacks' movement to the internet demonstrated their desire to regain control from corporate media organizations, taking back both the creative side of popular culture (production) and the economic side of popular culture (profit). Migration to the internet also enabled them to exercise control over the distribution of Black popular culture to audiences.

In a similar fashion, the internet can provide a means for directors to regain control of the content, financing, production, dissemination, and exhibition of their films. Such a Black cinema collective might well put pressure on Hollywood at a level that would shock the industry out of its racial politics or possibly supplant the industry in the production of popular movies about African American lives and cultures. Of course, threats to net neutrality serve the interests of the prevailing class to maintain the status quo of marginalization of insurgent visions and voices. These new attempts at oppression and persistent maneuvers to undermine more egalitarian online discourses would also need to be fought and overcome to ensure that the web remains a viable alternative to existing cultural production power structures.

A Black cinema collective would benefit from an ensemble of vested community members to realize the mission of community-based, large-scale movie production. Herman Gray writes of the *jazz left*, the model of local cultural practices that produce jazz music—from cultural workers such as music teachers, marching-band directors, and choir leaders to institutions such as churches, civil organizations, and other venues for performance.[23] The jazz left is situated on the margins, outside the mainstream, and beyond dominant institutions, cultural centers, authorities, and power. It creates an alternate entry point for exploring cultural practices and productions. Black cinema could use a parallel cultural move that develops local cultural practices to produce cinema.

Myriad independent film festivals support diverse filmmakers, from the Urbanworld Film Festival in New York City to the BronzeLens Film Festival in Atlanta to ImageNation Cinema Foundation in Harlem and many others. ImageNation, for example, was "founded with the goal of establishing a chain of art-house cinemas, dedicated to progressive media by and about people of color. . . . We foster media equity, media literacy, solidarity, cross-cultural exchange and highlight the humanity of Pan-African people worldwide."[24] Filmmakers use these festivals and their resources to establish their craft and exhibit movies outside Hollywood.

Beyond film festivals, communities would reap immense rewards from the efforts of film directors, screenwriters, producers, and educators who forge initiatives that enhance cinema production and appreciation: developing youth art and technology cultures, taking on trainees with apprenticeships, creating more youth internships with cinema-production companies, increasing enrollment in film schools, and building community institutions—with sound stages, technical equipment, and other tools—for the purposes of fostering education and improving overall filmmaking craft.

A focus on developing the craft is important, as the underdevelopment of Black cinema has critically weakened its force and quality. Christopher Scott Cherot discusses his perception of the quality of Black filmmaking:

> The thing very few people talk about, as minority filmmakers we really need to raise the bar for what we consider to be good Black filmmaking. I don't think we've done that yet. That's not my opinion, that's just the way it is, unfortunately. . . . All folks of color, all minorities who want to be in this business, should ask themselves, "What is the best product I can make that will also appeal to audiences yet still retain my integrity as a filmmaker?" That's a difficult question to ask. I think in order for us to move up to the next level . . . we can say Oscars aren't recognizing Black movies, but we at the same time we need to make better Black movies. I don't think we're there yet.[25]

At times, interests in improving conditions in Hollywood compete with investments in attaining technical mastery of film apparatus. Cherot recognizes places where Black filmmaking can improve for the betterment of directors' craft.

Rather than making racial inequality, cinema has the potential to promote racial equality. Though shaking off the encumbrances of the Hollywood Jim Crow involves tireless labor, it is the only way to ensure that the cultural past, present, and history of all racial groups becomes entrenched within the narratives and myths of American cinema. It should come as no surprise that the road to independence and true expression of creative freedom is littered with rocky opposition. If successful, a Black cinema collective poses a viable challenge to white hegemonic popular-culture industries. The collective also provides a model for other marginalized racial groups to combat their disadvantaged positions in the popular-cinema industry. New collectives are certainly vulnerable to media conglomerates' counterattacks, whether that means rival buyouts, co-optation, or pursuit with litigation.[26] However, in no way should pressure from conglomerates thwart progress toward the goal of a more egalitarian cinema.

A Black cinema collective forges a way forward for directors to overcome the Hollywood Jim Crow and ultimately to ensure that their voices, narratives, and identities are inscribed in American cinema of the twenty-first century. A Black cinema collective bridges the path to overcome an incomplete integration and oppressive symbolic exclusion in Hollywood cinematic production and to rise to full inclusion in the moviemaking industry. Therefore, a resilient Black cinema collective must arise, thrive, and ultimately resist co-optation pressures if African Americans are to wholly and indelibly disassemble Hollywood's racial hierarchies. As a stand-alone force, the progressive politics of a Black cinema collective is a strategy to pursue regardless of stagnation or change within Hollywood. A move toward a Black cinema collective provides an advance toward full citizenship for Black Americans in the United States, a roadmap to equality for other marginalized racial groups, and a victory for all.

Conclusion

Hollywood's Racial Politics

Surrounding the election of Barack Obama as the first U.S. president who is African American, discussions arose about whether the United States was becoming a postracial nation where race no longer mattered and racial preference, discrimination, or prejudice no longer existed.[1] Current research demonstrates that racial inequality persists despite the rise of postracial discourses. Indeed, explicit racism, the racial logic of Jim Crow, is back in full force. This book has investigated the ways that Hollywood workers reify racial difference and engage in explicit racism as part of regular business practice. Uncovering the roots and epistemologies behind everyday meanings and practices in the film industry helps to illustrate why racial patterns exist and illuminate ways to resolve inequities.

Understanding the Hollywood Jim Crow starts with breaking down the racial order of contemporary society. Through law and custom, whites in power have stratified U.S. society along racial divisions. In the Jim Crow era, racism was unabashedly justified on the outright basis of an ideology of white supremacism. At the onset of the post-civil-rights era, explicit racial discrimination was outlawed, but implicit racism ushered in a new racial ideology and consequently mechanisms, discourses, terminology, and practices that reproduced racial inequality were covert or invisible. In particular, during the late 1960s, the development of colorblind discourses eclipsed the blatant state-sanctioned Jim Crow laws. The racial practices of centuries ago continued under a veil of colorblindness, wherein race is not believed to be a relevant aspect of social life but other factors besides race are said to have more influence on an individual's opportunities and outcomes. In the current moment, colorblindness has given way to a new wave of explicit racism that uses race as a factor but couples it with other explanations in order to justify unequal racial outcomes.

Contemporary Hollywood disavows an ideology of outright racism in favor of a market rationale that movies with white casts and directors are more marketable and have the potential to attract larger audiences than do movies with Black, Asian, or Latino/a casts and directors. In other words, Hollywood decision-makers invoke racist ideas about cultural selection to suggest that movies with white casts and directors, as cultural products, are more acceptable and favored by global audiences. Rather than simply being just about race, the reasons provided for racial discrimination are couched as both cultural and economic.

Similar to the Jim Crow order of the past, the logic of the Hollywood Jim Crow assumes racial difference, acts on that difference to stratify groups, and produces a result of unequal outcomes. Under the Hollywood Jim Crow, the assumption that Black is unbankable, not universal, and financially risky serves as a basis for disadvantaging Black directors and movies and privileging white directors and movies. Racial hierarchies based on the "unbankable" label are a prime example of how racial distinctions are made in explicit fashion in Hollywood, with racist sentiments outwardly expressed as the basis for advantage and disadvantage. Hollywood insiders apply the "unbankable" assumption uniquely to African Americans and other racial minority groups and not to whites. This is a significant shift from racial discourses that have dominated the post-civil-rights period, when social norms rendered overt practices of racial hierarchy, hostility, bigotry, and bias illegal and immoral. Now explicit practices of racial hierarchy govern everyday decision-making in Hollywood. Economic and cultural logics are deployed to defend practices of explicit racial bias.

As Hollywood insiders make predictions about box-office performance and decisions about movies, race is a primary sorting mechanism. Prior to any observed outcomes, race—and imagined relationships between directors, casts, and audiences—is embedded into discussions about profit potential. The racial argument is couched in terms of market logics, using language about profit. Hollywood's racial logic shapes distribution strategies. Distribution is significant in its role of imagining and creating audiences for movies. As justification for patterns of distribution, films are raced by actors and directors. Audiences are also raced through market segmentation. Hollywood insiders imagine and create segmented audiences for the consumption of Black films.

In fact, the very definition of potential success and failure of Hollywood movies is socially constructed in a way that is biased toward the box-office performance of white movies. Industry gatekeepers perpetuate the myth that foreign audiences, especially, desire white movies more than Black movies and that Black movies do not perform well in foreign markets. Ironically, however, whites are no longer the majority share of moviegoers in the United States, nor are they the primary focus of the exportation of Hollywood movies globally. Notwithstanding this discrepancy, this production logic of a racialized box office is still pervasive among Hollywood insiders. It is not only permitted but routine, everyday practice in cinematic decision-making. Moreover, in the highly concentrated film market, only a few dozen movies receive most of the box-office revenue. But the performance of these select movies, and the accompanying goal to make at least two-thirds of box-office revenue overseas, becomes the normative industry standard that Hollywood insiders use to justify racial inequality in film distribution. Within the context of global white supremacism, one role of media is to cultivate a language that normalizes, justifies, and facilitates widespread societal complicity with racial difference. One could argue that the recent shift to focus on the foreign box-office profit is a language developed to simultaneously account for the rising box office of Black films and the falling box office of white films in the domestic market. In any case, foreign-market revenue became the new gold standard to measure cinematic worthiness, without regard for the racial origins and implications of the standard.

Essentially, we are back to square one with blatant, explicit racism that once belonged to the Jim Crow era in the center of everyday business practices in the movie industry. This time, however, the explicit racism is backed with cultural and economic rationales. On the face of it, society is beyond the notion of seeing color, since color presumably only matters as it relates to economics and not for its own sake. Economic logics and cultural explanations give Hollywood insiders plausible deniability, to allege they would not invoke race if it were not linked to economics and culture.

The "unbankable" label has detrimental implications for directors' careers and prevents Black movies and directors from maintaining a permanent foothold in the film industry, due to their difficulty receiving big budgets, distribution, and financial support. Disproportionate representation at major studios and on big-budget films has direct consequences for who gets ahead, who gets promoted, and who reaches the highest levels of commercial success within the film industry. Rather than acknowledging these differences in production budgets and studios, white directors are, instead, probably perceived as being more competent than African Americans are at directing. Internalizing this perception without taking into account the groups' disparate access to resources for cinematic production can lead to studio executives justifying the hiring of white directors more often than Black directors on future movies, while privileging the career trajectories of white directors and negatively impacting the career trajectories of Black directors.

The films that Hollywood devalues, labels unprofitable, and casts low expectations on are the very films around which African Americans typically shape their film-directing careers. The slippery slope of projecting low expectations on Black-directed cinema leads to disadvantages for Black directors. With Black directors assigned to films with low expectations and production values, the entrapment cycle begins, relegating them to marginal movies and limiting their career paths in Hollywood. Segregation into different film genres has implications for the kinds of stories that appear about African Americans in Hollywood films and the types of narratives that are excluded. Black Americans' inclusion in all genres of media production is important to instill diverse voices in mass-distributed popular-culture stories. To prevent the monopolistic dominance of Hollywood narratives, it is not only important to include characters from various Black voices and perspectives, such as in sci-fi cinema, but also not to privilege some aspects of African American experiences—ghettos or performance cultures—over others. Marginalization of Black stories and directors maintains a prevalence of whiteness in content and production in the film industry and thwarts progress toward making the United States, and its constitutive film institutions, more racially inclusive, contrary to the purported societal norm of racial equality.

When movies that display Black identities, social experiences, or cultures are economically disadvantaged and labeled unbankable, Hollywood studios express little interest in investing in and supporting them with big budgets for production and distribution. The burden puts immense pressure on Black movies and directors to perform at the box office, or else a negative stigma will be attached to any underperformance. If Black directors are unsuccessful, they are marked as racial outcasts, yet white directors' lack of success is not ascribed to race but is rather viewed as nonracial. Black directors' position in the film industry remains precarious despite their multitudinous achievements. Black movies and directors that perform well are overlooked and explained away as being "flukes"—exceptions rather than the rule. The "unbankable" label encompasses all Black-cast films and overshadows prominent directors to relegate them to positions of entrenched disadvantage along the movie-production process. Black movies and directors need an integration without stigma. Dismantling the Hollywood Jim Crow would mean removing the racial stigma to ensure that Black movies and directors are accepted and represented within all areas and at all levels of film production.

Stark power disparities shape who can or cannot access different levels of cinematic production. Marginalized racial groups have little command over the production and content of mainstream cinema. This lack of control over images makes it difficult to control image and ideological production of mass media, improve work conditions, or challenge stereotypes that influence social behavior. Since civil-rights-era protests for racial inclusion in U.S. society, more Black Americans have participated in directing for Hollywood studios. Still, racial disadvantage remains a prevalent concern among film scholars, media critics, and film professionals. Specifically, doors to the upper echelon of opportunities in Hollywood remain closed to Black Americans and other U.S. racial minority groups. An essential part of diversifying the American cultural canon requires making the film industry truly representative of the nation's multicultural citizens.

Different racial groups, however, require different approaches to solving problems with representation in Hollywood. Asian and Latino/a directors have begun making inroads via integrating into the hierarchy of big-budget movies and tent-pole franchise films. Yet Latino/a directors are especially underrepresented relative to their portion of the population. Of all racial minority groups, Black directors are most ghettoized on small-budget movies. Collectively, women from marginalized racial groups are underrepresented and lack inclusion on Hollywood's core cultural products. In fact, white Europeans receive far more access to directing big-budget movies than do directors from racial minority groups. Certainly that dynamic deserves further attention to understand where Hollywood executives could target initiatives for improving representation, if they aspire to dispose of organizational practices of racial bias and form a more racially inclusive film industry.

The disproportionate benefits and disadvantages of the Hollywood Jim Crow do not end at the doors of the film industry but also affect societal racial inequality and permeate individual lives. The Hollywood Jim Crow trickles down through individuals and families to entire neighborhoods and international communities via the spread of global media messages. An industry-wide hierarchy of directors and movies along racial lines has far-reaching implications for other spheres of social life.

A slippery slope leads to accepting the argument that Black films are unbankable and then using that argument to justify unequal allocation of resources and rewards. If the explicit language of racial inferiority and superiority and the disparate treatment of racial groups on the basis of economic and cultural logics is accepted as a social norm and practice, this precedent could lead down a path to convenient applicability to culture industries and other sectors. The argument that a movie with a Black director or cast would not sell to foreign audiences is not far from explaining away any form of racial discrimination in culture industries as audience preferences. Sports teams, for example, could determine who plays not on the basis of talent, skill, and acumen but on the basis of jersey sales in a given fiscal year. Sales and marketing consultants, university administrators and presidents, and broadcast and radio news correspondents, to name a few occupations, all have to connect with consumer audiences, viewers, and listeners—sometimes seeking out funds, donations, or philanthropy. Using Hollywood's economic logic, a university board of trustees could make the argument that a racial-minority president is expected to be unbankable—unsuccessful at fundraising—an assessment that could establish a perpetual norm of racially homogeneous leaders for years to come, buoyed by the justification that white presidents are preferred by alumni and the prediction that they will make more money for the university. Beyond culture industries, further linkages to Hollywood's racial logic can be drawn to occupations in which work involves being able to forge connections to audiences, constituents, and consumers.

Race structures in the film industry represent a microcosm of a massive and complex system of racial inequality in the United States. Broadly, the Hollywood Jim Crow and the Black integration project into Hollywood can be extrapolated to illustrate the limitations that Black Americans face in white-dominated elite occupations in contemporary U.S society. The more we look, Jim Crow hierarchies of racial advantage and disadvantage appear across many sectors of U.S. industries—from academia to health care. Black Americans' marginalization and symbolic exclusion in cinematic production draws familiar parallels to their relegation to limited areas of work and stalled progress in high-paying positions in other elite occupations. Furthermore, a racial order keeping Black Americans at a distance from institutional fulcrums has implications for societal understanding of African Americans' roles in U.S. occupational structures, often locating them at the bottom rather than atop or spread evenly throughout career ladders, obstructed by glass ceilings as opposed to transcending them.

Upholding the Hollywood Jim Crow, at any costs, means leaving white executives' mentality toward the profit motive unchallenged, even at the expense of racial discrimination. The result normalizes precarious employment for Black Americans but without labeling racial bias as the culprit. Instead, racial inequality is said to be a natural outcome of market forces and audience preferences. Explicit racial bias is permitted so long as it is couched in the language of economic sensibility and bottom-line profit. Thus, a vital aspect of challenging Hollywood and other institutions that do not adhere to social norms of racial equality, perhaps the most essential act, is possessing the conviction to challenge the profit motive. In these neoliberal and neoconservative political times, it is widely accepted that profit lords over other ends. National football teams and supermarkets alike pack up and move house, from city to city, in search of more and better profits, and criticism for their actions is sparse due to the acceptance of capitalist misadventures as the way of life. Indeed, film directors, in order to perform their craft, have to make arguments to studio executives and financiers to suggest that their movies will be immensely profitable. If there is any hope of ending the Hollywood Jim Crow, it would require less kowtowing to the bottom line. From a moral standpoint, the film industry serves a purpose for distributing national cinema to domestic and global audiences. From a practical outlook, industries such as Hollywood receive public government support, funded by citizens. Film studios should bear a responsibility to the people who support them with their tax dollars and patronage.

The U.S. government should be involved in ensuring racial equality in Hollywood operations and practices, for the simple reason that the public sphere generously aids the private sphere. The film industry receives no small amount of support from the U.S. government. Taxpayers of all races contribute money to the film industry via government assistance to Hollywood studio productions. The state helps ensure not only the survival but also the prosperity of the film industry. Hollywood movies are protected and defended by the state. National, state, and local film commissions offer incentives to attract film productions to their localities. Economic incentives for film companies include tax rebates, hotel discounts, and free services—such as research or government liaisons for screenwriters. Beyond tax breaks and incentives, the U.S. government provides aid to the film industry, protecting it in international treaty negotiations, encouraging countries to open their markets to Hollywood movies, and penalizing countries that do not comply with this agenda.[2] In addition, close ties exist between the government and Hollywood companies; for instance, Ronald Reagan was a Hollywood actor before becoming president, and Bill Clinton had close friends in Hollywood.

Unfortunately, the federal government does not hold Hollywood accountable for its racial bias. Instead, the government responds to allegations and legal challenges with laissez-faire inaction. For example, following the civil rights movement, Hollywood was referred to the Justice Department for its racial inequality and exclusion in ownership, distribution, and production. In the 1960s, the Justice Department threatened legal action against Hollywood, but later, in 1970, following negotiations, it dropped its legal action against Hollywood to instead settle on a two-year voluntary agreement to increase the film industry's minority employment to a goal of 20 percent. With no long-term, formal policy, a short-term increase during the two-year period was short-lived.[3] In this way, the government is complicit with the status quo. A lack of consequences for industries with stark racial disparities in employment makes inequality and hierarchy difficult to overcome. Hollywood's virtual immunity to legal challenges mirrors why racial inequality persisted in prior Jim Crow systems.

Ideally, the government should have a hand in curbing racism, but it has too often demonstrated the very opposite: complicity with the construction and maintenance of racial inequity. As prior research has elucidated, Jim Crow systems and practices are legalized, with government having a hand in perpetuating and condoning racial inequality.[4] In this regard, the Hollywood Jim Crow is no different. Despite Hollywood's unequal treatment on the explicit basis of race and its blatant defiance of the norm of racial equality, its unflinching adherence to faulty economic and cultural logics receives full government backing.

Currently there are few checks and balances to prevent the persistence of racial inequality in Hollywood. The U.S. government's silence of the subject of racial inequality is coupled with its complicity in aiding film-industry institutions that foster unequal practices. If private industries are to receive tax breaks, public money, and support from federal, state, and local governments, they should be beholden to the tenets of racial equality in society and not only to their private profits. Across many industries, companies and corporations—from Wall Street and the financial industry to the National Football League and the sports business to Silicon Valley and tech firms—have a tenuous relationship with the pursuit of racial equality, though all are dependent on government handouts to make profits. Dedication to social equality should be a pertinent factor in determining which institutions receive government support. People should hold their government accountable to all citizens in every possible manner. The Hollywood Jim Crow that regularly marginalizes, discriminates against, and stigmatizes racial minorities would face swift challenges if it were universally condemned and not aided and abetted by official government channels.

Additional studies of the Hollywood film industry would be useful to further understand its contours of inequality and to develop approaches to mitigate racial disparities. Research, for example, can investigate the role of social networks in producing unequal outcomes for racial groups. Standard industry practices, such as using social networks to hire new employees, may at times produce racially patterned outcomes, with or without stakeholders directly invoking a stain of Blackness to rationalize their decisions. In addition, in-depth qualitative field studies can provide up-close information on how day-to-day processes within the film business result in widespread inequality. Interviews with industry decision-makers and ethnographies of film-development deals and productions would give first-person accounts of film-industry practices. Analyses of relevant movie-project documents would provide deeper context into the ways race seeps into everyday business operations. Such studies can further investigate the degree to

Figure C.1. Black-directed movies *Black Panther* and *Wrinkle in Time* headline showings at Beechwood Cinema in Athens, Georgia. Photo by author, March 14, 2018.

which racial considerations shape the filmmaking process by providing unique insight into the inner workings of day-to-day life in the film-industry workplace and demonstrating how race is situated in decision-making through production, distribution, and exhibition. Moreover, theatrical distribution is only one stage of the distribution window for motion pictures. Besides theatrical releases, motion pictures also find distribution in other markets, including home video, cable and broadcast television, public libraries, prisons, schools, airlines, colleges, hotels, hospitals, railroads, and churches. Future studies can examine whose movies and which directors are showcased across several motion-picture markets and whether the extent of racial inequality is magnified or lessened in various arenas. While the theatrical market is highly visible, investigations of inequality in distribution within other markets will provide a broader picture of how racial differences manifest throughout the distribution process.

At this juncture, as the Jim Crow structure of Hollywood comes to light, it is to be expected that the visibility of racial minorities will peak and their opportunities will increase momentarily, so as not to put the hierarchical system on full display. As Tyler Perry describes, "Hollywood always has a wave, and in that wave comes films about people of color. It's just a wave that happens and once it crests, it gives a way."[5] After the wave, Black directors inevitably become crestfallen, when another drought in opportunity sets in. Hollywood is on the cusp of a monumental wave with unprecedented big-budget movies for Black men and women: *The Fate of the Furious* (2017), *Black Panther* (2018), and *Wrinkle in Time* (2018). The global sensation of *Black Panther* shattered numerous records and proved, once again, that Black stars, casts, and stories can and do draw audiences—both nationally and globally. It remains to be seen, however, whether these movies and other successful films will genuinely inspire enough changes in the film industry to radiate optimism about the future of race in Hollywood.

To end the cycle of the Hollywood Jim Crow—of racial inequality making, marginalization, segregation, and stigmatization—all interested parties must exert persistent pressure on Hollywood studios to effect change, whether it is change from within Hollywood with racial minorities occupying more positions with decision-making power or outside Hollywood with a Black cinema collective of insurgent cinematic production. Dismantling the Hollywood Jim Crow and enabling racial minorities to gain lucrative work opportunities and shape popular cinema from positions of influence means reshaping existing power dynamics in the industry while challenging myths about the conventional logics of media production and control.

ACKNOWLEDGMENTS

Before this book was even an idea, my interest in sociological research was piqued by the Sociology Department at the University of Notre Dame and specifically the guidance of Rory McVeigh and Bill Carbonaro. Along the way, I received support and guidance from colleagues and friends in the Sociology and Africana Studies Departments and the Cinema Studies program at University of Pennsylvania, the Sociology Department at University of Memphis, and the Sociology Department and Institute for African American Studies at the University of Georgia.

Camille Z. Charles is an excellent mentor who supported my desires to push the boundaries of sociology and engage in interdisciplinary fields of cinema and media studies, communications, and Africana studies. Mia Mask introduced me to the study of cinema from a scholarly perspective. Michael X. Delli Carpini, Tukufu Zuberi, and Onoso Imoagene provided much-needed support during the early stages of this project. The group of devoted media and diversity scholars who participated in the University of Southern California Annenberg Summer Institute on Race and Diversity provided an interactive forum for feedback and exchange of ideas. The anonymous reviewers gave thoughtful comments that helped improve the book tremendously.

The team at New York University Press made this book idea a reality. Ilene Kalish showed enthusiasm about this book from the start. Ellen Chodosh openly welcomed me to the press. Maryam Arain helped answer all of my questions. Alexia Traganas moved the book smoothly through production. Others working for the press contributed in numerous ways.

Writing this book was a long process that would not have been possible without the support of colleagues, friends, and family, for whom I am ever grateful.

APPENDIX

DATA AND METHODOLOGY
The book includes quotes from and references to conversations between Hollywood insiders that were obtained via WikiLeaks (WL) in a collection of correspondences that included more than 173,132 emails to and from more than 2,200 Sony Pictures Entertainment email addresses. While referencing the correspondences in the book, pseudonyms are used in place of actual names of senders and recipients. This allows the focus of the analysis to remain on the collective sentiments about race and cinema production within the system of Hollywood rather than on individual people and statements. The following is a list of webpages for the email quotations included in the book:

WL. 2017a. https://wikileaks.org/sony/emails/180342.
WL. 2017b. https://wikileaks.org/sony/emails/20848.
WL. 2017c. https://wikileaks.org/sony/emails/40707.
WL. 2017d. https://wikileaks.org/sony/emails/33055.
WL. 2017e. https://wikileaks.org/sony/emails/27578.
WL. 2017f. https://wikileaks.org/sony/emails/37024.
WL. 2017g. https://wikileaks.org/sony/emails/60405.
WL. 2017h. https://wikileaks.org/sony/emails/60032.
WL. 2017i. https://wikileaks.org/sony/emails/46051.
WL. 2017j. https://wikileaks.org/sony/emails/123081.
WL. 2017k. https://wikileaks.org/sony/emails/124558.
WL. 2017l. https://wikileaks.org/sony/emails/37267.
WL. 2017m. https://wikileaks.org/sony/emails/33572.
WL. 2017n. https://wikileaks.org/sony/emails/56694.
WL. 2017o. https://wikileaks.org/sony/emails/75001.
WL. 2017p. https://wikileaks.org/sony/emails/185733.
WL. 2017q. https://wikileaks.org/sony/emails/195225.

WL. 2017r. https://wikileaks.org/sony/emails/183162.
WL. 2017s. https://wikileaks.org/sony/emails/44786.

DATA COLLECTION

Theatrical releases, or movies released to cinemas, reach the widest audiences and are believed to have the greatest influence on mass popular culture compared to other methods of cinematic distribution. For these reasons, the book takes theatrically released movies as the primary objects of interest. Only the first theatrical run is included. The data do not include reissues, or later nonconsecutive releases of a movie in subsequent years, to avoid counting the same film multiple times. Janet Wasko in her book *How Hollywood Works* categorizes movies by theatrical release patterns in the U.S. market: exclusive releases have under 10 play dates, limited releases have 11 to 599 play dates, and wide releases have 600 or more play dates. The focus of the book is movies that have wide releases of 600 or more play dates. In a few cases of groups that are vastly underrepresented, for example, women from racial-minority backgrounds, some limited releases are included to provide a picture of their level of inclusion as directors of Hollywood movies.

Frequent mergers and acquisitions between established companies, the emergence of new companies, and the disappearance of old companies make tracking information on racial inequality in film companies a challenge. The film companies included in this book are major players in the film industry that have distributed at least fifty movies since 2000. Other companies can be influential but shift in and out of relevance and so are not deemed pivotal for this analysis. In total, just over thirteen hundred "Hollywood" movies make up the bulk of the primary analysis. Here, "Hollywood" is defined as movies distributed by the major film companies' key distribution arms: Sony, Universal, 20th Century Fox, Disney (Buena Vista), Warner Brothers (and Warner Brothers / New Line), and Paramount (and Paramount/DreamWorks). Other movies included in subsequent analyses are distributed by the following studio independent and independent companies: Lionsgate, New Line Cinema, Metro Goldwyn Mayer (MGM), Focus Features, Sony Screen Gems, Fox Searchlight, and Miramax.

A number of prior studies use data from the Internet Movie Database (IMDb, www.imdb.com) and Box Office Mojo (www.boxofficemojo

.com). These online databases contain information on contemporary movies, directors, film organizations, and box-office receipts. The production budgets, domestic box-office receipts, and foreign box-office receipts are estimates that are accurate at the time of collection but are subject to change due to changes in reporting of information from film organizations. The aggregate data provide an overall picture of racial inequality in the film industry that is resistant to any minor changes in reporting of individual film statistics.

Race was coded as Black, white, Asian, Latino/a, or other. Most Black, Asian, and Latino/a directors made references to racial or ethnic identity. Black directors typically identified as African American or Black. Asian directors commonly identified as Asian or mentioned ties to Asian countries, sometimes in addition to American nationality. Latino/a directors identified as Hispanic/Latino/a or mentioned ties to Central/South American ethnic or national heritage. White directors, on the other hand, often referenced ties to ethnicity—European, American, or other nationality—but less often made direct references to a white racial identity. For Hollywood movies, the analysis includes 1,194 white-directed movies, 65 Black-directed movies, 33 Asian-directed movies, and 11 Latino/a-directed movies.

LINKS TO SELECT FIGURES

Figure I.1. Antoine Fuqua at the premiere of *The Magnificent Seven*: https:// www.flickr.com/photos/tonyshek/29659104992/.

Figure 1.2. 1963 March on Washington: https://www.flickr.com/photos /pingnews/286476812.

Figure 2.1. Variety headline: https://www.flickr.com/photos /montclairfilmfest/34480432196/.

Figure 3.2. Ava DuVernay at the Ultimate Disney Fan Event: https://www .flickr.com/photos/disneyabc/35136570223/.

Figure 4.1. "She's Back" billboard ad: https://www.flickr.com/photos /perspective/20570542574/.

Figure 5.1. John Singleton at a Canadian entertainment cultural showcase: https://www.flickr.com/photos/cfccreates/8470517347/.

Figure 6.1. Carver Theater in downtown Birmingham, Alabama: https://www .flickr.com/photos/string_bass_dave/29170652293/.

NOTES

INTRODUCTION

1. WL 2017a. Steve and other first-name-only references are pseudonyms from quotes obtained from emails of people affiliated with a major film studio. Details for all references to WikiLeaks (WL) emails can be found in the appendix. Spelling and grammar are as written in emails, with occasional minor edits for purposes of clarity.
2. Caldwell 2008; Dueze 2010; Ortner 2013; Perren 2012; Wasko 2003.
3. Gray 2016: 246.
4. Hesmondhalgh and Saha 2013.
5. Hughey 2014; Lipsitz 1998; Quinn 2013.
6. DiMaggio 1987; Maguire and Matthews 2012.
7. Quinn 2013: 198.
8. Bonilla-Silva 2014: 3.
9. Bonilla-Silva 2014.
10. Michelle Alexander (2010) weaves in this analogy in her book *The New Jim Crow*. During the New Jim Crow, corporate media and public policies, such as the Rockefeller and Reagan laws, manufactured narratives of inferiority in the law and white public opinion to support the allegation that Blacks were more morally deficient and used more drugs than whites. Subsequently, under this New Jim Crow era, a substantial number of Black people are labeled "criminals" and are subjected to legal discrimination. First, they are disproportionately targeted, stopped, frisked, arrested, charged, and imprisoned. Second, when they come out of jails and prisons and reenter society, a cycle of unequal outcomes, from unemployment to unstable housing to poor health, follows to diminish their opportunities and life chances. Whites, on the other hand, due to their privilege, are far less likely to find themselves embroiled in the carceral cycle and doubly are advantaged by a decreased competition for jobs that is a result of imprisoning large numbers of African Americans.
11. Wasko 2003: 4.
12. Wasko 2003: 12.
13. Collins 2009.
14. Shohat and Stam 1997.
15. Schatz 2013.
16. Watkins 1998: 84.
17. Guerrero 1993; Reid 2005; Smith and Choueiti 2011.

18. Oliver and Shapiro 1995; Baradaran 2017.
19. Caldwell 2008.
20. Caldwell 2008: 345.
21. W. Bielby and D. Bielby 1994; Caves 2000.
22. Rehling 2009.

CHAPTER 1. REPRESENTATION AND RACIAL HIERARCHY

1. WL 2017b.
2. Higgins 2018.
3. Ciras 2017.
4. Ciras 2017.
5. Belton 2017.
6. Waxman 1996.
7. "Celebrities Who Are Democratic" 2016.
8. Pendakur 2008: 191.
9. Quinn 2013.
10. Quinn 2011: 3.
11. Davis and Dee 1998: 388.
12. U.S. Bureau of Labor Statistics 2015.
13. Western 2006.
14. Smith, Choueiti, and Pieper 2014; Yuen 2004, 2010, 2017.
15. W. Bielby and D. Bielby 1999; D. Bielby and W. Bielby 2002; Erigha 2015, 2016a, 2018; Hunt, Ramón, and Price 2014; Hunt and Ramón 2015; Smith and Choueiti 2011.
16. Smith, Choueiti, and Pieper 2014.
17. Tim Story, talk at University of Southern California Annenberg School of Communication, March 29, 2013.
18. Rock 2014.
19. Reid 2005.
20. Havens (2013) discusses the circulation of Black television around the world.
21. Hall 1973.
22. Morales 2012c.
23. McHenry 2016.
24. Hughey 2014: 126.
25. Ware 2017a.
26. Ibid.
27. Golding 2017.
28. Ibid.
29. Tillet 2012.
30. WL 2017b.
31. Horn and Smith 2013.
32. Yuen 2017.
33. Feinberg 2014.

34. Penrice 2017.
35. Bowser, Gaines, and Musser 2001; Reid 1993, 2005.
36. Reid 1993.
37. Bowser, Gaines, and Musser 2001; Reid 2005: 8–9.
38. Cripps 1993; Simpson 1990; Yearwood 2000.
39. Simpson 1990.
40. Guerrero 1993.
41. Erigha 2015; Hunt, Ramón, and Price 2014; Smith and Choueiti 2011; Smith, Choueiti, and Pieper 2014.
42. Morales 2013b.
43. Smith, Choueiti, and Pieper 2014.
44. Couch and Fairlie 2010.
45. Gray 2016.
46. Gray 2016: 246.
47. Ruef and Fletcher 2003: 477.
48. Winship 2004: 297.

CHAPTER 2. LABELING BLACK UNBANKABLE

1. WL 2017c; Duke 2014.
2. WL 2017c.
3. Feagin, Vera, and Batur 2001: 186–187.
4. WL 2017c.
5. WL 2017c.
6. Quinn 2012: 479–480.
7. Reid 2005.
8. Caves 2000; W. Bielby and D. Bielby 1994.
9. WL 2017d.
10. WL 2017e.
11. WL 2017f.
12. WL 2017g.
13. WL 2017h.
14. WL 2017i.
15. WL 2017j.
16. WL 2017d; WL 2017k.
17. WL 2017l.
18. WL 2017f.
19. WL 2017m.
20. WL 2017n.
21. WL2017o.
22. WL 2017f.
23. Gettell 2014.
24. Morales 2012a.
25. Morales 2011c.

26. Morales 2013a.
27. Morales 2012b.
28. Morales 2012a.
29. Shohat and Stam 1997: 183.
30. Caves 2000: 146.
31. W. Bielby and D. Bielby 1994.
32. Alex Stedman, "Leaked Sony Emails Reveal Jokes about Obama and Race," *Variety*, December 10, 2014, www.variety.com.
33. D. Bielby and W. Bielby 2002; Hunt, Ramón, and Price 2014.
34. Rock 2014.
35. Maldonado 2009.
36. D. Bielby and W. Bielby 2002; Hunt, Ramón, and Price 2014.
37. One exception is Forrest Whitaker directing *Hope Floats* (1996), a romance drama starring Sandra Bullock and featuring a majority-white cast.
38. Quinn 2011; Hughey 2014; Lipsitz 1998.
39. Sam Bidder, "Sony Leak: Studio Exec Calls Kevin Hart a Greedy Whore," *Gawker*, December 10, 2014, www.defamer.gawker.com.
40. WL 2017i.
41. WL 2017h.
42. WL 2017h.
43. WL 2017f.
44. Brent Lang, "You Can't Track Black: How Box Office Predictions Fail Diverse Movies," *Variety*, September 23, 2015, www.variety.com.
45. Quinn 2013: 198.
46. Morales 2011b.
47. Cripps 1978; Als 2010.
48. Hunt, Ramón, and Price 2014.
49. Greene 1994; Guerrero 1993; Reid 2005.
50. WL 2017p.
51. Cieply 2013.
52. Cieply 2013.
53. WL 2017m.
54. Cunningham 2014.

CHAPTER 3. DIRECTING ON THE MARGINS

1. Morales 2014.
2. Reid 2005: 15.
3. Barot and Bird 2001; Maldonado 2009; Bonilla-Silva and Lewis 1999.
4. Wasko 2008: 44.
5. Morales 2012d.
6. Schatz 2008, 2009, 2013.
7. Garnham 1987: 32.

8. WL 2017c.
9. These averages are derived from 1,194 white-directed, 65 Black-directed, 33 Asian-directed, and 11 Latino-directed movies.
10. Erigha 2016b.
11. Talbert 2010.
12. Morales 2011b.
13. Morales 2011b.
14. Danielle 2017.
15. Garnham 1987: 31.
16. Wasko 2003: 56.
17. Wasko 2003: 80.
18. Rhines 1996: 9.
19. Wasko 2003: 122.
20. Balio 2013; Elberse 2013; Schatz 2008, 2009, 2013.
21. Schatz 2009.
22. Lee 2015.
23. Saha 2017: 315.
24. W. Bielby and D. Bielby 1999.
25. Schatz 2009; Scott 2004.
26. Cieply 2013.
27. WL 2017q.
28. WL 2017g.
29. WL 2017r.
30. WL 2017s.
31. Wasko 2003.
32. Bogle 1991.
33. Cieply 2013.
34. WL 2017q.
35. Sperling 2013.
36. Ibid.
37. Morales 2014.
38. Hunt, Ramón, and Price 2014; Rehling 2009.
39. Scott 2004.
40. Rock 2014.
41. Smith, Choueiti, and Piper 2014. Their study examined the top-one-hundred-grossing films each year over a six-year period.
42. Donalson 2003.
43. Ava DuVernay, talk at University of Southern California Annenberg School of Communication, March 29, 2013.
44. Burks 1996.
45. Bobo 1998; Burks 1996; Collins 2009.
46. Collins 2009.

CHAPTER 4. MAKING GENRE GHETTOS

1. WL 2017d.
2. Rhines 1996: 87.
3. Talbert 2010.
4. Cripps 1978; Reid 1993.
5. Bobo 1998; Jones 1991; Leonard 2006; Mask 2000; Ndounou 2014; and Reid 2005.
6. D. Bielby and W. Bielby 2002; Yuen 2010.
7. Guerrero 1993, 1995.
8. Quinn 2013: 204.
9. Friedman 2011.
10. Watkins 1998.
11. Irene Cara, Willie D. Burton, and Russell Williams II's Oscars were shared awards. See Mapp 2008.
12. Burton's was a shared award.
13. Chow-White, Deveau, and Adams 2015.
14. Keegan 2007; Quinn 2013.
15. Bernardi 1998; Guerrero 1993; Nama 2008; Pounds 1999; and Roberts 2000.
16. Fradley 2013.
17. Critics argue, however, that *Sleight* perpetuates controlling stereotypes. Besides the drug-dealer role, Bo also toes the line of a "magical Negro" who has a white female love interest and only develops his powers via the assistance of a "white savior" teacher figure. For example, see Ware 2017b.
18. Nama 2008: 148.
19. Rehling 2009.
20. Chow-White, Deveau, and Adams 2015.
21. Morales 2012b.
22. Metcalfe 2012.
23. Tim Story, talk at University of Southern California Annenberg School of Communication, March 29, 2013.
24. Peterson and Anand 2004.
25. Guerrero 1993.
26. Shohat and Stam 1997.
27. Rutledge 2001.
28. W. Bielby and D. Bielby 1994.
29. Rutledge 2001.
30. Morales 2012a.
31. WL 2017c.
32. Wasko 2003: 27.
33. Nama 2008: 149.
34. Caves 2000.
35. Collins, Hand, and Snell 2002; Hirsch 1972.
36. WL 2017c.
37. Reynolds 2011.

38. Thompson 2014.
39. Lang and Kelley 2017.

CHAPTER 5. MANUFACTURING RACIAL STIGMA

1. Du Bois 1903: 1.
2. Du Bois 1898.
3. Alexander 2010.
4. Sperling 2013.
5. Metcalfe 2012.
6. Du Bois 1913: 138.
7. Bonilla-Silva 2015: 74.
8. Cieply 2013.
9. Morales 2011c.
10. Morales 2013c.
11. Du Bois 1903
12. Morales 2013a.
13. Morales 2011b.
14. Morales 2012a.
15. Rhines 1996.
16. Nama 2008.
17. For a discussion of Shonda Rhimes as a creator of crossover television shows, see Erigha 2015.
18. Ndounou 2014: 180–181.
19. Lubiano 1991: 258.
20. Lubiano concedes, however, that studio funding does not always mean compromise and that nonstudio funding does not always mean subversion or empowerment. While these exceptions are not impossible, she believes they are highly improbable.
21. Hall 1992.
22. Rock 2014.
23. Feagin, Vera, and Batur 2001.
24. Cruse 1967.
25. Collins 2004: 168.
26. Sexton 2009.
27. Aldridge 2011.
28. Guerrero 1993: 182.
29. Palmer 2011: 34.
30. Morales 2011b.

CHAPTER 6. REMAKING CINEMA

1. Bonilla-Silva 2015.
2. Hunt and Ramón 2015.
3. Quinn 2011: 12.

4. Morales 2012d.
5. Anderson 2015.
6. Schatz 2008.
7. Morales 2011a
8. Rhines 1996.
9. Bonilla-Silva 2015.
10. Quinn 2012: 479.
11. Morales 2012d.
12. West 1990: 94.
13. Hall 1992.
14. Cripps 1993; Yearwood 2000.
15. Ava DuVernay, talk at University of Southern California Annenberg School of Communication, March 29, 2013.
16. Array, n.d.
17. Morales 2012a.
18. Rock 2014.
19. Cripps 1978.
20. Morales 2012c.
21. Metcalfe 2012.
22. Watkins (2001: 391) examined the website Rapstation.com, run by Chuck D, the leader of the rap group Public Enemy.
23. Gray 2005.
24. ImageNation Cinema Foundation, n.d.
25. Morales 2011a.
26. Watkins 2001: 392.

CONCLUSION

1. Michael Dawson and Lawrence Bobo (2009) discuss postracial discourses during the Obama presidency.
2. Wasko 2003: 181.
3. Quinn 2012: 481.
4. Alexander 2010.
5. Morales 2013b.

REFERENCES

Aldridge, Leah. 2011. "Mythology and Affect: The Brands of Cinematic Blackness of Will Smith and Tyler Perry." *University of Southern California Journal of Film and Television* 31 (1): 41–47.

Alexander, Michelle. 2010. *The New Jim Crow: Mass Incarceration in the Age of Color-blindness.* New York: New Press.

Als, Hilton. 2010. "Mama's Gun: The World of Tyler Perry." *New Yorker*, April 26. www.newyorker.com.

Anderson, Tre'vell. 2015. "Spike Lee on Hollywood Diversity: 'We Don't Have a Vote. We're Not in the Room.'" *Los Angeles Times*, November 17. www.latimes.com.

Array. n.d. "Our Story: About Array." Accessed November 12, 2017. www.arraynow.com.

Balio, Tino. 2013. *Hollywood in the New Millennium.* London: British Film Institute.

Baradaran, Mehrsa. 2017. *The Color of Money: Black Banks and the Racial Wealth Gap.* Cambridge, MA: Harvard University Press.

Barot, Rohit, and John Bird. 2001. "Racialization: The Genealogy and Critique of a Concept." *Ethnic and Racial Studies* 24 (4): 601–618.

Belton, Danielle. 2017. "At the AAFC Awards, Black Artists of TV and Film Invest in One Another." *The Root*, February 9. www.theroot.com.

Bernardi, Daniel. 1998. *"Star Trek" and History: Race-ing toward a White Future.* New Brunswick, NJ: Rutgers University Press.

Bielby, Denise D., and William T. Bielby. 2002. "Hollywood Dreams, Harsh Realities: Writing for Film and Television." *Contexts* 1 (4): 21–27.

Bielby, William T., and Denise D. Bielby. 1994. "'All Hits Are Flukes': Institutionalized Decision Making and the Rhetoric of Network Prime-Time Program Development." *American Journal of Sociology* 99:1287–1313.

———. 1999. "Organizational Mediation of Project-Based Labor Markets: Talent Agencies and the Careers of Screenwriters." *American Sociological Review* 64:64–85.

Bobo, Jacqueline. 1998. *Black Women Film and Video Artists.* London: Routledge.

Bogle, Donald. 1991. *Toms, Coons, Mammies, Mulattoes and Bucks: An Interpretative History of Blacks in American Films.* New York: Continuum.

Bonilla-Silva, Eduardo. 2014. *Racism without Racists: Color-Blind Racism and the Persistence of Racial Inequality in America.* 4th ed. Lanham, MD: Rowman and Littlefield.

———. 2015. "More than Prejudice: Restatement, Reflections, and New Directions in Critical Race Theory." *Sociology of Race and Ethnicity* 1 (1): 73–87.

Bonilla-Silva, Eduardo, and Amanda Lewis. 1999. "The New Racism: Racial Structure in the United States, 1960s–1990s." In *Race, Ethnicity, and Nationality in the United States*, edited by Paul Wong, 55–101. Boulder, CO: Westview.

Bowser, Pearl, Jane Gaines, and Charles Musser, eds. 2001. *Oscar Micheaux and His Circle: African-American Filmmaking and Race Cinema of the Silent Era*. Bloomington: Indiana University Press.

Burks, Ruth Elizabeth. 1996. "Imitations of Invisibility: Black Women and Contemporary Hollywood Cinema." In *Mediated Messages and African American Culture: Contemporary Issues*, edited by Venice T. Berry and Carmen L. Manning-Miller, 24–39. Thousand Oaks, CA: Sage.

Caldwell, John Thornton. 2008. *Production Culture: Industrial Reflexivity and Critical Practice in Film and Television*. Durham, NC: Duke University Press.

Caves, Richard. 2000. *Creative Industries: Contracts between Art and Commerce*. Cambridge, MA: Harvard University Press.

"Celebrities Who Are Democratic, Liberal." 2016. *Newsday*, November 8. www.newsday.com.

Chow-White, Peter A., Danielle Deveau, and Philippa Adams. 2015. "Media Encoding in Science Fiction Television: *Battlestar Galactica* as a Site of Critical Cultural Production." *Media, Culture & Society* 37 (8): 1210–1255.

Cieply, Michael. 2013. "The International Fate of *12 Years*: Steve McQueen's Film Is a Box-Office Test Case." *New York Times*, October 28. www.nytimes.com.

Ciras, Heather. 2017. "Here Is What the Cast and Crew of 'Moonlight' Had to Say about Their Oscar Win." *Boston Globe*, February 27. www.bostonglobe.com.

Collins, Alan, Chris Hand, and Martin C. Snell. 2002. "What Makes a Blockbuster? Economic Analysis of Film Success in the United Kingdom." *Managerial and Decision Economics* 23:343–354.

Collins, Patricia Hill. 2004. *Black Sexual Politics: African Americans, Gender, and the New Racism*. New York: Routledge.

———. 2009. *Black Feminist Thought: Knowledge, Consciousness, and the Politics of Empowerment*. 3rd ed. Boston: Unwin Hyman.

Couch, Kenneth A., and Robert Fairlie. 2010. "Last Hired, First Fired? Black-White Unemployment and the Business Cycle." *Demography* 47 (1): 227–247.

Cripps, Thomas. 1978. *Black Film as Genre*. Bloomington: Indiana University Press.

———. 1993. *Making Movies Black: The Hollywood Message Movie from World War II to the Civil Rights Era*. New York: Oxford University Press.

Cruse, Harold. 1967. *The Crisis of the Negro Intellectual: A Historical Analysis of the Failure of Black Leadership*. New York: Morrow.

Cunningham, Todd. 2014. "5 Reasons Why Denzel Washington's 'Equalizer' Exploded at the Box Office." *The Wrap*, September 29. www.businessinsider.com.

Danielle, Britni. 2017. "Talking to the Women of *Everything, Everything* about #BlackGirlMagic." *Splinter*, May 19. http://splinternews.com.

Davis, Ossie, and Ruby Dee. 1998. *With Ossie and Ruby: In This Life Together*. New York: Morrow.

Dawson, Michael C., and Lawrence D. Bobo. 2009. "One Year Later and the Myth of a Post-Racial Society." *Du Bois Review: Social Science Research on Race* 6 (2): 247–249.

DiMaggio, Paul. 1987. "Classification in Art." *American Sociological Review* 52:440–455.

Donalson, Melvin. 2003. *Black Directors in Hollywood*. Austin: University of Texas Press.

Du Bois, W. E. B. 1898. "The Study of Negro Problems." *Annals of the American Academy of Political and Social Science* 11:1–23.

———. 1903. *The Souls of Black Folk*. London: Longmans, Green.

———. 1913. "Socialism and the Negro Problem." *New Review: A Weekly Review of International Socialism* 1 (5): 138–141.

Dueze, Mark. 2010. *Managing Media Work*. Thousand Oaks, CA: Sage.

Duke, Alan. 2014. "Denzel Blacklisted! Sony Warned Not to Cast Washington in Big Flicks Because Black Leads 'Don't Play Well'—Latest Shocking Email Leak." *Radar Online*, December 17. www.radaronline.com.

Elberse, Anita. 2013. *Blockbusters: Hit-Making, Risk-Taking, and the Big Business of Entertainment*. New York: Holt.

Erigha, Maryann. 2015. "Race, Gender, Hollywood: Representation in Cultural Production and Digital Media's Potential for Change." *Sociology Compass* 9 (1): 78–89.

———. 2016a. "Black, Asian, and Latino Directors in Hollywood." In *Race and Contention in Twenty-First Century Media*, edited by Jason Smith and Bhoomi K. Thakore, 59–69. London: Routledge.

———. 2016b. "Do African Americans Direct Science Fiction and Blockbuster Franchise Movies? Race, Gender, and Contemporary Hollywood." *Journal of Black Studies* 47 (6): 550–569.

———. 2018. "On the Margins: Black Directors and the Persistence of Racial Inequality in the Twenty-First Century." *Ethnic and Racial Studies* 41 (7): 1217–1234.

Feagin, Joe R., Herman Vera, and Pinar Batur. 2001. *White Racism: The Basics*. New York: Routledge.

Feinberg, Scott. 2014. "Oscar Voter Reveals Brutally Honest Ballot." *Hollywood Reporter*, February 26. www.hollywoodreporter.com.

Fradley, Martin. 2013. "What Do You Believe In? Film Scholarship and the Cultural Politics of the *Dark Knight* Franchise." *Film Quarterly* 66 (3): 15–27.

Friedman, Ryan Jay. 2011. *Hollywood's African American Films: The Transition to Sound*. New Brunswick, NJ: Rutgers University Press.

Garnham, Nicholas. 1987. "Concepts of Culture: Public Policy and the Cultural Industries." *Cultural Studies* 1 (1): 23–37.

Gettell, Oliver. 2014. "'No Good Deed': Five Reasons for Its Surprising Box-Office Success." *Los Angeles Times*, September 15. www.latimes.com.

Golding, Shenequa. 2017. "John Singleton's Tupac Shakur Script Surfaces, Features a Jail Gang Rape Scene." *Vibe*, July 10. www.vibe.com.

Gray, Herman. 2005. *Cultural Moves: African Americans and the Politics of Representation*. Berkeley: University of California Press.

———. 2016. "Precarious Diversity: Representation and Demography." In *Precarious Creativity: Global Media, Local Labor*, edited by Michael Curtin and Kevin Sanson, 241–253. Berkeley: University of California Press.

Greene, Dennis. 1994. "Tragically Hip: Hollywood and African-American Cinema." *Cineaste* 20 (4): 28–29.

Guerrero, Ed. 1993. *Framing Blackness: The African American Image in Film*. Philadelphia: Temple University Press.

———. 1995. "The Black Man on Our Screens and the Empty Space in Representation." *Callaloo* 18 (2): 395–400.

Hall, Stuart. 1973. *Encoding and Decoding in the Television Discourse*. Birmingham, UK: Centre for Contemporary Cultural Studies.

———. 1992. "What Is This 'Black' in Black Popular Culture?" In *Black Popular Culture: A Project*, edited by Michele Wallace and Gina Dent, 21–37. Seattle: Bay.

Havens, Timothy. 2013. *Black Television Travels: African American Media around the Globe*. New York: NYU Press.

Hesmondhalgh, David, and Anamik Saha. 2013. "Race, Ethnicity and Cultural Production." *Popular Communication* 11 (3): 179–195.

Higgins, Bill. 2018. "Hollywood Flashback: A Snubbed Spike Lee Trashed Wim Wenders at Cannes in 1989." *Hollywood Reporter*, May 12. www.hollywoodreporter.com.

Hirsch, Paul. 1972. "Processing Fads and Fashions: An Organization-Set Analysis of Cultural Industry Systems." *American Journal of Sociology* 77 (4): 639–659.

Horn, John, and Doug Smith. 2013. "Diversity Efforts Slow to Change the Face of Oscar Voters." *Los Angeles Times*, December 21. www.latimes.com.

Hughey, Matthew. 2014. *The White Savior Film: Content, Critics, and Consumption*. Philadelphia: Temple University Press.

Hunt, Darnell, and Ana-Christina Ramón. 2015. *2015 Hollywood Diversity Report: Flipping the Script*. Los Angeles: Ralph J. Bunche Center for African American Studies at UCLA.

Hunt, Darnell, Ana-Christina Ramón, and Zachary Price. 2014. *2014 Hollywood Diversity Report: Making Sense of the Disconnect*. Los Angeles: Ralph J. Bunche Center for African American Studies at UCLA.

ImageNation Cinema Foundation. n.d. "Mission." Accessed November 12, 2017. www.imagenation.us.

Jones, Jacquie. 1991. "The New Ghetto Aesthetic." *Wide Angle* 13:32–43.

Keegan, Rebecca Winters. 2007. "The Legend of Will Smith." *Time*, November 29. www.time.com.

Lang, Brett, and Seth Kelley. 2017. "How Too Many Aging Franchises Wrecked the Summer Box Office." *Variety*, July 11. www.variety.com.

Lee, Ashley. 2015. "Ava DuVernay's Advice on Hollywood: 'Follow the White Guys, They've Got This Thing Wired.'" *Hollywood Reporter*, July 18. www.hollywoodreporter.com.

Leonard, David. 2006. *Screens Fade to Black: Contemporary African American Cinema*. Westport, CT: Praeger.

Lipsitz, George. 1998. *The Possessive Investment in Whiteness: How White People Profit from Identity Politics*. Philadelphia: Temple University Press.

Lubiano, Wahneema. 1991. "But Compared to What? Reading Realism, Representation, and Essentialism in *School Daze, Do the Right Thing*, and the Spike Lee Discourse." *Black American Literature Forum* 25 (2): 253–282.

Maguire, Jennifer, and Julian Matthews. 2012. "Are We All Cultural Intermediaries Now? An Introduction to Cultural Intermediaries in Context." *European Journal of Cultural Studies* 15 (5): 551–580.

Maldonado, Maria. 2009. "'It Is Their Nature to Do Menial Labour': The Racialization of 'Latino/a Workers' by Agricultural Employers." *Ethnic and Racial Studies* 32 (6): 1017–1036.

Mapp, Edward. 2008. *African Americans and the Oscar: Decade of Struggle and Achievement*. 2nd ed. Lanham, MD: Scarecrow.

Mask, Mia. 2000. "Buppy Love in an Urban World." *Cineaste* 25 (2): 41–45.

McHenry, Jackson. 2016. "Leslie Jones Responds to Criticism of Her MTA Worker *Ghostbusters* Character by Sharing a Message from an MTA Worker." *Vulture*, March 5. www.vulture.com.

Metcalfe, Nasser. 2012. "Exclusive: Tyler Perry Talks *Madea's Witness Protection*." *Black film.com*, June 27. www.blackfilm.com.

Morales, Wilson. 2011a. "Christopher Scott Cherot's Return to the Big Screen." *Black film.com*, March 13. www.blackfilm.com.

———. 2011b. "Exclusive: John Singleton Talks *Abduction*." *Blackfilm.com*, April 14. www.blackfilm.com.

———. 2011c. "*35 and Ticking* Director Russ Parr." *Blackfilm.com*, May 19. www.black film.com.

———. 2012a. "Exclusive: Director Reginald Hudlin Talks *Boomerang* 20 Years Later, *Black Panther*, and Producing *Django Unchained*." *Blackfilm.com*, July 1. www.black film.com.

———. 2012b. "Exclusive: Tyler Perry Talks *Good Deeds*." *Blackfilm.com*, February 17. www.blackfilm.com.

———. 2012c. "Neema Barnette Talks *Woman Thou Art Loosed: On the 7th Day*." *Black film.com*, April 12. www.blackfilm.com.

———. 2012d. "Spike Lee Talks *Red Hook Summer* and Black Cinema." *Blackfilm.com*, January 20. www.blackfilm.com.

———. 2013a. "David E. Talbert Talks *Baggage Claim*." *Blackfilm.com*, September 25. www.blackfilm.com.

———. 2013b. "Exclusive: Tyler Perry Talks *A Madea Christmas*, David Fincher's *Girl Gone*, and Year in Black Cinema." *Blackfilm.com*, December 11. www.black film.com.

———. 2013c. "Lee Daniels Talks *Lee Daniels' The Butler*." *Blackfilm.com*, August 9. www.blackfilm.com.

———. 2014. "Exclusive: Tim Story Talks *Think Like a Man Too*." *Blackfilm.com*, June 18. www.blackfilm.com.

Nama, Adilifu. 2008. *Black Space: Imagining Race in Science Fiction Film*. Austin: University of Texas Press.

Ndounou, Monica White. 2014. *Shaping the Future of African American Film: Color-Coded Economics and the Story Behind the Numbers*. New Brunswick, NJ: Rutgers University Press.

Oliver, Melvin, and Thomas Shapiro. 1995. *Black Wealth, White Wealth: A New Perspective on Racial Inequality*. New York: Routledge.

Ortner, Sherry B. 2013. *Not Hollywood: Independent Film at the Twilight of the American Dream*. Raleigh, NC: Duke University Press.

Palmer, Lorrie. 2011. "Black Man / White Machine: Will Smith Crosses Over." *Velvet Light Trap* 67:28–40.

Pendakur, Manjunath. 2008. "Hollywood and the State: The American Film Industry Cartel in the Age of Globalization." In *The Contemporary Hollywood Film Industry*, edited by Paul McDonald and Janet Wasko, 182–194. Malden, MA: Blackwell.

Penrice, Ronda Racha. 2017. "Cheryl Boone Isaacs Put the Oscars on a Path toward Diversity: Will Her Successor Continue the Trend?" *The Root*, February 26. www .theroot.com.

Perren, Alisa. 2012. *Indie, Inc.: Miramax and the Transformation of Hollywood in the 1990s*. Austin: University of Texas Press.

Peterson, Richard A., and N. Anand. 2004. "The Production of Culture Perspective." *Annual Review of Sociology* 30:311–334.

Pounds, Micheal C. 1999. *Race in Space: The Representation of Ethnicity in "Star Trek: The Next Generation."* Lanham, MD: Scarecrow.

Quinn, Eithne. 2011. "Sincere Fictions: The Production Cultures of Whiteness in Late 1960s Hollywood." *Velvet Light Trap* 67:3–13.

———. 2012. "Closing Doors: Hollywood, Affirmative Action, and the Revitalization of Conservative Racial Politics." *Journal of American History* 99 (2): 466–491.

———. 2013. "Black Talent and Conglomerate Hollywood: Will Smith, Tyler Perry, and the Continuing Significance of Race." *Popular Communication* 11:196–210.

Rehling, Nicola. 2009. *Extra-Ordinary Men: White Heterosexual Masculinity in Contemporary Popular Cinema*. Lanham, MD: Lexington Books.

Reid, Mark. 1993. *Redefining Black Film*. Berkeley: University of California Press.

———. 2005. *Black Lenses, Black Voices: African American Film Now*. Lanham, MD: Rowman and Littlefield.

Reynolds, Simon. 2011. *Retromania: Pop Culture's Addiction to Its Own Past*. London: Faber and Faber.

Rhines, Jesse Algernon. 1996. *Black Film / White Money*. New Brunswick, NJ: Rutgers University Press.

Roberts, Adam. 2000. *Science Fiction: The New Critical Idiom*. New York: Routledge.

Rock, Chris. 2014. "Chris Rock Pens Blistering Essay on Hollywood's Race Problem: It's a White Industry." *Hollywood Reporter*, December 3. www.hollywoodreporter.com.

Ruef, Martin, and Ben Fletcher. 2003. "Legacies of American Slavery: Status Attainment among Southern Blacks after Emancipation." *Social Forces* 82 (2): 445–480.

Rutledge, Gregory. 2001. "Futurist Fiction & Fantasy: The Racial Establishment." *Callaloo* 24 (1): 236–252.

Saha, Anamik. 2017. "The Politics of Race in Cultural Distribution: Addressing Inequalities in British Asian Theatre." *Cultural Sociology* 11 (3): 302–317.

Schatz, Thomas. 2008. "The Studio System and Conglomerate Hollywood." In *The Contemporary Hollywood Film Industry*, edited by Paul McDonald and Janet Wasko, 13–42. Malden, MA: Wiley-Blackwell.

———. 2009. "New Hollywood, New Millennium." In *Film Theory and Contemporary Hollywood Movies*, edited by Warren Buckland, 19–46. New York: Routledge.

———. 2013. "Conglomerate Hollywood and American Independent Film." In *American Independent Cinema: Indie, Indiewood, and Beyond*, edited by Geoff King, Claire Molloy, and Yannis Tzioumakis, 127–139. New York: Routledge.

Scott, Allen J. 2004. "Hollywood and the World: the Geography of Motion-Picture Distribution and Marketing." *Review of International Political Economy* 11 (1): 33–61.

Sexton, Jared. 2009. "The Ruse of Engagement: Black Masculinity and the Cinema of Policing." *American Quarterly* 61 (1): 39–63.

Shohat, Ella, and Robert Stam. 1997. *Unthinking Eurocentrism*. New York: Routledge.

Simpson, Donald. 1990. "Black Images in Film: The 1940s to the Early 1960s." *Black Scholar* 21 (2): 20–29.

Smith, Stacy L., and Marc Choueiti. 2011. *Black Characters in Popular Film: Is the Key to Diversifying Cinematic Content Held in the Hand of the Black Director?* Los Angeles: Annenberg School for Communication and Journalism.

Smith, Stacy, Marc Choueiti, and Katherine Pieper. 2014. "Race/Ethnicity in 600 Popular Films: Examining On Screen Portrayals and Behind the Camera Diversity." Media, Diversity, & Social Change Initiative, Annenberg School for Communication & Journalism, Los Angeles.

Sperling, Nicole. 2013. "*Best Man Holiday*: Does Its Success Change the Future of Black Film?" *Entertainment Weekly*, November 18. http://insidemovies.ew.com.

Talbert, Marcia. 2010. "ACTION!" *Black Enterprise*, May 25. www.blackenterprise.com.

Thompson, Derek. 2014. "The Reason Why Hollywood Makes So Many Boring Superhero Movies." *Atlantic*, May 13. www.theatlantic.com.

Tillet, Salamishah. 2012. *Sites of Slavery: Citizenship and Racial Democracy in the Post–Civil Rights Imagination*. Durham, NC: Duke University Press.

U.S. Bureau of Labor Statistics. 2015. "Employment Status of the Civilian Population by Race, Sex, and Age." www.bls.gov.

Ware, Lawrence. 2017a. "Racial Progress in Film Remains Slow Drag 30 Years after *Hollywood Shuffle*." *The Root*, March 2. www.theroot.com.

———. 2017b. "*Sleight* Is an Imperfect Magic Trick Well Worth the Ride." *The Root*, May 1. www.theroot.com.

Wasko, Janet. 2003. *How Hollywood Works*. London: Sage.

———. 2008. "Financing and Production: Creating the Hollywood Film Commodity." In *The Contemporary Hollywood Film Industry*, edited by Paul McDonald and Janet Wasko, 43–62. Malden, MA: Wiley-Blackwell.

Watkins, S. Craig. 1998. *Representing: Hip Hop Culture and the Production of Black Cinema*. Chicago: University of Chicago Press.

———. 2001. "A Nation of Millions: Hip Hop Culture and the Legacy of Black Nationalism." *Communication Review* 4:373–398.

Waxman, Sharon. 1996. "Hollywood Reeling from Article's Accusation of Racism." *Washington Post*, March 12. www.washingtonpost.com.

West, Cornel. 1990. "The New Cultural Politics of Difference." *October* 53:93–109.

Western, Bruce. 2006. *Punishment and Inequality*. New York: Russell Sage Foundation.

Winship, Christopher. 2004. "Veneers and Underlayments: Critical Moments and Situational Redefinition." *Negotiation Journal* 20 (2): 297–309.

Yearwood, Gladstone L., ed. 2000. *Black Cinema Aesthetics: Issues in Independent Black Filmmaking*. Athens: Ohio University Press.

Yuen, Nancy Wang. 2004. "Performing Race, Negotiating Identity: Asian American Professional Actors in Hollywood." In *Asian American Youth Culture, Identity, and Ethnicity*, edited by Jennifer Lee and Min Zhou, 251–267. New York: Routledge.

———. 2010. "Playing 'Ghetto': Black Actors, Stereotypes, and Authenticity." In *Black Los Angeles: American Dreams and Racial Realities*, edited by Darnell Hunt and Ana-Christina Ramón, 232–242. New York: NYU Press.

———. 2017. *Reel Inequality: Hollywood Actors and Racism*. New Brunswick, NJ: Rutgers University Press.

INDEX

Abduction, 89, 155

About Last Night, 59–61, 73–74, 102

Academy Awards: Best Director, 29; Best Documentary Feature, 28; Best Picture, 23–24, 28–29, 162; Black directors and, 23–24, 27–29, 39; for music, 120–21; #OscarsSoWhite, 38–39; representation and, 23–26, 162; for technical workers, 27–28; 2014, 23–24; 2017, 27–28

Academy of Motion Picture Arts and Sciences: Boone Isaacs leading, 39–40, 46; liberalism of, 30–31; racial makeup of, 38–40, 168; representation and, 23–31, 37–40, 46, 162

actors. *See* Black actors

advertising: budget, 85; distribution and, 91, 166; unbankable label and, 57–63, 74, 80

AFFRM. *See* African American Film Festival Releasing Movement

African American Critics Association Award Ceremony, 29

African American Film Festival Releasing Movement (AFFRM), 173

After Earth, 124

agencies. *See* talent agencies

Akil, Mara Brock, 168

Alexander, Michelle, 143, 199n10

Ali, 99, *101*

Allain, Stephanie, 97

Allen, Debbie, 168

Aronofsky, Darren, 106

Asian directors, 29, 87, 89, 94, 124, 185

ATL, 118, 173

audiences: imagined, 53–63, *58*, 182; Latino/a, 57–59, 61–63; movie messages interpreted by, 35–36; segmentation of, 58–62, 182; stigma influencing, 160; white, 1–3, 9, 120, 128, 151. *See also* Black audiences

Baby Boy, 29, 154

Bad Boys II, 99, *101*

Baggage Claim, 64, 148–49

Barbershop franchise, 72, *100*, 132, *134*, 144

Barnette, Neema, 35, 88–89

Bay, Michael, 99, *101*, *136*

Be Cool, 46, 72

Benjamin, Andre, 72, 155

Berg, Peter, 106–7

Best Man Holiday, 43, 56–57, 104, 132, *134*, 144

Best Picture: *Moonlight* winning, 28–29, 162; *12 Years a Slave* winning, 23–24, 162

Bielby, Denise, 33, 67, 92–93

Bielby, William, 33, 67, 92–93

big-budget movies: Black directors and, 85, 87–89, 91, 105, 110–11, 113, 151–56, 185; tent-pole franchises, 130–38, *134–36*, 140, 156

Black actors: crossover stars, 151; directors and, 19, 97–103, *100–101*; female, 108; as human and universal, 161; production budgets and, 100–101, *100–101*; representation of, 33; as unbankable, 19, 52–56, 59–60, 62, 68–73, 77–80, 88, 149

Black audiences: *The Magnificent Seven* and, 1–3; targeted, 41, 55, 57, 59, 62–63, 80; unbankable label and, 55, 57, 59, 62–63, 72–73, 75, 77–78, 80

Black cinema collective: distribution and, 172–77; need for, 21–22, 171–80, 191–92

Black cinema paradox, 158

Black directors: Academy Awards and, 23–24, 27–29, 39; Black actors and, 97–101, *100*; in cinema collective, 171–80; distribution and, 89–97, *94–96*, 113, 166–67; focus on, 16–17; Hollywood insiders on, 83–84, 86–87, 98, 101–5, 107, 112–13; lower ranking of, 83–84, 112–14; marginalization of, 83–89, 93–105, *100–101*, 108–9, 112–13; oeuvre of, 21, 153, 155, 158; production budgets of, 19, 82, 84–89, 91, *96*, 96–97, 100, *100*, 105–7, 110–11, 113, 151–56, 185; as racialized other, 163–64; racial stigma and, 141–45, 147–61, *150*; representation of, 15–16, 27–37, 39–51, 93–97, 113, 116–17, 120, 123, 125–30, 132, 139–40, 155–56, 162–63, 185; in television, 167–68; as unbankable, 12, 19–21, 49, 52, 54–56, 63–74, 77–81, 83–84, 97, 109, 113, 118, 142–44, 182–85. *See also* female Black directors; genre ghettos

Black Film Boom, 42

"Black films," label of, 57, 147

Black Panther, 99, 123, 133, 161, *190*, 191; DuVernay and, 91–92; unbankable label and, 69, 75

Black problem, racial stigma and, 20–21, 142–45, 160

Black producers, 28, 40–41

Black writers, 33, 69–70, 92–93

Blaxploitation era, 42, 123

blockbuster movies. *See* big-budget movies

Bonilla-Silva, Eduardo, 7–8, 146

The Book of Eli, 124–25

Boone Isaacs, Cheryl, 39–40, 46

box office: barriers, foreign market, 11, 101–8, 113, 141, 161, 183, 186; mentality, race attached to, 3–4, 128. *See also* unbankable label

Boyz N the Hood, 29, 42, 153

Bray, Kevin, 168

The Brother from Another Planet, 125

budgets. *See* production budgets

Burton, Willie D., 120–21

The Butler, 43, 57, 68, 147–48

Carr, Steve, 99, *101*

Cherot, Christopher Scott, 166, 179

Chism, Tina Gordon, 173

Chu, John, 87

citizenship. *See* cultural citizenship

civic representation, 18, 25, 26, 37–40, 51

colorblindness, 7–9, 16, 54, 126, 181

comps analysis, 56–57

Condon, Bill, 99, *101*

Conglomerate Hollywood, 15

Coogler, Ryan, 39, 69, 132–33, *135*

core agencies, 92–93

Crazy Sexy Cool: The TLC Story, 168

Creed, 69, 133, *134*

crossover success, 151–55, 159

Cruse, Harold, 157

Cuarón, Alfonso, 29

cultural citizenship: Black cinema collective and, 180; representation and, 18, 25, 25–26, 37–40, 50, 180

cultural representation pyramid, 25, 25–27

dance movies, 119–20

Daniels, Lee, 43, 115, 147–48, 168

Dash, Julie, 108

Daughters of the Dust, 108

Davis, Ossie, 31–32

Dawson, Michael, 206n1

Dear White People, 102, 168

deep texts, 17
del Toro, Guillermo, 87
Democratic Party, 30–31
demographic parity, 44–46, 50
digital technologies, Black cinema collective using, 177–78
directors: Asian, 29, 87, 89, 94, 124, 185;
Best Director award for, 29; Black
actors and, 19, 97–103, *100–101*;
Latino/a, 29, 87, 89, 94, 124, 185; racial
inequality and, 83, 88, 92, 96–97; role
of, 83. *See also* Black directors; white
directors
Disney, 91, 94, *94*, *96*, 97
distribution: advertising and, 91, 166;
Black cinema collective and, 172–77;
Black directors and, 89–97, *94–96*, 113,
166–67; deal, 90; foreign market, 19,
38, 93, 102, 104, 107–8; independent
movies, 90–92, 95; representation
and, 93–94, *94–96*; significance of,
182; white directors and, 92, *94–95*,
96–97, 113
Dixon, Ivan, 42
Django Unchained, 64, 68, 78
DJ Pooh, 121
Dope, 82
Do the Right Thing, 26
double consciousness, 148
Dr. Do Little 2, 99, *101*
Dreamgirls, 99–100, *101*, 121
Drumline, 72, 167, 173
A Dry White Season, 42, 108
Du Bois, W. E. B., 20–21, 142, 145–48, 160
DuVernay, Ava, 104–5, 168; *Black Panther*
and, 91–92; company of, 172–74; *13th*
directed by, 28; *Wrinkle in Time* di-
rected by, *110*, 110–11

Elba, Idris, 56, 115
Empire, 168
employment, racial gap in, 15–16, 32–33,
176

The Equalizer, *134*; Fuqua directing, 1,
53, 79, 133, *135*; unbankable label and,
61–62, 79; Washington, Denzel, in, 1,
52–54, 79, 86
Everything, Everything, 112
executives. *See* studio executives

Fabrick, Howard, 54
faith-based movies. *See* religious movies
Famuyiwa, Rick, 82, 85
Fantastic Four franchise, 73, 87, 124, 132–
33, *134*
Fast & Furious franchise, 87–88, 191; genre
ghettos and, 132–33, *134–36*; racial
stigma and, 154–55
female Black directors: double disadvantage of, 20, 84, 108–12, *110*, 114, 185;
representation of, 42–43, 185
Fences, 28, 36
film festivals, 90, 173, 178
film studios, three-tiered system of, 91.
See also specific studios
Fishburne, Laurence, 125, 153
foreign market: box-office barriers, 11,
101–8, 113, 141, 161, 183, 186; distribution, 19, 38, 93, 102, 104, 107–8;
unbankable label and, 53–55, 62–63,
66, 75, 78–80, 101
Foster, Bill, 41
Four Brothers, 155
The Fourth Kind, 124
Foxx, Jamie, 78, 121
franchise movies. *See* tent-pole franchises
Franklin, Carl, 116
Franklin, Devon, 46, 170
Fruitvale Station, 69
Fuqua, Antoine, 43, 87; *The Equalizer*
directed by, 1, 53, 79, 133, *135*; *The Magnificent Seven* directed by, 1–3, *2*, 7

gatekeepers: role of, 4, 6, 14, 163, 183; sci-fi,
126–30, *127*

genre ghettos: defined, 116; Hollywood insiders and, 115–16, 118, 128, 130–32, 139–40; marginalization in, 116, 124–26, 128–32, 137–40; music, 20, 116–23, 139, 177; racial hierarchies in, 20, 116, 120, 123, 126, 129, 131–32, 138–40, 184; sci-fi, 20, 117, 123–31, 139; tent-pole franchises and, 20, 130–38, *134–36*, 140, 156; unbankable label and, 116–18, 126, 140; westerns and, 1–3, 7

Get Out, 75

Ghostbusters (2016), 35

Girls Trip, 75, 144

government regulation, 188–89

Gray, F. Gary, 88, *100*; genre ghettos and, 117, 121–22, 133; unbankable label and, 72, 75

Gray, Herman, 44–45, 178

Guerrero, Ed, 42, 116, 158

Hall, Regina, 57, 74–75

Hall, Stuart, 34, 156, 171

Hamri, Sanaa, 109, 111, 121, *135*, 168

Hancock, 46, 124

Hardy, Rob, 168

Harlem Globetrotter, 57

Harris, Leslie, 42, 108

Hart, Kevin, 57, 69, 73–74

Harvey, Steve, 60, 62

Hayes, Isaac, 120

The Help, 100, 103–4

Hemingway, Anthony, *100*, 168

Henson, Taraji P., 56, 115, 154

Herbie Fully Loaded, 110–11, 133, *134*

Hidden Figures, 28, 100

Higher Learning, 153–54

Hitch, 141

Hollywood insiders: on Black directors, 83–84, 86–87, 98, 101–5, 107, 112–13; genre ghettos and, 115–16, 118, 128, 130–32, 139–40; on *The Magnificent Seven,* 1–3, 7; power of, 164–65; racial logic of, 1–7, 9, 16–19, 48–49, 58, 62, 68, 80, 112, 126, 137, 181–82, 186; racial stigma manufactured by, 21, 141, 143, 145, 147, 149, 160; studies of, 189–90; on *12 Years a Slave,* 24–25, 37–38; unbankable label used by, 52–67, 73–74, 80–81, 182–86; whiteness and, 24, 54, 56

Hollywood Jim Crow. *See specific topics*

Hollywood liberalism, 30–31, 49

Hollywood Shuffle, 13, 36, 42

Honey, 119, *134*

Hudlin, Reginald, 130, 150–51; on institution building, 175–76; unbankable label and, 63–64

Hudson, Jennifer, 99, 121

Hughes, Albert, 124

Hughes, Allen, 124

human and universal defense, 144–49, 161

Hunt, Darnell, 33, 39–40, 106

Hunter, Paul, 124

I, Robot, 124

I Am Legend, 124

I Can Do Bad All by Myself, 76, 77, *134*

Ice Cube, 39, 117, 122, 153

Idlewild, 117–18

I Like It like That, 42–43, 108

imagined audiences, 53–63, *58*, 182

Iñárritu, Alejandro González, 29

independent movies, 172; distribution, 90–92, 95; sci-fi, 125; small-budget, 85

inequality. *See* racial inequality

Inglourious Basterds, 78

Inside Man, 152

institution building, need for, 175–76

integration: incomplete, 20–21, 156–60, 163, 169, 180, 187; in remaking of cinema, 162–63, 168–72, 180

international audience. *See* foreign market

I Will Follow, 173

Jackson, Peter, 138

Jackson, Samuel L., 78, 154

Jakes, Bishop T. D., 46
jazz left, 178
Jenkins, Barry, 28–29, 162
Jenkins, Patty, 111
Jim Crow systems: defined, 4, 9–10; rules of, 10. *See also specific topics*
Johnson, Noble, 41
Joyner, Tom, 60, 62
Just Another Girl on the I.R.T., 42, 108

The Karate Kid reboot, 46
King Arthur, 87
Knowles, Beyoncé, 30, 99
Kosinski, Joseph, 106

Lassiter, James, 123
Latino/a audiences, 57–59, 61–63
Latino/a directors, 29, 87, 89, 94, 124, 185
Lawrence, Martin, 71, 99
Lee, Ang, 29
Lee, Malcolm D., 43, 75, *100*, 104; genre ghettos and, 132, *135*; on racial stigma, 144
Lee, Spike: movies directed by, 13, 26, 42, 84–85, 91, *100*, 150, 152, 176; production budgets of, 84–85, 152; on studio executives, 165, 170
Lemmons, Kasi, 43, 109, 111
liberalism, of Hollywood, 30–31, 49, 162
Lin, Justin, 87
Love and Basketball, 43, 111
Lubiano, Wahneema, 155, 205n20

Madea movies: as franchise, 132, *134*; Perry creating, 43, *76*, 76–77, *100*, 126–27, *127*, 132, *134–35*, 152
The Magnificent Seven, 1–3, *2*, 7
Mann, Michael, 99, *101*
March on Washington, 32
marginalization: directing and, 83–89, 93–105, *100–101*, 108–9, 112–13; in genre ghettos, 116, 124–26, 128–32, 137–40; major pains from, 89–97, *94–96*;

marketing and, 85, 89, 93, 98, 106, 109; overview of, 4, 6, 10–12, 14, 16, 18–19, 22, 184–85, 187, 189, 191; with racial stigma, 141, 143; remaking of cinema and, 163, 170–71, 174, 178–80; representation and, 27–29, 33–34, 37, 39–40, 48–49; with unbankable label, 54, 67, 80–81
marketing, 116, 153, 159, 186; marginalization and, 85, 89, 93, 98, 106, 109; unbankable label and, 55, 57–64, 72–73
mark of the plural, 65
Martin, Darnell, 42–43, 108
mass incarceration, 13, 143, 162, 199n10
McG, 137
McQueen, Steve: *12 Years a Slave* directed by, 23–25, 27, 37–38, 43, 68, 79, 146, 162; unbankable label and, 79
Meghie, Stella, 89, 112
Micheaux, Oscar, 40–41, 172, 176
middle-budget movies, 85, 87
Moonlight, 28–29, 162
Moore, Kenya, 101–2
Murphy, Eddie, 71, 99, 151
music genre: Academy Awards for, 120–21; ghetto, 20, 116–23, 139, 177

NAACP. *See* National Association for the Advancement of Colored People
Nama, Adilifu, 126
National Association for the Advancement of Colored People (NAACP), 41
Negro problem, 20–21, 142–45, 160
New Jim Crow, 13, 143, 199n10
Noah, 106
No Good Deed, 56, 58–63, 79, 115
Nolan, Christopher, 138
noncore agencies, 92–93
Norbit, 99, *101*
The Nutty Professor II: The Klumps, 99, *101*
Nyong'o, Lupita, 77–78

Obama, Barack, 30, 145; postracialism and, 8, 181; unbankable label and, 68–73, *70*
Oblivion, 106
oeuvre, of Black directors, 21, 153, 155, 158
online marketing campaigns, 59–60
#OscarsSoWhite, 38–39
Osunsanmi, Olatunde, 124

Packer, Will, 102
Palcy, Euzhan, 42, 108
Paramount, *70*, *134*, *136*, 138; distribution by, 91, *94*, 94–96, *96*; marginalization and, 87, 91, *94*, 94–96, *96*, 100–101, 106
pariah status, 143–44, 149
Parks, Gordon, Jr., 42
Parks, Gordon, Sr., 42
Parr, Russ, 63, 147
Pascal, Amy, 54
Patton, Paula, 148–49
Peele, Jordan, 75
Perry, Tyler, 56, 145, 191; Madea movies of, 43, *76*, 76–77, *100*, 126–27, *127*, 132, *134*–35, 152; sci-fi gatekeepers and, 126–30, *127*; studio of, 170, 172–74; success of, 19, 63–64, 75–77, *76*, 104, 127, 176
Pinkett Smith, Jada, 30, 75
Poetic Justice, 153
Poitier, Sidney, 30, 151
postracialism, 7–9, 54, 181, 206n1
Prince-Bythewood, Gina, 43, 109, 111
producers, Black, 28, 40–41
production budgets: Black casts and, 100–101, *100–101*; of Black directors, 19, 82, 84–89, 91, *96*, 96–97, 100, *100*, 105–7, 110–11, 113, 151–56, 185; defined, 84–85; Lubiano on, 155, 205n20; of middle-budget movies, 85, 87; small, 85–89, 91, 185. *See also* big-budget movies
progress, symbols of, 27–31

Queen Latifah, 60, 73, 75, 87, 117
Quinn, Eithne, 31, 165, 169

raced movies, imagined audiences of, 56–63, *58*
race movies, 40–41, 77, 176
race politics: film industry shaped by, 3, 11–12; U.S., 3, 7, 11–12, 27, 47, 181, 187
racial grammar, 146
racial hierarchy: genre ghettos and, 20, 116, 120, 123, 126, 129, 131–32, 138–40, 184; in Jim Crow systems, 4–5, 9–14, 53, 83–84, 100, 116, 128–29, 141, 162–63, 181–82; racial stigma and, 141–43, 149, 161. *See also* representation, racial hierarchy and
racial inequality: construction of, 3–11, 13–19, 92, 116; directors and, 83, 88, 92, 96–97; representation and, 26–27, 31, 33, 44–48, 51; unbankable label and, 53
racialization, theory of, 83
racial stigma, manufactured: Black directors facing, 141–45, 147–61, *150*; Black problem and, 20–21, 142–45, 160; by Hollywood insiders, 18, 141, 143, 145, 147, 149, 160; human and universal defense against, 144–49, 161; incomplete integration and, 156–60; marginalization with, 141, 143; overview of, 141–42, 160–61; pariah status, 143–44, 149; racial hierarchy and, 141–43, 149, 161; Singleton and, *150*, 150–51, 153–55, 160; unbankable label and, 141–44, 149, 160, 163–64
Ray, 100, *101*, 121
Red Hook Summer, 176
Red Tails, 57, *100*
Rees, Dee, 39, 168
regulation, governmental, 188–89
Reid, Mark, 82
religious movies, 46, 77, 170
remaking, of cinema: Black cinema collective, 21–22, 171–80, 191–92; integration, 162–63, 168–72, 180; marginalization and, 163, 170–71, 174, 178–80;

overview of, 162–64; as uphill climb, 164–69, *167*

representation, racial hierarchy and: Academy and, 23–31, 37–40, 46, 162; of Black directors, 15–16, 27–37, 39–51, 93–97, 113, 116–17, 120, 123, 125–30, 132, 139–40, 155–56, 162–63, 185; civic, 18, 25, 26, 37–40, 51; cultural citizenship and, 18, 25, 25–26, 37–40, 50, 180; distribution and, 93–94, *94–96*; hierarchical, 18, 25, 26–27, 40–44, 47–51; inequality and, 26–27, 31, 33, 44–48, 51; Jim Crow systems and, 27, 40, 48–49; marginalization and, 27–29, 33–34, 37, 39–40, 48–49; measurement of, 44–49; numeric, 18, 25, 26, 31–37, 44–46, 50–51; overview of, 11, 14–16, 18, 20–21, 23–27, *25*, 49–51; pyramid, *25*, 25–27; stereotypes and, 29, 36–37; in studio executives, 46, 164–65; symbolic, 18, *25*, 25–31, 44, 46, 50–51, 157, 160–61; at talent agencies, 166

Republican Party, 30

Rhimes, Shonda, 168

Rhines, Jesse, 166

Ride Along, 56–57, 69, 102, 132–33, *134*

Robbins, Brian, 99, *101*

Robinson, Angela, 110–11, 133, *135*

Rock, Chris, 30, 33–34, 69, *100*, 176; on Black female actors, 108; on racial stigma, 156–57

Rosewood, 154

Rutledge, Gregory, 129

Save the Last Dance, 119

Scary Movie franchise, 43, 132–33, *134*, 144

Schatz, Thomas, 15, 91

Schultz, Michael, 42

sci-fi movies: gatekeepers, 126–30, *127*; genre ghettos and, 20, 117, 123–31, 139

Segal, Peter, 99, *101*

segregation: Jim Crow, 9–10, 13, 48, 122, 162, *167*; legacy of, 10, 48. *See also* genre ghettos

Selma, 91, 121

Sexton, Jared, 158

Shaft, 120, *134*, 154

Shakur, Tupac, 36, 121, 153

She's Gotta Have It, 13, 42

Simien, Justin, 102, 168

sincere fictions, 53–54

Single Mom's Club, 76, *76*, 152, 160

Singleton, John, 77, 133, *135*, 168; production budgets of, 88–89; racial stigma and, *150*, 150–51, 153–55, 160; representation and, 29, 36–37, 42

The Sisterhood of the Traveling Pants 2, 111, 121, *134*

slavery, 10, 13, 47–48, 162. See also *12 Years a Slave*

small-budget movies, 85–89, 91, 185

Smith, Jaden, 46, 124

Smith, Stacy, 33, 43

Smith, Will, 30, 46, 71, 99, 141; as crossover star, 151; in sci-fi movies, 123–24

social-media promotions, 61, 73–75

social networks, exclusion from, 128, 189

social-problem films, 30, 42

Sony Pictures, 46, 52, 54, 66, *70*, 73; genre ghettos and, 130, 132, *134*; marginalization and, 86, 91, 94–96, *94–96*, *100–101*

Star Trek franchise, 87, 127, 131, 161

Star Wars franchise, 77–78, 130–31, 133, 136, 161

stereotypes: failures becoming, 65; genre ghettos and, 139; guise of, changing, 103; in music genre, 117; representation and, 29, 36–37; in *Sleight*, 204n17

stigma, racial. *See* racial stigma, manufactured

Stomp the Yard, 72

Stone, Charles, III, 72, 167

Story, Tim, 33–34, 64, 72–73, 105; genres and, 124, 128, 132, *135*; production budgets of, 87

Straight Outta Compton, 75, *100*, 117, 122, 133

studio executives: Lee, S., on, 165, 170; movies linked by, 64–67; representation in, 46, 164–65

Sullivan, Kevin Rodney, *100, 135*

Talbert, David E., 64, 148–49

talent agencies: representation at, 166; writers at, 92–93

Tarantino, Quentin, 78

Taxi, 73, *134*

television: ads, 59–60; Black directors working in, 167–68; Black writers working in, 69–70; music-genre shows, 121

tent-pole franchises: genre ghettos and, 20, 130–38, *134–36*, 140; racial stigma and, 156

Think Like a Man series, 104; genre ghettos and, 132, *134*; unbankable label and, 56–57, 64, 68, 72–74

34th Street Films Studio, 173–74

Three-Fifths Compromise, 145–46

Townsend, Robert, 13, 36–37, 42

Trois, 101–2

True Grit, 1, 78

Tsujihara, Kevin, 46

Turn It Up, 117–18

12 Years a Slave: Best Picture won by, 23–24, 162; Hollywood insiders on, 24–25, 37–38; McQueen directing, 23–25, 27, 37–38, 43, 68, 79, 146, 162

20th Century Fox, 42, *70*, *100–101*; distribution by, 91, 94–96, *94–96*; genre ghettos and, 124, *134, 136*

Tyler Perry Studios, 170, 172–74

unbankable label: advertising and, 57–63, 74, 80; on Black actors, 19, 52–56, 59–60, 62, 68–73, 77–80, 88, 149; Black audiences and, 55, 57, 59, 62–63, 72–73, 75, 77–78, 80; on Black directors, 12, 19–21, 49, 52, 54–56, 63–74, 77–81, 83–84, 97, 109, 113, 118, 142–44, 182–85; foreign market and, 53–55, 62–63, 66, 75, 78–80, 101; genre ghettos and, 116–18, 126, 140; Hollywood insiders using, 52–67, 73–74, 80–81, 182–86; imagined audiences and, 53–63, *58*; linking of movies and, 63–68; marginalization with, 54, 67, 80–81; marketing and, 55, 57–64, 72–73; Obama and, 68–73, *70*; overview of, 12, 19–21, 52–56; racial inequality and, 53; racial stigma and, 141–44, 149, 160, 163–64; remaking cinema and, 164; snubbed home runs and, 73–80, *76*; whiteness and, 54, 56, 58, 67, 71, 81

unemployment, racial gap in, 32–33

Universal, 42, *70*, 75; genre ghettos and, 124, *134, 136*, 138; marginalization and, 87, 91, 94, *94–95, 96, 97, 100–101*, 106

Van Peebles, Mario, 115, 168

Van Peebles, Melvin, 42

veneer of consensus, 49

Verbinski, Gore, 88

Wan, James, 87, *136*

Wang, Wayne, 87

Warner Brothers, 42, 46, *70*; distribution by, 91, 94, *94, 96, 97*; genre ghettos and, 124, *134, 136*, 137–38

Washington, Denzel, 124, 149, 152; in *The Equalizer*, 1, 52–54, 79, 86; in *The Magnificent Seven*, 1, 7

Wasko, Janet, 11, 83, 90

Wayans, Keenan Ivory, 39, *100*, 133, *135*

western genre, 1–3, 7

Whedon, Joss, *136*, 137

White, Sylvain, 72
white audiences, 1–3, 9, 120, 128, 151
white directors: Black casts and, 97–101,
    101; distribution and, 92, *94–95*, 96–
    97, 113; genres and, 124, 137; produc-
    tion budgets of, 87–88, *96*; unbank-
    able label and, 71, 80
whiteness, 84, 98, 184; doctrines of,
    6; Hollywood insiders and, 24, 54,
    56; normalized, 56, 146, 149, 156;

unbankable label and, 54, 56, 58, 67,
    71, 81
white supremacism, 6, 11, 65, 98, 181, 183
Why Did I Get Married?, 76, 77
Williams, Spencer, 40–41, 77
Wonder Woman, 111
Woo, John, 87
The Wood, 82
Wrinkle in Time, 110, 110–11, *190*, 191
writers, 33, 69–70, 92–93

ABOUT THE AUTHOR

Maryann Erigha is Assistant Professor of Sociology and African American Studies at the University of Georgia. She writes and teaches courses about race, film, media, and technology. Her published work appears in the scholarly journals *Ethnic and Racial Studies*, the *Journal of Black Studies*, the *Black Scholar*, *Sociology Compass*, and the *Du Bois Review: Social Science Research on Race*.

CPSIA information can be obtained
at www.ICGtesting.com
Printed in the USA
LVHW091510041219
639413LV00001B/3/P

9 781479 886647